NAVIGATING MINISTRY CHALLENGES

David A. Davis
John Lukomski
Robert Riggert
Todd Kollbaum
Don Neuendorf
Ron Garwood
Michael Walther
Jesse Yow
Ray Hartwig
Billy Brath
Joshua Duffy

CONCORDIA PUBLISHING HOUSE · SAINT LOUIS

3558 S. Jefferson Avenue, St. Louis, MO 63118-3968
1-800-325-3040 • cph.org

Manufactured in the United States of America

Library of Congress Cataloging-in-Publication Data

Names: Davis, David A.; Lukomski, John; Riggert, Robert; Kollbaum, Todd; Neuendorf, Don; Garwood, Ron; Walther, Michael; Yow, Jesse; Hartwig, Ray; Brath, Billy; Duffy, Josh..

Title: Navigating ministry challenges

Description: Saint Louis, MO : Concordia Publishing House, [2021] | Summary: "Contributors share their wisdom about the practical side of ministry: work/life balance, governing a church, managing people, and other challenges pastors encounter. Pastors new to parish ministry will benefit from learning from those who have gone before them, who have served in parishes of all shapes and sizes. Experienced pastors will learn from their peers, giving them fresh tips and tools for parish ministry"-- Provided by publisher.

Identifiers: LCCN 2021034210 (print) | LCCN 2021034211 (ebook) | ISBN 9780758667144 (paperback) | ISBN 9780758667151 (ebook)

Subjects: LCSH: Pastoral theology.

Classification: LCC BV4011.3 .N39 2021 (print) | LCC BV4011.3 (ebook) | DDC 253--dc23

LC record available at https://lccn.loc.gov/2021034210

LC ebook record available at https://lccn.loc.gov/2021034211

---

1 2 3 4 5 6 7 8 9 10 30 29 28 27 26 25 24 23 22 21

TABLE OF CONTENTS

CHAPTER 1

THE PASTOR AND CONGREGATION

Rev. David A. Davis

INTRODUCTION

Two of my biggest surprises in life came from my childhood friends Rusty and Mike. In both cases, the surprise was that they hit back. We were kids together in the neighborhood—rode bikes, shot baskets, played football. And a couple of times, we got into fights.

While not at all the biggest kid, I figured I could hold my own. I knew where I wanted to land my blows; I had a strategy for the fight. But I had not counted on one thing: they hit back. Oddly, I felt betrayed. "Hey, that hurts!" And that threw off everything. Things went from bad to worse—blood, pain, embarrassment. I got the worst of it!

Starting a chapter about unexpected challenges that pastors face when working with lay leaders with an analogy to a fistfight might not be the best idea in the world. Then again, it might be just the right idea for three reasons.

First, one of the things that causes escalating conflict between pastors and lay people is that lay people respond in a way, sometimes very strongly, that the pastor never considered. As pastors, we are trained to know, to strategize, to lead. We are not so well trained to respond constructively when others see things differently. We are surprised. Unprepared for a "counterpunch" or a counterpoint, we get thrown off and feel betrayed.

Second, too often we then respond blow for blow, point for point, argument for argument. Things only get worse. Conflict. Anger. Hurt. Brothers and sisters in Christ become combatants. Others draw up sides. People gather around to see who will win and who will lose.

Third, the best thing to do when it looks like a fight is about to break out is seek reconciliation. I would have been far better served to have made peace with Rusty and Mike. In the end, there were no winners. The fight did nothing to repair the friendship. And other friends were now divided, having taken sides. As messy as fights between friends are, fights between a pastor and his people are even more so. Jesus teaches the importance of reconciliation in Matthew 5:25: "Come to terms quickly with your accuser while you are going with him to court." Or the voters assembly. Indeed, Jesus teaches the importance of reconciliation throughout the Gospels as an outgrowth of His Gospel.

There will be surprises between pastors and their lay leaders. There will be challenges. There will be disagreements. What follows should help such experiences be an occasion for the Gospel instead of a fistfight.

NOTE: All examples that follow are fictitious in their specifics but accurate in their points. Most are compilations of various situations. No real names are used. Some are from congregations I served. Some are from stories I have heard from other pastors.

SHEEP NOT ALLIGATORS:

What do I do with difficult people?

Kevin loved the neighboring congregation. He couldn't say enough good things about their preacher. He always wished we had the kind of music that they did. He would explain to me great insights about how our church could be so much better if we were more like the neighboring church. He seemed to assume I had never read or thought or tried anything to make our church "better." With a pleasant demeanor, he would take the floor at a board meeting or leave a voicemail on my phone to explain how our congregation was lacking in this or that area.

But he was too busy to serve. He was too busy to get involved. He was too busy to help. I regretted that he was, apparently, too busy to transfer. Boy, did he bug me!

It is important for pastors to remember what Jesus said to Peter: "Feed My sheep." Without much searching, you can find numerous places in the New Testament where God's people, in one way or another, are referred to as sheep or lambs.

Not once does Jesus call His people alligators. Try a search. Not once. Neither should you. It's not easy, but we should do all we can to keep in mind that our members are 1 Corinthians 8:11 and Romans 14:15 kinds of people—ones for whom Christ died.

One of the biggest challenges that pastors face is dealing with people. Many a pastor has said, "Being a pastor would be easy if it weren't for the people." Even though our people confess together every week that they are poor, miserable sinners, too often we pastors get frustrated when they live it out. Why should we be surprised when people live out both sides of being sinners and saints?

We expect them to be saints even when we keep picking music they don't like. We expect them to be saints even when they have been at a contentious board meeting too late in the evening. We expect them to be saints even when we or someone else in the church inadvertently (or advertently?) hurts them. We expect them to be saints even when they are struggling with problems at home or work.

Difficult people are a fact of ministry. I remember reading material early in my ministry that helped focus on EGR people: *extra grace required*. Some sheep require more kindness, understanding, and grace than others.

There are four things that you should consider when you run into difficult people.

→ First, never demonize difficult people.

The morning get-together of the staff was supposed to be for a devotion. At times, it was more of an exorcism. Jim, a longtime elder, had complained to one of the staff members that on Sundays, the staff members were not spending enough time talking with congregants following worship services. While Jim thought he was being helpful, that staff member reported the complaint to the rest of the staff members, and together they spent the first ten minutes of morning devotion time condemning him for sinning against the staff and breaking Matthew 18.

I have seen congregations in which any dissenter was viewed as a betrayer. I have seen difficult people belittled behind their backs. I have seen people with disagreements labeled alligators. It is crucial that you refrain from such labels. Avoid demonization. Remember they are Jesus' sheep. Remember they are people for whom Christ died. Or as my mother used to say, "That person is someone's little boy or girl."

→ Second, take time to listen to difficult people.

Gretchen pointed out things that were wrong. It was her strong suit. She thought she had a special gift of discernment in explaining what was wrong with everything that came up. I grew frustrated. I groaned when she took the floor at a meeting. But after a while, I decided to listen, to see what merit there was in her comment. And for all the negativity, there tended to be some positive point to her statements. In treating her well and with dignity, others came to see that the church (in this case, church meetings) was a safe place even when there are dissenters.

Build relationship with them. Assume that even your most ardent opponent is seeking the good of the congregation. Just because they view things differently than you do does not mean they are evil or intend you harm. A huge part of being a pastor is being able to patiently listen to people and even learn from them. In fact, the more you befriend your most ardent detractors, the stronger your leadership influence will become.

→ Third, pray for difficult people.

Ben betrayed me. He made promises he didn't keep. As chairman, he was a big talker—all show and no go. When I tried to call him on it, he let me know how busy he was and how difficult his life was. He really messed things up for me. But I determined to pray for him, not against but for him. While that did not change the situation, it shaped my heart.

This may sound like too simple a solution. This may sound like too "pastor-ish" a solution. But it is biblical. We are to pray for those who persecute us. We are to pray for our enemies. God tends to answer such prayer with a softening heart of the pray-er toward the pray-ee.

If you are running into conflict with people or struggling with personality problems, keep in mind that Satan is delighted. Satan celebrates bringing division and divisiveness into Jesus' congregations. Hoisting the shield of faith to quench such arrows and then becoming fervent in prayer will go a long way to having better relationships with even the most difficult person. God invites pastors to bathe the baptized in prayer. Instead of writing people off, write their names down on your prayer list.

→ Fourth, find the right place for the difficult person.

Henry could not play well with others. He was abrasive and domineering at meetings. He really meant well; it just never sounded like it. And when people did not see it his way, he became even more difficult. But he could teach. Once he was employed as a teacher in the congregation instead of a board member, he was much less irritated and irritating.

Some people can't play well with other boys and girls. But put them on a particular project to work on instead of a committee, and they thrive. Some people are terrible at follow-through—big ideas but crummy follow-through. Put them on a team with others who can help keep deadlines. Focus on deploying people by their natural abilities and their spiritual gifts.

Pastors must develop people skills. This is an area that cannot be learned at the seminary. It can only be learned with patience, practice, and prayer. At the heart of learning to deal well with others, especially difficult people, is coming to a greater realization of God's grace to the pastor himself.

> Therefore the kingdom of heaven may be compared to a king who wished to settle accounts with his servants. When he began to settle, one was brought to him who owed him ten thousand talents. And since he could not pay, his master ordered him to be sold, with his wife and children and all that he had, and payment to be made. So the servant fell on his knees, imploring him, "Have patience with me, and I will pay you everything." (Matthew 18:23–26)

One of the things that will become ever clearer to you as a pastor is how crucial it is that you are a forgiven sinner. While you will give great effort to consecrated improvement for Kingdom work, no matter how hard you try, you will sin. Your only hope is God's continued grace, mercy, and patience.

> *And out of pity for him, the master of that servant released him and forgave him the debt.* (Matthew 18:27, italics added for emphasis)

The foundation for your ability to serve as pastor is God's forgiving heart toward you.

> But when that same servant went out, he found one of his fellow servants who owed him a hundred denarii, and seizing him, he began to choke him, saying, "Pay what you owe." So his fellow servant fell down and pleaded with him, "Have patience with me, and I will pay you." He refused and went and put him in prison until he should pay the debt. When his fellow servants saw what had taken place, they were greatly distressed, and they went and reported to their master all that had taken place. Then his master summoned him and said to him, "You wicked servant! I forgave you all that debt because you pleaded with me. And should not you have had mercy on your fellow servant, as I had mercy on you?" And in

> **anger his master delivered him to the jailers, until he should pay all his debt. So also My heavenly Father will do to every one of you, if you do not forgive your brother from your heart.**
> (Matthew 18:28–35)

As pastors, we are called to be quick to forgive people and be patient with them when they sin against us. If we are to forgive sins with patience, how much more should we be patient with them when they are simply being difficult?

Keep in mind the power of names. Adam was tasked with naming things. God revealed Himself by name. God calls us by name. Names, titles, words have power. Call a child "dumb" often enough and he will be.

Pastors must keep in mind the power of names. Even the most troublesome members are children of God, beloved. They are and should be labeled sheep. Never, ever alligators.

HEY, THAT'S A GOOD IDEA!

Why don't people more readily get on board with my good ideas?

I have known very few pastors who are not creative. For most pastors, new ideas and thoughts for ministry occur with great regularity. Between the work of the Holy Spirit and the fact that pastors spend their days focused on the congregation, we should not be surprised that every pastor is part "Mr. Idea Man."

The ideas come pouring out. And it can be frustrating when people around us do not readily accept our new ideas. "Hey, I'm the pastor!"

Early in my ministry, I had a great idea. It seemed obvious that our congregation needed a great big gym for the community and a classroom wing for our burgeoning education program. Obvious. To me. Not to everyone else. In fact, no matter how much I tried to sell my idea, I couldn't get the congregation, especially a couple of key lay leaders, on board.

The thinking was sound. The need was clear. The opportunity was endless.

"Hey, that's a good idea! I'm the pastor!"

One day when I was out for a jog, it dawned on me that if I kept playing my cards the way I was, there was a good chance we wouldn't build anything at all. So I gulped down my pride, and I opened my ears, and within eighteen months, we had a classroom wing—that part of the good idea became a reality. Part of it was better than none of it.

Focusing on the following five words will help you have more success and less frustration with your good ideas: *patience*, *pride*, *point*, *plan*, and *park*.

Patience: New ideas take time to blossom. Although we live in a culture that worships the new, the now, and constant change, people generally, institutions specifically, and local congregations very specifically can be slower to adopt change than you would think. Change calls for patience. Keep in mind that you are focused on the problems and solutions that surround your new idea all day long. Your people have other fish they are frying while you are cooking up change. Give them time to come around. Others have said, "Ministry is more marathon than sprint."

Pride: It is easy to get your nose out of joint when others don't quickly see the keen insight and strong intellect that has birthed your new idea. And when they don't, you feel hurt, offended, attacked, even sinned against. Keep the Eighth Commandment in mind. Don't automatically assume they have it out for you; put the best construction on their reaction. Gulp down your pride. They are not attacking you; they are thinking. They are using their brains to assess what you have in mind. Don't succumb to the pride of ownership. New ideas ultimately are hatched much more quickly with collaborative thinking. Lay people know much and should be listened to. In the long term, you will be more likely to get your ideas instituted if you check your pride and open your ears. Like chewing the cud, a pastor's pride has to be swallowed often.

Point: Keep the point in mind. This grows from the point above on pride. When it comes to a good idea, the point is not who is right; the point is what is right. Focus on what is right. When you depersonalize the issue, you and others can be far more objective in your assessment of the idea under consideration. In theology, there is, of course, a time to think on the objective and a time to think on the subjective side of a topic. When sorting through new ideas, the more you focus on the objective idea and the less you get caught up in the "subjective" person who raised it (or who is shooting it down), the better.

Plan: New ideas almost never win the day the first time you surface them. If you have a good idea, it is wise to shop it around. Run it up the flag pole. Send up a trial balloon. Test the market. (Yes, these are trite sayings, but they are sound pieces of advice.) Early in my ministry, a mentor pastor told me that all new ideas get shot down at least three times before they are approved. I have made it my practice to let my new ideas get shot down in nonofficial ways a number of times before they ever come up for a vote. If you plan to involve others in conversation, keep focused on *what* not *who*, exert patience, and let your idea get shot down unofficially a few times, you have a much better chance of having that idea approved on the first ballot.

Park: There is one other thing about good ideas. Sometimes no matter how skillfully you work with others to mold and shape that idea, it just isn't the right time. There is no shame in parking a good idea on the shelf for a bit. There are some new ideas that aren't bad ideas at all; they just need to be parked for a while. They can be like pyrophile plants whose seeds lay dormant for a very long time and only come to life with fire and heat. Good ideas can sit for some time. They aren't going anywhere. It may take a hot issue later to bring them to life.

Keep in mind the Gospel, the ultimate "new idea." Think about how often God's plan had been rejected. Think about how patient God was with His people. Think about how God parked the plan (and His people) in Babylon. Think about how the disciples three times dismissed Jesus' plan for death and resurrection. But God's plan was right. God's plan was not about ego. And not only did God's "new idea" win the day, it continues to win souls for eternity.

Here's the rest of my story. I really was disappointed that my idea of building a gym and classroom at my first congregation didn't win the day. But because I was able to work well with the congregation and let them help shape and develop the idea in a way that made more sense to them, they not only approved that classroom wing on the first ballot, they were also much more open to subsequent ideas, including planting new congregations, developing small group ministry, and building a staff. We never built the gym, but by God's grace, we built ministry while maintaining unity.

When you find yourself frustrated trying to win the day with your new ideas, take both a breath and the long view. I served with one of the most effective churchmen I ever knew in a very big change project in our district. The change included overhauling a long-standing governance system and reshaping the process for staffing the district. We traveled the district. We spoke. We listened. We refined. He told me, "Good ideas will win the day; they do not need to be sold." He was right. Following the points outlined above, that big idea won the day on the first ballot.

THE BALANCE OF "BUSINESS"

> *How do you balance congregation as a business but not a business?*

How is a congregation like a family but different from a family? How is a congregation like a school but different from a school? How is a congregation like a social service agency but different from a social service agency? Considering the dynamics and characteristics of families, schools, and social service agencies can do much to inform and enhance a congregation's ministry. Balance is key.

The same is true when we ask the question, "How is a congregation like a business but different from a business?"

I forget who it was the first time, but there have been a number of times that I have heard pastors speak disparagingly about the church as a business by pronouncing the word "bid-den-ness." Funny, but a little naive, or at least overstated. It comes from a point of view that the business world and its tools are irrelevant and even antithetical to the work of the local congregation.

I clearly remember sitting in a Marketing 101 class I was auditing after I had left the seminary and had started at my first congregation. Of all things, the emotion of anger came over me. It made me angry to think that there were people in my congregation who knew all about marketing and other business practices but were not applying them to our life as a congregation. They were glad to employ such ideas to make money for their businesses but not for our work of reaching and edifying lost souls. Or, far more charitably, perhaps no one had ever helped them make a connection.

Without a doubt, there are business aspects to the local congregation. It is a business in the eyes of the state (Romans 13) and must have articles of incorporation, a constitution, and follow governmental regulations (as long as they do not go against God's Word). As such, it can benefit from employing many best practices from the business world. Two insights follow.

All truth is God's truth. Truths about how organizations run smoothly, how workers can grow in effectiveness and efficiency, and how people can be cared for are no less true because they have been discovered in the realm of a business setting and not in a Bible study. A business truth is not by definition a taboo truth that should not be applied in the context of congregational life. Truth is truth.

God works through means. Catchy music helps draw people's attention to a product. Well-kept yards and clean bathrooms make for a good impression on people. Personal follow-up on recent visitors and regular customers keeps people coming back to the same place of business. Well-organized agendas keep participants engaged. These are not ungodly means to distort or twist people's reactions. They are means that reflect that humans are, rightly understood, sentient beings. They are means through which people are related to as people. If car dealerships, funeral homes, and hamburger joints use such means for their businesses, why would we ignore them as we busy ourselves with our Kingdom work?

But there is more to consider.

The bottom line makes the difference. The key difference between the business world and the local congregation is the bottom line. The Church's bottom line is not money.* We want to be involved in seeking and saving lost people. We focus on raising up and building up the saints. When push comes to shove in a local congregation, people, not money, must be the bottom line. We do not seek to succeed financially at all costs; we seek to love God and love our neighbor.

This makes measurements difficult. It is easy to measure money—count it up. But measuring people's spiritual development, counting up changes in heart, or tracking growth in biblical insight proves very difficult. A key divergence between the business world and congregational life centers in the area of measurements. It is here that congregations and their leaders might make decisions that do not make business sense. We keep working in some areas, investing resources and expending energy on things that would not happen in a business setting.

God's upside-down principles often prevail. Greatness is found in humbleness. Strength is found in weakness. Firstness is found in lastness. Wisdom is found in foolishness. Giving is better than receiving. While following business principles that address human nature, organizational theory, economic prudence, and the like have their place in a local congregation's work, God has a special interest in and power for the local congregation. God's power often accomplishes astonishing things in the most unlikely ways. Defying logic, precedence, and statistics, God acts in ways in the midst of His people that would make the most astute business executives scratch their heads. Humbleness, weakness, lastness, foolishness, and giving may not seem to be a prudent path for the business executive, but they are the ways of the Kingdom.**

This should not encourage local congregations herewith to eschew generally accepted business principles but rather ultimately to look to the power of God at work through the Means of Grace—grace with a big *G*—even as we employ the means of grace—grace with a small *g*. This does not give us license to ignore the gifts and insights God provides to the business community; it gives us encouragement when, on the surface, it looks like our "business" is failing.

Consider working with business people to hear about their experience and apply it to congregational life when it is obedient to Christ. Congregations generally tap professional teachers to help with Sunday School and confirmation class. We tap RNs and LPNs to serve as parish nurses. We tap members who are plumbers to fix the water tap.

Why wouldn't we want to engage members with experience in business to apply their vocational expertise to the mission and ministry of the local congregation?

Don't forget about being busied with prayer. While the business world certainly is free to pray, the Church, its congregations, and congregants should be ever busied with prayer. Martin Luther had some very astonishing things to say about the power of prayer. Read his introduction to the Lord's Prayer in the Large Catechism. And Jesus had plenty to say about prayer! All the business of the local congregation will benefit from being busied with prayer.

And don't forget 1 Corinthians 12. Paul identifies the Church as a corporation, the Body of Christ. Like a body, like a business, the Church has systems that will work better when properly organized, integrated, and focused.

The local congregation a business? In fact, the most important business, corporation, in the world.

*Do a quick Google search about businesses and the bottom line. You will see that it is a false notion that the only thing businesses are really concerned about is the bottom line. Many of the finest businesses are driven by something different, something more.

** Again, do a Google search about business success and these characteristics, and you will find that they characterize many successful businesses. See Adam Grant's *Give and Take* as an example.

WOE, THESE PEOPLE KNOW MORE THAN I DO

What happens when there are people in your congregation who know more than you do?

I knew I was in trouble at the interview. This was my fourth congregation. I had stayed current. I had read widely. I had even kept up on my Greek. One of the members of the interview committee asked me to talk about my position on the homoousion controversy. I blanched on the inside, but on the outside, I said something like, "Say something more about that." It had been a long time since seminary.

As he talked, by the grace of God, something clicked within the inner recesses of my mind. I said, "I think you have that a little wrong. You are asking about the *filioque* issue." Whew!

I got by on that one, but right then and there, I vowed never to fake anything I didn't know. There were some learned people around here who knew serious things. If I faked something, someone would call me on it. It turned out the congregation was comprised of all sorts of doctors (MDs and PhDs), lawyers, and other very learned people.

It would almost always be the case that I would not be the smartest person at any meeting of church members. And that was okay.

There was a time that a pastor was one of the most educated people in the congregation. He occupied one of the three literate professions: doctor, lawyer, pastor. (These professions were also characterized by the pledge of confidentiality.) That is certainly not the case today.

One of the worst situations a pastor can put himself in is to think that he always needs to be the smartest, most learned person in the congregation. This is a fool's errand and a pointless competition.

You do not need to know it all. Remember, the members around you are part of the Body of Christ. The Holy Spirit gives gifts to each one as He determines—and that includes mental capacity and intellectual acuity. Do not be in competition with them; celebrate the gifts, intellectual and other, that God has distributed to your people. Benefit from what others know. Let iron sharpen iron.

My congregation was working on a major change. It was a big project. One of our members teaches about change and organizations at the university level. He is recognized as a leader in his field. While I already had what I thought was a lot of experience as a change agent, lunches with him—picking his brain, recalibrating my thinking—proved invaluable. And the project would have gone even better if I had done more so.

Don't fake it. Don't pretend that you know things that you don't. You will be found out. Even more important than winning a reputation for knowing things is winning one for being trustworthy.

I once preached a stellar Christmas Eve sermon that included a masterful illustration with an allusion to allspice. The only problem was that

I really didn't know what allspice was; I thought it was a combination of many spices. I faked it as if I were a master baker. It turned out that the father of one of the parishioners was a spice dealer, and that parishioner called me out on it (good-naturedly) at the door. The story ends well; later she brought me a container of it.

There is no shame or guilt in admitting you don't know or that you were wrong. You might need to eat a little crow now and then, but with a little salt, you can acquire a taste for it. In fact, people will have more confidence in what you say if, now and again, you admit your ignorance or error on a topic. Remember it is God—not you—who is omniscient.

One of my friends led a weekend conference for my congregation. It was to be an in-depth study of Scripture. He had traveled far and wide as a Bible teacher, recognized nationally for being gifted and knowledgable. He was keenly adept at applying interesting insights from Jewish teachers. But what most impressed me was that when one of the participants stumped him with a question, without a bit of shame or embarrassment he answered, "How should I know? I don't know everything!"

Do not equate either academic degrees or station in life with intelligence. I have known some highly degreed people who knew little outside of their limited area of excellence. Through the years, some of the smartest people in my congregations have been farmers, custodians, and tree trimmers. Listen and learn from all.

Pete went through high school. He never really had a full-time job. He was a handyman. He was a farmer. He did a little of this and a little of that. He was also a little shy. I spent a number of times out in his barn listening and learning. Inadvertently, he taught me lessons about stewardship (raise money for the congregation by asking God's people for it), human nature (don't be overawed by people's position in the community), and temperance (too much of his homemade wine caused headaches). He was one of the wisest people I have known.

Beware of pride. Pastors receive a rigorous academic experience. Pastors learn a lot: theology, languages, history, literature, and more. All that serves as a strength—and an important one at that. But remember, many tragic figures in literature are undone by pride in their strength.

They are undone by their strong suit. Be grateful for your learning. Employ it rigorously. But do not flaunt it. Remember your education and intellect are to serve the Gospel, not yourself.

Henry had become very successful. His congregation boomed. He was asked to write for professional publications. He was a leading voice in the larger church. People looked up to him, sought his counsel and advice. As time went on, his ministry started to flounder. He became distracted by the fruits of his labor instead of concentrating on the work at hand. His attention to spiritual and personal discipline became lax. He started taking shortcuts and living on his reputation. People suggested this. People suggested that. He didn't listen. They didn't know. He was the expert. His ministry foundered.

A pastor's calling includes truth telling, information sharing, broad-range teaching, well-informed preaching, and organizational thinking. There is much to know, but no one knows it all. Remember you are called to be a pastor in the Lord's Church, not a Renaissance man. Or as you can find on any number of posters, "If you are the smartest person in the room, you are in the wrong room." You are probably also mistaken.

LONELINESS AND ISOLATION

How do you balance being a friend and being a pastor?

My first congregation was extremely friendly. We were welcomed with open arms. Our children had other little children to play with. People invited us for Friday pizza. Saturdays could include either afternoons at someone's pool in the summer or college football at someone else's house in the fall.

But Sunday afternoons could be particularly lonely. Sunday tended to be a family day. While we were included in many activities throughout the week, Sundays were different. The members were with their extended family in the small community where they had grown up; ours was two and a half hours away.

Be patient.

Lifelong friendships take a lifetime to develop. When you arrive at your first congregation or when you first arrive at a subsequent congregation, friendships there start at zero. The deep connections you had with seminary classmates will not be duplicated with members anytime soon. The rich relationships you and your spouse had with other seminary couples cannot be replaced in a fortnight.

Relationships take time to develop. Shared experience, good or bad, plus regular interaction, plus care for one another over time equals a deep relationship. Serving together on boards, planning retreats, visiting at hospital beds, conducting weddings, officiating at funerals, and enjoying casual gatherings will bring deep friendships to fruition in time.

Keep in mind that the members of the congregation already have relationships with one another, many of them deep and long-lasting. The introduction of a new pastor and his family will cause some disruption to the social setting of the congregation. Somewhere I heard that whenever a new person joins a group, the group "goes back to zero." It will take some time for the congregation to sort things out and for a social equilibrium, with your place in it, to return.

Be careful.

Some counsel pastors not to make friends within their congregation. Given the biblical call to love one another deeply (1 Peter 4:8), that sounds unbiblical. It also seems counterintuitive, absurd, and, if the Holy Spirit does what the Holy Spirit does to a body, impossible. Of course, some cautions are important to keep in mind so those friendships reflect that the relationship between a pastor and members of his congregation is that of Christ's under-shepherd with His sheep (John 10).

You should be careful. Some seek friendship with the pastor to gain position over or information about others. Some seek friendship with the pastor because they want greater influence in the congregation or in the community. Some seek friendship with the pastor because they have alienated everyone else. Be on guard about dual-purpose friendships.

Be careful with confidentiality. Not only do shared interests and experiences characterize friendships, so do honesty and openness.

While every pastor must develop a clear reputation for both honesty and openness, pastors must maintain confidentiality. We are vowed to do so. But we are also tempted within friendships, especially at a dinner party with alcohol, to share things that must remain privileged information for the pastor. In building friendships within a congregation, you must scrupulously maintain pastoral confidentiality.

Be careful regarding partiality. You will naturally be drawn to some people more than others for friendship. Some personalities connect better with one person instead of another. Some connections have inherently more shared interests and experiences. Let your friendships develop according to those normal processes. Do not build relationships based on the status, influence, or financial situation of particular members. Such partiality is prohibited by the Word of God (James 2).

Also, in a related manner, keep an eye on your relationships with congregational friends in public, congregational settings. When you are in a congregational setting, you are the pastor for the congregation. Do not let your deeper friendship with some interfere with your responsibility to the whole.

Be expansive.

To have all your friendships and social relationships within the congregation makes you vulnerable to a myopic view of life and will stunt your impact for the greater Kingdom. Make sure that you build relationships with people outside your congregation.

Develop friendships in your community. Keep in mind the distinction between a congregation and a parish. A congregation is a group of believers committed to grow in Christ with one another in a given area. It is characterized by a building in which it meets. A parish is a general area where that congregation exists and includes not only the committed but also those who are members of other congregations and those who are unbelievers. It is characterized by a zip code. Make sure that you build friendships with others in your parish: neighbors, participants on a sports team, parents of your children's friends, and so on.

Maintain friendships with colleagues and seminary classmates. These friendships can be places where you have a greater sense of openness regarding the rigors and challenges of pastoral ministry. These friends understand in a way others may not. And with these friends, you can be open in a way you cannot be with members. Such friendships also offer an opportunity for accountability.

Enrich your friendship with your wife and children. Congregations come and go. People move. People leave. Family relationships last for life. Take time to enrich your relationships with those closest to you. There was a time that pastors were almost encouraged to ignore their family for the sake of the congregation. Today we are almost encouraged to "wear our family on our sleeve" or as a badge of honor. The sweet spot is somewhere in the middle and finding it is crucial.

Be inviting.

Some pastors are more gregarious or extroverted than others. Some are more reticent and introverted than others. While I have not done an expansive research study, it seems that there is a stronger introverted stripe running through the pastorate than people might guess.

In any case, all pastors should at some point be inviters, initiators, or instigators of friendships. Don't wait for others to reach out and get a conversation or an activity or a project started; extend an invitation. Keep in mind that some members may be interested in friendship with you, but they may be intimidated by your office.

If you find yourself or your family in a particularly lonely situation, reach out and extend an invitation.

Be resigned.

When all is said and done, there are some very lonely times for pastors. There are some burdens we must bear by ourselves, some responsibilities that can fall to no one else.

There is a sense in which the congregation is never ours. Even if a pastor stays for a very long time in a given congregation, there will be people who were already friends together before his arrival and whose friendship with one another will transcend the pastor's leaving or retiring. Such a dynamic can spread a hidden veil of loneliness over what are true and deep friendships. The spirit of "pretty soon, Pastor, you will be moving on" leaves all friendships just a bit less.

That is the calling. I wonder if Abram and Sarai still missed family back in Haran even after they became Abraham and Sarah. Psalm 84:5 instructs our hearts for pilgrimage, "Blessed are those whose strength is in You, in whose heart are the highways to Zion." While Ecclesiastes affirms that two are better than one and that a three-strand cord is not easily broken (Ecclesiastes 4:9–12), Proverbs comforts us that there is a Friend who sticks closer than a brother (Proverbs 18:24).

And be thankful!

Over time, friendships will come and become deep. When we live and serve in the context of a Christian congregation, the Holy Spirit will be at work to shape us in the image of the triune God as we build deep and, by God's grace, eternally abiding friendships.

HOMEMAKER REALITY

> *What happens when leaders and pastors have crossed expectations?*

I have to admit I was ticked. No one had shown up to shovel the walk before the evening service. It wasn't like it was that much to take care of. In fact, I had always liked shoveling snow. But tonight? I am a pastor now, and I am about to lead and preach an Advent service. Do these people really expect me to shovel too? I did not go to the seminary only to have to shovel snow.

I even remember sending off an angry note (this was before the days of email but after the days of carrier pigeons).

Did they really expect me to shovel, or had they not signed someone up to do it, or was the person who signed up to do it delayed at work?

What were the expectations regarding the shoveling of snow?

It is difficult to count the number of different tasks that go into being a pastor, especially the sole pastor of a normal-size congregation. The closest comparison to the multifaceted work of a pastor is a homemaker.

Think of what a homemaker must be, often all in the same day: cook, dietician, child psychologist, plumber, seamstress, nurse, chemist, artist, chauffeur, critter control specialist, detective.

The same is true of a pastor. First, there are the various tasks of the office:

→ Preacher
→ Teacher of adults
→ Teacher of teens
→ Teacher of children
→ Teacher of new members
→ Theologian
→ Apologist
→ Hospital visitor
→ Spiritual leader
→ Pastor caregiver to couples
→ Pastoral counselor to the grieving

Then there are other tasks that rightly or wrongly often fall to the pastor:

→ Business manager
→ Marketer
→ Community organizer
→ Psychologist
→ Plumber
→ Electrician
→ Computer scientist
→ Graphic artist
→ Secretary
→ Snow shoveler

That is a lot to expect of one man. And there is more. Not only are there many expectations of the pastor, not everyone has the same expectations. Some members expect this but not that. Others expect that but not this. And the pastor might have expected neither or both.

More than multiplicity of expectations, crossed expectations cause the real problems between pastors and leaders. There are four keys to keeping expectations uncrossed.

Insist on an annual review. Pastors should sit down with the board of elders, the governing board, or whatever group oversees him to discuss expectations, performance factors, and other duties for the coming twelve months. Put this down on paper. This exercise will enable pastor and leaders to agree on a goalpost. The pastor should not be intimidated by this; he should insist on it.

Working through expectations in this manner will help pastor and leaders be both objective and proactive. Putting this all down on paper at once will give everyone a better idea of the pastor's breadth of responsibilities and an opportunity to narrow such a list into a manageable scale. Even the most hopeful congregation does not really expect its pastor to be Superman. Doing this together also forestalls conflict later. When a pastor is faithfully fulfilling agreed-upon expectations, conflict and complaint will be minimized.

This review should be revisited and, if necessary, renegotiated every six months.

Feed members' expectations into whatever board deals with that review. If a congregation has 100 members, there are 100 different sets of expectations of the pastor. If a congregation has 250 members, there are 250 different sets of expectations of the pastor. No pastor can please everyone. Some die trying. Others harden themselves against input.

Instead of trying to meet or legitimizing everyone's expectations of the pastor, the pastor should work with the board that oversees him to sort out expectations that assorted congregational members may have. If they are legitimate, then the board and pastor can adjust what was agreed upon at the annual review. If they are not legitimate, the board can provide cover for the pastor in the face of members' complaints.

Search your own motivation for what you expect of yourself and why. When you are notified that a member is in the hospital, do you drop everything and go visit? What if you find out she has already been there four days? Or what if you find out it is for a routine overnight test?

What if you find out that the person's elder was just there for a time of prayer? Are you visiting because of that person's real need for you or because you need to visit to convince yourself you are a good pastor? Whose need is being served?

When worship is over, you have had some time to visit with people, and you see people lingering in the narthex, but you know you have a family outing planned soon. Do you still wait until everyone is gone so you can lock up? Why do you expect that you need to be the last one out? Does anyone else expect that?

When you see the list of meetings on the weekly calendar, do you bemoan the week ahead because of all the meetings you expect yourself to attend? How crucial are you at each of those meetings? Are there some meetings that you could just pop into without sitting down? Are there some meetings that will happen just fine without you, but you think a good pastor would be there?

Many of the expectations on a pastor that make his work particularly onerous are ones that he, and no one else, has placed on himself.

Meet or exceed expectations. My favorite book title of all time is *It Takes So Little to Be Above Average* by Florence Littauer. While being driven by false expectations or being driven crazy by too many expectations, a pastor should seek both to meet and exceed legitimate expectations.

If he and the board have agreed on what is expected, accomplishing and living up to those expectations is crucial. It is an instance of letting your yes be yes and your no be no. To meet agreed-upon expectations engenders trust and confidence.

And exceed those expectations too. This may sound like undoing everything that was just written since the beginning of this section, but the pastor, while not opening up a Pandora's box of endless expectations, should have a spirit of saying, "What's the most I can do?" and not, "Hey, I did what you expected." A little more. A little better. A little quicker. A little nicer. When a pastor voluntarily exceeds what was agreed upon with a heart of service and not a neurotic need to please or be affirmed, he models Jesus. Properly understood, exceeding expectations is an example of the Gospel.

This is in the spirit of underpromise and overdeliver.

It has been many years since I crabbed about snow shoveling. Through those years, I sought to clarify with my boards and then accomplish what was expected. At the same time (admittedly imperfectly), I have sought to do a little more, to exceed those expectations with a free spirit.

Recently, we had a clogged toilet at church. We have a lot of different washrooms, and somehow this one had not been tended for some time—apparently a long time. It was nasty. We have plumbers on call, and the sexton was tasked with contacting one to come and fix it. We have no expectation of the pastor serving as plumber. I needed to do nothing, and no one would think the less. I could let it go, and there would be no conflict with or complaint about the pastor's job performance.

In the meantime, with no one expecting it and with a plugged nose, a clear conscience, and even a joyful spirit, I got a pail and flushed it the old-fashioned way.

WHEN A LEADER GOES BOOM

> *What happens when a leader disappoints you through moral failure?*

The call came early on a Saturday morning. "Pastor, can I come to the church to talk with you." It was one of my leaders. He sounded subdued.

Late that morning we met. He was ashamed. He had been to a business party the night before and, having worked all day without much to eat, ended up with too much alcohol in his system. He flipped his company car on the way home. He spent the night in jail.

I love this man.

There were two immediate reactions in my heart. First, what can I do to affirm this man of God while, hopefully, protecting and maintaining his place of leadership? And second, wow, if *he* did this, who is safe? Am I?

As I remember, we had a very poignant time of Confession and Absolution. The Gospel was at work.

Every one of your leaders is a 2 Corinthians 4:7 sort of person. We are all cracked pots. We all have feet of clay.

But it is hard when a leader goes boom. It may be alcohol or drugs. It may be embezzlement at church or work. It may be an affair. It may be a divorce. It may be child molesting. It may be apostasy. It may be an emotional meltdown that ends in a very messy resignation. It may be suicide.

There is a very good chance you will see them all.

Your reaction should be two-pronged. First, you must deal with the individual and that situation. Second, you must protect yourself from the same failure.

Dealing with the individual and the situation

Above all, this must be a place for the Gospel. You must seek to lead the person, by the Word and the Holy Spirit, to Confession and Absolution. This can be one of the most beautiful experiences of your ministry.

Second, you must balance confidentiality and the protection of the congregation. While private sins confessed to the pastor must remain private, public sins, especially those against a congregation, should be dealt with publicly but with as much decorum and modesty as possible. This is a time to carefully apply the Eighth Commandment. While the offense may be true enough, to follow the Eighth Commandment, knowledge of the offense should only be shared in a way and in the arenas where it might build up the body. You must guard against gossip.

Third, if there are legal implications, you must acknowledge the legal system as a Romans 13 servant of God. As citizens of a community, involving the court system may serve to protect others. Too many congregations sweep a known legal offense under the rug in a quest to maintain the congregation's reputation, only to have the situation be exacerbated later.

Fourth, because all leaders are of the flesh, when one fails, the congregation should provide safeguards against others falling into the same temptation and a reoccurrence by the same leader.

A congregation I knew had a treasurer embezzle a large amount of money. The congregation confronted the member but to no avail. With a heart hardened against the truth, the congregation was compelled not only to file charges but also to excommunicate the member. Sometime later, the former treasurer finally repented and was reinstated as a member. But as the brother pastor said, "We never put him in charge of the money again."

When there has been some sort of a moral failure of a leader, it is incumbent upon the other leaders to review policies and procedures of the congregation to safeguard others from temptation. For instance:

→ **Always make sure that at least two people are involved in counting the offering.**

→ **Do not allow only one or two people in the building by themselves.**

→ **Limit alcohol at congregational functions.**

→ **Discourage travel with two members of the opposite sex by themselves.**

→ **Conduct background checks of all who are involved with ministry to minors.**

Protecting yourself from the same failure

Whenever I have had a leader go through some sort of moral failure, it has shaken me. And not just because I was surprised or disappointed in the person. It has shaken me because I have thought, "Is no one immune? Am I immune?"

The answer is no.

The failure of a leader should serve as a warning to you to be on your guard. Scripture counsels us, "Therefore let anyone who thinks that he stands take heed lest he fall" (1 Corinthian 10:12). Paul quotes the psalmist, "None is righteous, no, not one" (Romans 3:10). Jesus warned, "Watch and pray that you may not enter into temptation" (Matthew 26:41).

The prince of this world has much to gain by leading a pastor into moral failure. This causes the demons too much glee.

Never think, "It can't happen to me." Instead, when you have a leader who goes boom, make sure you check where the detonators are in your life.

→ **Never counsel someone of the opposite sex in the building by yourself.**

→ **Never handle any of the congregation's cash.**

- → Decline a petty cash fund. Insist instead on a credit card monitored by another.
- → Be careful of whom you touch and how.
- → Limit your alcohol use.
- → Avoid sharing intimate details of your personal life.
- → Maintain a strong relationship with your wife.
- → Install pornography controls on your computer.

Every congregation is comprised of sinners and saints. In fact, every congregant is a sinner and saint. As pastor, you must be fully aware of this and seek to forestall moral failures by praying for your leaders, instituting moral safeguards, and keeping your eyes open to warning signs.

CONCLUSION

Jim taught me one of the most crucial lessons about being a pastor, and he wasn't a pastor. In fact, our conversation had nothing to do with pastoring; it had to do with the home rental company Jim ran with his grandmother. Together they had about one hundred properties.

He and I were talking about his work of fixing up properties and how, no matter what, he always ran into some sort of problem, something he had not anticipated. Every project came with a curveball.

That surprised me. I had only ever been sort of handy with projects around the house: painting, carpentry, minor electrical or plumbing repairs, and even more minor small engine repair. There were things I had gotten decent at, but it seemed like I always ran into something I had not anticipated, a curveball. Through the years, I had come to conclude that I was inept as a repairman.

I had not realized that the problem had more to do with the nature of projects and not so much my ability or lack thereof. It turned out that even the most seasoned veteran, Jim, was always running into something that he had to think his way through or backtrack or refigure or even ask for help.

Expect that as pastor.

This chapter focuses especially on unexpected challenges at the beginning of a pastorate. As a pastor, you should expect that no matter how seasoned you become, there will always be a new challenge to face or an old challenge that has a new wrinkle. Do not conclude that because you are always facing challenges that you are somehow not cut out to be a pastor; remember my friend Jim.

Keep in mind that his job is like your job, which is ultimately like most jobs in this respect: unexpected challenges will continue. But by the grace of God at work through Word and Sacrament, with attention to prayer and by employment of the sorts of tactics chronicled throughout this chapter, you will be up to the task.

And God's name will be hallowed, His kingdom will come, and His will will be done.

CHAPTER 2

THE PASTOR AND MULTIPOINT PARISHES

Rev. John Lukomski

Since I'm a little slow on the uptake, when I was asked to write a chapter on unexpected challenges in a multipoint parish, I wondered, "How is that possible?" If it's unexpected, you, the reader, wouldn't know about it, and certainly, I, the author, wouldn't know it either. After all, it's unexpected. Then it dawned on me that they probably wanted me to write about the unexpected challenges that I faced in my forty years of ministry in a dual-point parish. Perhaps someone could learn from the things I did right or, more likely, the things I did wrong. Far be it from me to prevent someone from learning from my mistakes (there would be a vast education there), but that approach is also fraught with danger. The problem is unexpected challenges are unique. Like a snowflake, they have hundreds of details that are specific to a given situation. As a reader, you will have to pray for the gift of discernment because, as similar as my experience may seem to yours, it is likely one detail may cause an entirely different outcome. I believe what I can do is share some guiding principles that I used in my unexpected challenges, especially those in a dual parish. Then we can look at specific issues as we see how these principles apply. Please note I use the word *principle* cautiously. We are not going to discuss rules or guidelines so much as a way of thinking. Perhaps a better way of saying it: a way of believing.

1. **Faith—Why no book can solve the challenges of a multipoint congregation, but the forgiveness of sins can.**

When facing an unexpected challenge, the first question is whether there is some way you can apply the Gospel. Our first response, when faced with a challenge, is to think we have to solve the challenge, and I suppose eventually you will. However, perhaps the reason God gave you this challenge is so you might have the opportunity to bring the Gospel to the situation. In some cases, it may be simply saying, "I forgive you." Or it may be witnessing to the God of steadfast love and mercy. Every challenge provides an opportunity to show people their Savior, Jesus. You might argue, "Is this always true? Aren't there some situations where it is just a matter of using reason and common sense to resolve a matter?" There are probably cases like that. Maybe your challenge is how to divide the office expenses between two parishes. I suppose it doesn't require a lot of theology to do that. Simply divide the expenses by the number of bulletins each church uses, and you have your answer. But you would hardly call that a challenge, would you? If a situation has an obvious solution, then just do it. But what about those challenges when the answer is not so clear-cut?

Let's look at an example from the Gospel of Mark 2:1–4:

> And when He [Jesus] returned to Capernaum after some days, it was reported that He was at home. And many were gathered together, so that there was no more room, not even at the door. And He was preaching the word to them. And they came, bringing to him a paralytic carried by four men. And when they could not get near him because of the crowd, they removed the roof above him, and when they had made an opening, they let down the bed on which the paralytic lay.

The challenge here was pretty obvious—getting their sick friend to see Jesus. The unexpected challenge was how to carry a stretcher into a room that was already overflowing with people. In this case, it was just a matter of thinking outside the box (or outside the room). Why not just cut a hole in the roof and lower the friend down? Creative, but fairly straightforward. It was Jesus, however, who added the unexpected Gospel: "And when Jesus saw their faith, He said to the paralytic, 'Son, your sins are forgiven'" (Mark 2:5).

The challenge seemed pretty obvious. The paralytic needed to be healed. Rather than solve the challenge, Jesus instead applied the Gospel, "Son, your sins are forgiven." Now, why would Jesus do that? To answer that question, we need to read a little earlier in the Gospel of Mark. It turns out that this wasn't the first time Jesus had been healing the sick in Capernaum. In the previous chapter, Mark tells how Jesus had come to Capernaum and cast out a demon in their synagogue. Mark writes, "That evening at sundown they brought to Him all who were sick or oppressed by demons. And the whole city was gathered together at the door. And He healed many who were sick with various diseases, and cast out many demons" (Mark 1:32–34).

But apparently not "all who were sick" were brought to Him, nor had "the whole city" gathered at His door. There was one big exception—the paralytic. Now it's not that Mark is confused or contradicting himself. It's just that the Greek word for "all" was sometimes a popular way of indicating a great number. Many had come to Jesus at His first visit. The question is why hadn't the paralytic availed himself of this obvious opportunity to be healed? There was, of course, the problem of transportation. He was a paralytic. How would he get to Jesus? No Uber at Capernaum. But that can't be the issue, for we know he had friends who would go to great lengths to help him. Perhaps the problem is how the Jews felt about illness and tribulation.

Consider Jesus' words in Luke 13:1–5: "There were some present at that very time who told Him about the Galileans whose blood Pilate had mingled with their sacrifices. And He answered them, 'Do you think that these Galileans were worse sinners than all the other Galileans, because they suffered in this way? No, I tell you; but unless you repent, you will all likewise perish. Or those eighteen on whom the tower in Siloam fell and killed them: do you think that they were worse offenders than all the others who lived in Jerusalem? No, I tell you; but unless you repent, you will all likewise perish.'" As Jesus talks about "worse sinners" and "worse offenders," He is commenting on the commonly held belief that if people suffered, it was because they had sinned in some way. Jesus' disciples show the same attitude in John 9:1–2: "As He [Jesus] passed by, He saw a man blind from birth. And His disciples asked Him, 'Rabbi, who sinned, this man or his parents, that he was born blind?'"

Perhaps this is the reason the paralytic had refused to go to Jesus the first time. Sure, Jesus was a great healer, but the paralytic was no ordinary blind man, lame man, or leper. He was a paraplegic, totally helpless, needing the aid of four men just to move. Certainly, with such a condition, his sins must have been great. No need to bother the master when your condition is beyond Jesus' help. Why would Jesus even want to help such a great sinner?

It is interesting Jesus notes the faith of the friends who brought the man. Faith doesn't concern itself with whether a person is worthy to come to Jesus. Believers simply want to bring their loved one to the Lord. And so they did. One can imagine the paralytic's response when there was no room for him to get in the house. There it is, another sign that God doesn't want to heal me. But faith does not consider signs and will not stop until forgiveness has been bestowed, so the faithful friends pressed onward. Jesus understood the man's first need was forgiveness. He spoke as only He could: "Son, your sins are forgiven." Mark tells us the point of this story is that "the Son of Man has authority on earth to forgive sins" (Mark 2:10). We need to remember that same authority has been given to us both as called pastors and also to all Christians in what the Lutheran Confessions call "the mutual . . . consolation of the brethren" (SA III IV). As Jesus said in Matthew 18:18, "Whatever you loose on earth shall be loosed in heaven." And again in John 20:23, "If you forgive the sins of any, they are forgiven them."

This is how we should handle every challenge. It's not just a matter of overcoming the difficulty, but it is first a matter of bringing the Gospel to everyone impacted by the challenge. Also, we should remember that the Gospel needs to be brought to us as well. How can we overcome the unexpected challenges unless we first know the Lord who also says to us in our doubts and confusions, "Son, your sins are forgiven"?

One day, out of the blue, I got a phone call from a complete stranger saying he was going to commit suicide. Talk about an unexpected challenge. These are the kind of phone calls that grab a pastor's heart, and I immediately went to this man's house. So I came to meet the person we will call Terry. Terry became a regular member and someone who needed frequent counseling. People in the community warned me that he was a consummate con man, but you know me; I have to give everybody the Gospel. Then things began to happen. First, some office equipment was stolen. We suspected Terry but had no proof. Months later, we caught him red-handed, sneaking into the church after Saturday services and taking all the cash out of the offerings, something he had apparently been doing for many months. It was particularly discouraging for the congregation because this whole time we had provided him food, helped with utility bills, and even bought him a new carburetor for his car. It was especially disheartening for me because I had spent countless hours counseling him. In the end, we banned him from coming on church property. You might think that was too harsh or that we should have given him a second chance. If so, please send me your church name and phone number. I will be certain that Terry gets your information.

Despite all of this, for nearly twenty years, I continued to talk to Terry. I soon realized for my own sanity, these conversations had to be highly structured: never in person, only once a week, and no longer than a half-hour. Give Terry an inch, and he was always ready to take a mile. And so the regular conversations continued. I am not trying to make myself out to be a saint. During those twenty years, my heart was often filled with thoughts about Terry that should not be in a pastor's heart. But I just felt he needed to know that there was a God who loved him. I would like to tell you that over time, Terry confessed his sins, became a faithful member, and everything ended happily ever after. Rather, when I retired and handed his care off to other capable pastors, I can't say there was any change at all. All I can do is trust God's promise in Isaiah 55:11: "So shall My word be that goes out from My mouth; it shall not return to Me empty, but it shall accomplish that which I purpose, and shall succeed in the thing for which I sent it."

For a moment, think about the Terrys in your life, the challenging persons in your dual perish, or even among your friends or family. There may be many things you need to say to those people: words of admonition, confrontation, calls to repentance. But wouldn't you agree they need to know God loves them? Perhaps they do need to repent first. But is your call to repentance so they can see you are right and they are wrong? Or does your call echo the heart of Jesus, who desires not the death of the wicked but that they would repent and live? Even the Terrys of this world need to hear "Son, your sins are forgiven."

Ironically, the Terrys of the world make us feel bad about ourselves as well. They fill our hearts with anger, resentment, and even doubt. This anger, resentment, and doubt remind us we are sinners too. And if that is so, don't we also need to hear Jesus say, "Son, your sins are forgiven"? Without those words, how can we ever share that forgiveness with others?

The first point in responding to unexpected challenges is to look for the opportunity to apply the Gospel to yourself and to all affected by the challenge. However, that is not the end of it. The Jesus that says, "Son, your sins are forgiven," is also the Jesus who says, "I say to you, rise, pick up your bed, and go home" (Mark 2:11). Where there is forgiveness, there should also be loving action. This brings us to our second principle:

2. **Love—The reason why the answer to unexpected challenges is not "best practices" but the "loving practice."**

Let's return to those four men who carried the paralytic to see Jesus. Mark says Jesus saw their faith. But how did Jesus see their faith? Well, okay, Jesus is the Son of God, so He sees the faith that is in every believer's heart. Let me rephrase that question. How would we see their faith? Obviously, through their sacrificial work. Trust me, it's not easy to carry someone, even with the help of three others. At least you have six men helping when there's a coffin to carry. And this doesn't take into consideration lifting him up on a roof and then gently lowering him to the ground. Faith was shown in the hard work they did for their paralytic friend. As Article XIII of the Smalcald Articles says, "Such faith, renewal, and forgiveness of sins are followed by good works" (paragraph 2). As we approach our unexpected challenges, it is not just forgiveness we must consider but also the works that follow forgiveness. As James tells us, "If a brother or sister is poorly clothed and lacking in daily food, and one of you says to them, 'Go in peace, be warmed and filled,' without giving them the things needed for the body, what good is that?" (James 2:15–16). But let's talk a little more about those good works.

When confronted by a challenge, it is natural to think we need to figure out what the right thing is to do. That's not a bad approach to take if the challenge directly impinges on the Law of God. For example, if the joint parish council says, "Pastor, we have found the perfect way to raise money—child sacrifice," certainly that would be unexpected, but the only challenge would be the courage to say no. "But Pastor, we already have several parents who have signed up to donate their children." The answer is still no. This is another reason to make sure you attend every joint parish council. But let's face it, most dual parish challenges do not involve child sacrifice or idolatry, or murder, or adultery, or thievery (although coveting, false witness, and lack of faith are often factors). What about the challenges where we do not have a clear word of God about what's right and wrong? And, by the way, I would caution you about assuming that there is a clear answer from the Word of God. If you have to take hours to gather your reasons and arguments to convince someone you know the right thing to do, then I would suggest maybe the situation isn't as simple as you think. The thing to remember is we're not just looking for the right thing to do but also the loving thing.

Years ago, our district wanted to hold a "Best Practices Conference." The gathering was to accomplish much the same purpose as this book: bring together a group of people who could speak about a variety of issues facing the church. It was a great idea, but I objected to the title because "best practices" is the language of the government and the corporation. Outside of the Ten Commandments, the Church doesn't know one best practice but a variety of loving practices.

Consider the practice of having bishops. Many churches throughout history have had bishops, but our denomination, The Lutheran Church—Missouri Synod, never has. Are we not following the best practice? The answer is found in the Lutheran Confessions, Smalcald Article X: "If the bishops would be true bishops and would devote themselves to the Church and the Gospel, we might grant them to ordain and confirm us and our preachers. This would be for the *sake of love and unity*, but not because it *was necessary*" (paragraph 1, emphasis mine). Note there are two acceptable practices: churches can have bishops or churches can be without bishops. The Confessions mention the church in Alexandria as an example of the latter. The question is not what is the best practice, but as the Confessions say, what practice fosters "the sake of love and unity."

We all know there are things called adiaphora. They are neither forbidden nor required, so obviously, we can't make a necessity or best practice out of them. But let me give you another example from the early history of the Lutheran Church. It is striking because it deals with a practice that is not adiaphora, but rather one that has a clear commandment of our Lord. This is the practice of celebrating the Lord's Supper in both kinds. For years, the Church had only given the bread to the lay people. I once had a collection of Roman Catholic sermons explaining why that was. The arguments ranged from a shortage of wine to the danger of spilling the wine to "there's no need to drink the wine since if you eat the body, you're getting the blood as well." Methinks they protest too much. The simple teaching of Lutheranism is that Christ said, "eat" and "drink." So as good Lutherans, we just do what Jesus tells us. Yet listen to these instructions that were given to pastors who would be visiting the churches in Saxony: "We must remember that the people are strongly accustomed to receive only one kind, and that there are not a few who on account of this custom are in serious doubt. So one has to let the day have its twelve hours and leave the matter in God's hands" (AE 40:290). Or consider this additional guidance:

> Secondly, where there are weak Christians, who as yet have not heard, or been sufficiently instructed and strengthened by the word of the gospel, and so out of weakness and terror of conscience rather than obstinacy cannot receive both kinds, one may allow these to take communion in one kind for the time being and where they ask for it the pastor or preacher may so administer it. The reason is this: In this way the doctrine of both kinds will not be weakened or compromised, but only the application or use of the doctrine will be temporarily postponed through Christian patience and love. (40:290–91)

It was not a matter of the best practice but a matter of what would be the practice of "Christian patience and love" at the time. True, it was assumed the Word would change the hearts of the hearers, and they would gladly receive both bread and wine. True, it was recognized that for some, it was not a matter of weakness but obstinacy. In those situations, other steps would need to be taken. But the point is this: sometimes the Church gave out both kinds, sometimes only one. The challenge was what was the loving thing to do at a certain time and place.

Particularly striking is this final comment to the visitors of Saxony: "Even nowadays God tolerates much in us and in others which is wrong or insufficient, as a weak faith and other defects, according to Romans 14 and 15" (40:291). So we, too, at times tolerate what is wrong or insufficient. Therefore, we are not always looking for the best practice but the most loving practice. By the way, in the end, our district never had the "Best Practices Conference." They didn't have enough people sign up. I smugly felt God had justified my complaint. Which confirms what I'm sure you already suspected, that God tolerates much in me which is wrong or insufficient.

But why all this emphasis on what is loving versus what is right? Because this is of particular importance when it comes to merging multiple parishes. Every parish has its own practices and traditions. Everyone always thinks their traditions are the right ones and the best ones. Actually, as long as the churches were going it alone, they probably were the best practices for that particular church. But now that two parishes are working together, it becomes a question not of the best practices but the loving ones.

Let's look at the first dual parish recorded in the Scriptures, the merging of the Jewish synagogue and the Gentile church. What advice did the Jerusalem Council give to this newly merging congregation?

> **Therefore my judgment is that we should not trouble those of the Gentiles who turn to God, but should write to them to abstain from the things polluted by idols, and from sexual immorality, and from what has been strangled, and from blood. For from ancient generations Moses has had in every city those who proclaim him, for he is read every Sabbath in the synagogues.** (Acts 15:19–21)

There was no question about the issues addressed by the Commandments. Nothing that might involve idolatry was allowed. Sexual immorality was forbidden (one can imagine the things that were acceptable to Roman culture). But what about this concern for the "strangled" and the "blood." The practice of the day was that animals were killed by strangling, precisely so the blood would remain in them. However, as the text says, this was an abomination to Jews. The words of Moses taught in "every city" and "synagogue" were, "But you shall not eat flesh with its life, that is, its blood" (Genesis 9:4). Hold on, isn't that part of the ceremonial law? Doesn't Paul say in Colossians that no one should judge us in such matters? What right does the Jerusalem Council have to require such things of us Gentiles? I mean, who doesn't enjoy a nice, rare porterhouse (except for my wife)? What we have here is precisely what the Confessions spoke of above. The issue of strangling and blood is not an issue of "necessity," but it is an issue of "love and unity." The council was not saying Gentiles had to follow such practice, but in love for their Jewish brothers in faith, they were invited to do so. (By the way, I wouldn't have had any objections if the council had asked me to give up eating snakes and horses, but give me my tasty pork steaks.)

The most striking thing is what is not mentioned in this apostolic pronouncement, the very issue the council had met to decide—circumcision. "But some believers who belonged to the party of the Pharisees rose up and said [concerning the Gentiles], 'It is necessary to circumcise them and to order them to keep the law of Moses'" (Acts 15:5). And yet the council doesn't even address that issue. It's easy to see this is a practical matter. Asking people to avoid bloody meat is one thing but asking them to be circumcised is another issue entirely. Circumcision is a great tradition if you practice it from birth. I was circumcised as a baby. I don't have any objection to it, although I might have had at the time. But asking grown male adults to be circumcised? If you don't think that would be a problem, review the story of Hamor and his son Shechem in Genesis 34. Trust me, if you are planning on making disciples of all nations, circumcision is going to make those evangelism visits particularly uncomfortable.

And yet it was not for practical reasons that the council did not require circumcision. Listen carefully to how Peter addressed the council in Acts 15:10–11: "Now, therefore, why are you putting God to the test by placing a yoke on the neck of the disciples that neither our fathers nor we have been able to bear? But we believe that we will be saved through the grace of the Lord Jesus, just as they will." The reason why circumcision is set aside is because we are saved by faith—not by any ritual, even a ritual established by God Himself. As the Lutheran Confessions say in Article XXVI of the Augsburg Confession regarding that passage in Acts, "Peter forbids burdening consciences with many rites, either from Moses or others" (paragraph 28). Here is why this is important.

To the world, the decision of the Jerusalem Council would seem to be a classic example of compromise (I'll follow one of your traditions if you follow one of mine). But compromise is essentially formalized selfishness (I'll let you have your way if you let me have mine). That is not at all what is going on here. Rather, we have an illustration of the two principles we have been talking about all along. We set aside the tradition of circumcision because we believe we will be saved through the grace of the Lord Jesus. We need no traditions; we just need (and have) faith. On the other hand, we will avoid blood in our meat not as a necessity but out of Christian love and a desire for unity. Faith. Love. These are the basics for solving unexpected challenges in a dual parish.

The biggest challenge of dealing with multiple parishes is the merging of their various traditions. Before we look at some specific examples of combining parish traditions, let's consider one last Bible passage:

> **Therefore let no one pass judgment on you in questions of food and drink, or with regard to a festival or a new moon or a Sabbath. These are a shadow of the things to come, but the substance belongs to Christ.** (Colossians 2:16–17)

There was a time when I would have thought this passage irrelevant to our discussion (unless, of course, the challenge was merging a Lutheran congregation with a Jewish synagogue). After all, isn't Paul simply telling us we are no longer bound by the Old Testament ceremonial laws? However, the Lutheran Confessions insist that this passage concerns much more than just Jewish rituals but also addresses all human traditions. In Article XV of the Apology of the Augsburg Confession, we are told, referring to Colossians 2, "Here he welcomes both Moses' Law and human traditions at the same time, so that the adversaries may not dodge these testimonies, according to their custom, on the ground that Paul speaks only about Moses' Law. He clearly testifies here that he is speaking of human traditions" (paragraph 30). And again in Article XXVII we are told, "When Paul denies that by Moses' Law people merit the forgiveness of sins, he withdraws this praise much more from human traditions. He clearly presents this in Colossians 2:16. If Moses' Law, which was divinely revealed, did not merit the forgiveness of sins, how much less do these silly observances, hostile to the civil custom of life, merit the forgiveness of sins!" (paragraph 14).

The clear teaching of Scripture is that no man or congregation can insist that their human traditions must be followed. "Therefore let no one pass judgment on you" (Colossians 2:16). We must always remember that while traditions can be outward symbols of unity, they have no impact on faith. As the Lutheran Confessions testify in the Apology of the Augsburg Confession, Articles VII and VIII,

> Righteousness of the heart is a spiritual matter, a matter of enlivening hearts. Clearly human traditions do not enliven hearts and are not effects of the Holy Spirit. Such efforts are love for one's neighbor, self-control, and so on. They are not tools through which God moves hearts to believe, as are the divinely given Word and Sacraments. Rather, traditions are customs that have no connection to the heart. They perish with the using, and we must not believe that they are necessary for righteousness before God. To the same effect Paul says, "For the kingdom of God is not a matter of eating and drinking but of righteousness and peace and joy in the Holy Spirit" (Romans 4:17). (paragraph 36)

Because of this, in matters of tradition, we should be willing to forgo our perceived rights in order to foster unity in the Church, as the Confessions say of the apostle Paul: "Paul yields and gives way to the weak concerning food and <the observance of> times or days (Romans 14:6)" (SD X 13). And so also Paul had his protégé Timothy circumcised so as to make his ministry more acceptable to the Jewish people they would evangelize. Yet at the same time, Paul publicly criticized any who required that Christians be circumcised, even his fellow Christian leaders Peter and Barnabas.

It might be helpful to do a Bible study on this passage with your parishes so they understand that traditions must give way to faith and love. For this is the greatest challenge of all. We all love our traditions and, moreover, we think they are the best way to do things. Why should they have their way while we have to give up our ways? It occurs to me maybe the most important part of Colossians 2 is not the words "let no one pass judgment on you" but rather "the substance belongs to Christ." Pray long and hard that the Holy Spirit (for He alone can do this) move your people to see the substance of a dual parish is the love of God in Jesus Christ. It is for this purpose we band together, that more people can receive Jesus' absolution; be washed clean of sin with the water of Baptism; eat and drink of the body and blood of the Lord for their forgiveness; and hear the story of Jesus' suffering, death and resurrection. By focusing on this substance of Christ, hopefully, our people will see that everything else is only shadows that we willingly forgo in Christian love.

3. Faith and Love in Practice in a Dual Parish

Having laid out these thoughts, let's look at how they apply to the practical challenges faced by two churches working together. Let's use the example we had earlier about dividing up the cost of printing bulletins. One could total the cost of printing the bulletins and then simply divide those expenses by the number of bulletins each congregation uses. That would be the simplest, fairest, and best way of doing it. But would it be the most loving way? It might be, but then again, it might not. If everything else is equal, it sounds like a plan. After all, if one church uses more bulletins, they are probably the larger congregation and would have more resources. But that is seldom the way things are in dual parishes. Often the smaller church has more resources and usually less overhead as well. Wouldn't it be better for the church with the most money to pick up the bulk of the expense? On the other hand, is that really fair to them? After all, it's not their expenses.

Can you see the focus is on the wrong issues? Concerns about fairness and capability should be secondary to an attitude of faith and love. I never had to deal with this issue in my dual parishes. Long before I became pastor, the congregations had decided that the smaller church in Darmstadt would pay a monthly fee to the larger church in New Athens to cover office expenses. How that amount was determined I have no idea, but I do know it didn't change significantly in the forty years I ministered there. Perhaps it should have. What I found comforting is this: every year when the budget committee would meet in New Athens, the question always was, "How is Darmstadt doing? Can they afford to give us what they've been giving us?" There was a genuine concern for how the other church was doing. Likewise, at Darmstadt's meeting, they would ask if they should be contributing more. More important than solving a problem is developing an attitude of love and concern for their sister church. How is this accomplished? I believe only by constantly preaching the Gospel.

Let's tackle a more difficult challenge. One of the thorniest problems in combining two churches is the question of worship times. Worship times are among the strongest traditions of a church. No one wants to change what were the preferred times of parents and grandparents and generations before. There is a simple solution. Just do what I did. Come to a dual parish after all those issues are decided. Even better, come to a dual parish like mine. The Darmstadt church was primarily a rural farm church. These people were used to getting up early in the morning to feed their chickens. They wanted the earliest worship time they could get. New Athens, on the other hand, was the town church. Most of their members, like me, stayed up late on a Saturday night and were more than willing to have a later church time. It worked out well for everybody. (By the way, I was also thankful those early risers at Darmstadt were willing to wait until 9:00 a.m. for church. The congregation I grew up in started at 8 a.m., and I certainly didn't want to do that for forty years.)

Unfortunately, that solution will not work out for most of you. New dual parishes are cropping up every year. I suspect that trend will continue as people move out of the rural areas to the urban centers. More and more churches are going to have to band together in order to survive. And more and more churches are going to have conflicting worship schedules. There are various ways this can work out. One solution that a local dual parish used was to simply switch church times annually. Starting in August, one church would have the early service and the other the late service. Every year, they would reverse those times. It seemed confusing to me. How do you notify the general community when your services change? What work is involved in altering bulletins, signage, and stationery? How many times did the pastor show up at the wrong church on the first Sunday in August? How many congregational members showed up at the wrong church the first Sunday in August? But it worked for them. Indeed, it became their established tradition.

As I said, in my own parishes, there was no conflict as far as Sunday worship was concerned, but there was the issue of midweek services. Our compromise was to simply alternate between both congregations. During Advent and Lent, we would alternate locations. The first

Wednesday at New Athens, the next at Darmstadt. Then, in Holy Week, one church would host Maundy Thursday and the other Good Friday. The next year, we would simply reverse that order. Admittedly, it was easy for us because our churches were only nine miles apart, so members could easily attend either congregation. Your congregations might not be as willing to give up a service, so other compromises might have to be made. For instance, you might alternate between an afternoon and evening service. Eventually, as our churches grew older and some of our senior members were reluctant to come out at night, we began offering an afternoon Good Friday service. We then alternated annually who sponsored the afternoon and evening worship.

It's interesting that the one worship occasion we didn't alternate was Christmas Eve. When I arrived, the tradition was established that Darmstadt had the earlier service and New Athens the later. I believe this tradition developed because Darmstadt never had much in the way of Sunday School whereas New Athens did. I don't know how many readers can remember that it used to be the tradition in many of our churches that Christmas Eve was also the big Sunday School program. It made sense for New Athens to have the later service so that families would have time to eat supper, get the kids dressed, and head out to one of the biggest services of the church year. But here is where I make my confession. As time went on, traditions began to change. More and more families left town over Christmas to visit their families. The Sunday School program got moved to the Sunday before Christmas. More and more people were wanting an earlier Christmas Eve service so they could worship and then join their families at home. And yet the tradition of our churches remained the same—Darmstadt early, New Athens late. I realize now that we probably should have reconsidered those Christmas Eve practices. In light of how our culture has changed in its attitude toward Christmas Eve worship, it might have been more loving for the churches to alternate worship times just like they did other holy days. However, the problem of long-standing traditions is they foster another doubtful administrative precept—if it ain't broke, don't fix it. I must admit that has been my operating principle for many years, but in retirement, I realize it probably wasn't the best practice. On the other hand, I'm not suggesting that we go out looking for more challenges. Lord knows plenty of challenges will come to you without your looking for them. But love may call us to change things, even if the change brings with it more challenges.

In all of this, you can see the importance of remembering the "substance belongs to Christ." If worship for us is all about the time we traditionally get together, then merging dual parishes are headed for conflict. But if we understand that worship is about people receiving the Word and Sacraments, that this Word and Sacrament literally changes people's lives, that it gives them the faith to make it through a world fraught with challenges—more than that, it provides them with an eternal dwelling place in their Father's house, that Word and Sacrament is literally the most important thing that happens in a person's life, then our concern won't be about what suits us, but what we can do so that more people will hear the good news of Jesus' forgiveness. Worship times need to be an issue of faith and love, not what works out best for us.

Speaking of worship, let's consider another possible challenge in dual parishes—worship styles. There was a time in our Synod when this wouldn't have been an issue at all. Pretty much every church followed pages 5 and 15 in *The Lutheran Hymnal.* Not to say we wouldn't have some special services now and then. There was LWML Sunday, Youth Sunday, Evangelism Sunday, Visitor Sunday, and Mission Sunday—all of which might have their own orders. But we all knew that eventually we'd return to good old *TLH.* Not so anymore. Now we have three different hymnals, plus a couple of supplements, that congregations may use. An even greater challenge is one of the churches might not be using a hymnal at all but some kind of contemporary service. How do you merge these differing worship traditions?

Maybe you don't merge them at all. Many large churches offer differing worship options: traditional liturgy, a blended service, and maybe even a full-blown contemporary worship service. Why can't we do the same thing in a dual parish? Let each church do its own thing. And certainly, that's one approach, especially if you apply my operating principle, "If it ain't broke, don't fix it." The question is, however, is this the loving thing to do? Especially in terms of the pastor, who will have to prepare two totally different worship services in addition to remembering which service he's supposed to do where. The question of what is loving not only concerns the two congregations but the pastor as well. I think it is important for churches to ask how their traditions impact their pastor. Large churches have a large staff, often two pastors and a full-time secretary or secretaries. Dual churches usually have no staff, one pastor, and are blessed if they have a part-time secretary. Is it fair to ask a pastor to have the responsibility of two congregations, plus the added work of preparing two completely different worship services? The answer to that question will probably be determined by the pastor. I know many pastors will simply do the extra work, thinking it's easier than trying to change things. My point here is that I think it's all right for a pastor to consider his own needs. I think it's all right for a pastor to ask his churches to change traditions if it will make his work easier. I think it's all right for a pastor to ask his congregations to do things that are loving toward him. Certainly, having a unified service is one of the most loving things a church can do.

Of course, broaching this subject goes back to what we've been saying all along. As with all challenges, it cannot be accomplished by the Law but by faith and love. Oh, you can demand these things, and, depending on your stubbornness (and the stubbornness of your people), you may get your way. But the results will never be God-pleasing. It never pleases God when people do good because they feel it's what they have to do. The truly God-pleasing work is that which is done willingly, people loving because Christ has loved them. As always, it is a matter of speaking the word of forgiveness and waiting for it to bear fruit. I'm simply saying it is no sin for a pastor to share his needs with his congregations, remembering what the Lord says: "You do not have, because you do not ask" (James 4:2).

One other challenge dual parishes have to wrestle with that other congregations don't is how to divide the pastor's salary. The amount to pay shouldn't be an issue. I suspect all districts have some sort of salary guidelines based on the pastor's education and years of experience. Most churches at least acknowledge them and strive toward them, even if it's only a certain percentage. With one church, it's just a matter of deciding how much to pay (hopefully somewhere else in this book you'll find advice on the challenge of raising that money). But how do two churches decide what to pay? And the even greater challenge is how do they divide up that amount?

The best way would be for them to have a joint financial committee that could analyze income and compare the budgets and needs of both parishes. Then they could come up with a fair division of financial responsibilities between the two congregations. No doubt that would be the best way, but I must admit it was never the way used by my two congregations. Other than the original call document (which I assume had to have some joint committee), everything they did salarywise was done independently of each other. Furthermore, they both used totally different methods to determine that figure. The larger church would figure the percentage increase from the district guidelines and use that percentage to determine my raise. The smaller parish would simply increase my salary by a specific dollar amount. It usually was always the same amount (although sometimes it might be higher if the farmers had a particularly good year). As a result, the only person who really knew my total salary was the treasurer of the large congregation, who had to file the forms for our synodical insurance and retirement.

You would think they would worry that with such an arrangement, I might be getting paid way beyond district scale, but it never seemed to be a concern to them. They both were just doing what they felt was loving. Of course, maybe they weren't concerned because they knew I wasn't being paid way beyond district scale. Whatever their thoughts, this method worked for them, and they provided well for me. My point, again, is that there may seem to be a best way for doing things. That way may seem to have the support of logic and reason. And there is certainly nothing wrong with using reason and logic. But remember there are usually several ways for doing things. As long as the method reflects faith and love, isn't that the best way? And the best way to bring that result is by keeping the focus on the Gospel of Jesus' love for us.

4. Unresolved Challenges

I'm concerned at this point you may be thinking, "Oh, yes, all you have to do is preach the Gospel, and everyone will live happily ever after." We all know that's not true. The problem is you are called to a congregation of saints but also sinners. They (and you) have not yet been perfected. As Paul says in Philippians 3:12, "Not that I have already obtained this or am already perfect, but I press on to make it my own, because Christ Jesus has made me His own." I want to make sure you understand I am not offering you a methodology that will guarantee you success against all odds. I have already told you the story about Terry. I could also tell you the story of Lucille, who always wanted to serve in the Sunday School, but unfortunately, she had no idea how to work with children. Or Mirabel, who thought every time the pastor left for vacation, the church should plan a surprise party for him when he came back. It only took a couple of years before both congregation and pastor were tired of surprises, but the challenge was how to explain that to dear Mirabel.

There are two points I want to make here. The first is that most challenges in dual parishes are not about issues but people. People are not problems to be solved, as much as you'd like to solve them. There was Fred, who always had some sort of leadership position in the church. He did so because he was always the first to volunteer. The problem with Fred was he had a way of rubbing people the wrong way. Heck, he had a way of rubbing his pastor the wrong way. It was only later I discovered Fred had always wanted to be a pastor, but his family's financial situation had kept him out of school. Now he was determined to be the pastor in charge despite the frustration of both congregation members and the actual pastor. Similar people show up in all churches. With a dual parish, you have twice the chances of encountering a Fred. In reflection, I had many Freds of various shapes and sizes, of both genders, in my forty years of ministry. The one thing I can assure you is that you cannot solve a Fred; you can only learn to tolerate, forgive, and love a Fred (with a great emphasis on tolerate). Indeed, the only one who can solve a Fred is

Jesus Himself. Even for Jesus, maybe the only way He can "solve" Fred is by taking him home to the place prepared for him in His Father's mansions.

That is the important thing to remember about the Freds of your world. God loves them dearly. He has one chief desire for them, which is that they be saved. To paraphrase C. S. Lewis from his essay "The Trouble with X," it is probably also good to remember God has one more additional Fred that He tolerates, loves, and forgives. And that is you (and me as well, so technically it's two more Freds). We have frustrated and exasperated people as well. Particularly, we frustrate the God who asks us to daily live in faith and love. And yet, as with all Freds, Jesus loves us and desires that we all join Him in those mansions.

This brings me to my second point about unresolved challenges, whether they be caused by people or issues. Maybe they're supposed to be unresolved. Maybe God sent these challenges to accomplish a greater purpose than just that we would overcome them. Challenges are our greatest opportunity to be strengthened in faith. Let's face it, when everything is going fine, we have little need for faith. We used to have seminary students serving at our churches. When discussing sermon prep, I would tell them sometimes sermons come easily, like falling off a log. Sometimes that's the case week after week, every message seeming to flow without labor. At this point, you begin to think it's because you're such a good preacher. How bright you are to see all of these pertinent insights in Scripture. Then, of course, preaching becomes incredibly difficult. Maybe because God gives you some scriptural nut that's hard to crack. Or maybe your schedule becomes filled with hospital calls and funerals, so you don't have that essential sermon prep time. In all of these challenges, God is reminding you that the effective preaching of the Gospel is not dependent on your skills but upon His Holy Spirit, who works faith when and where it pleases Him. Indeed, that is another challenge that He might place in your life. Your preaching actually goes well, but you don't see any fruit of your preaching. All of this is God using challenges so that you might have faith in Him and not in yourself.

At the beginning of the Reformation, Luther found that many of the parishes in his area were in sad shape. Visitors were sent out to the region of Saxony to shore up the teaching throughout the church. These visitor articles included the following teaching:

> To the third part of Christian life, that is, the doing of good works, belongs also the knowledge of how one shall meet tribulation.
>
> First, we are to teach the people that all tribulation, not only of the spirit, but also of the body, is sent from God, whether it is poverty or illness, danger to children, peril of possessions, or hunger. God would thereby admonish us and awaken us to penitence. As we read in I Cor. 11 [:32]: "But when we are judged by the Lord, we are chastened so that we may not be condemned along with the world."
>
> Now it is not enough to know that God sends such experiences. We must also teach that in the midst of these tribulations we are to call upon Him and confidently believe that He will help, as we have explained above in regard to prayer. So God says in Psalm 49 [Ps. 50:15]: "Call upon me in the day of trouble; I will deliver you, and you shall glorify me." (AE 40:287)

Maybe your challenge isn't meant to be solved. Maybe it is intended to draw you to faith and prayer.

Not only do challenges bring us opportunity for faith but also for love. There is a movement in our day that emphasizes "random acts of kindness." Now I have nothing against kindness. No doubt, kindness is something our world could use a lot more of. But you mustn't confuse kindness with what Jesus calls the "greater love" (John 15:13). The greater love always involves sacrifice. This is the kind of love that flows out of challenges. Challenges call for us to be more than nice to people. Challenges call us to sacrifice our time, our resources, and even our own selves. This challenge of the "greater love" not only impacts us but God as well.

Consider that in the first chapter of Genesis, according to the Hebrew, it is Elohim who is at work. The Jewish rabbis will tell you the sense of the name *Elohim* is "the God of absolute power." No doubt the God of Genesis 1, the God called Elohim, is a God of greater love. The next time you read Genesis 1, note how everything Elohim does is with people (you and me) in mind. Have you ever noticed that after God calls the light good, it's not until day three that Scripture declares that emphatic phrase, "And God saw that it was good"? Why does He wait until day three? Because up to that point, there is no place for man to dwell. There is nothing but light and dark, heaven and water. It is only in day three that there is land for man to live and prosper upon. And God saw that it was good *for us.*

And yet, Adam and Eve in the garden, where all had been provided for them, did not yet know the "greater love" of God. It was a great place to be, a land where your every need was taken care of, from food to companionship. Still, there was no sacrifice required of Elohim in providing these things. All He had to do was speak the word and all these things came into being. The same is true of Jesus. Remember how the disciples thought it was such a great challenge when Jesus was surrounded by five thousand hungry men (and who knows how many hungry women and crying children)? "Jesus said to Philip, 'Where are we to buy bread, so that these people may eat?' Philip answered Him, 'Two hundred denarii worth of bread would not be enough for each of them to get a little'" (John 6: 5, 7). Likewise, Andrew chimed in, "There is a boy here who has five barley loaves and two fish, but what are they for so many?" (John 6:9). To them, feeding such a crowd was an insurmountable challenge. Yet Jesus fed all of them and still had baskets of fragments left over. But then again, this required no sacrifice on Jesus' part. As God, He daily feeds millions of people, not even counting the creatures to whom He gives their food in due season. Feeding five thousand is no big deal for the One who does "satisfy the desire of every living thing" (Psalm 145:16). Jesus did this and all of His miracles in love, just as Elohim had created the world in love. Yet in all of this, we did not yet know His "greater love." Why? Because in none of these things was there any real sacrifice involved; there was no real challenge.

We all know the story of the rich child who has everything. His father has given him the finest of designer clothing, a luxurious house with a swimming pool, the best of foods, and a Maserati convertible to boot.

And yet he whines, "My father doesn't love me." We would judge him as ungrateful, and we would be right. And yet the son has a point. None of these gifts necessarily means the father loves the son, for none of these gifts involve sacrifice for a rich father. Perhaps God intentionally allowed Adam and Eve to fall into sin so He could show them the "greater love" He has for them. In order for Elohim, the God of absolute power, to show His greater love, He must become the weakest of all creatures. He must experience hunger and loneliness. He must sweat blood and pray, "Father . . . remove this cup from Me" (Luke 22:42). He must cry out, "My God, My God, why have You forsaken Me?" (Matthew 27:46). Only in the sacrifice of the cross can we know the breadth, length, height, and depth of the love of Christ. Only when a man lays down his life for us can we know His "greater love" for us. We cannot know God's love completely as Elohim. We can only know the completeness of God's love in Jesus.

We are quick to recite the passage, "Walk in love, as Christ loved us" (Ephesians 5:2). But let us never forget the weight of these words. Let us never forget the sacrifice that was involved in Christ loving us. Let us never forget the sacrifice that will be required of our love. This is precisely what challenges bring to our lives. Challenges do not ask us just to be nice to people. Challenges call for us to love people sacrificially with that "greater love" of Christ.

But I do not want to simply bring us back to the Law. I do not want to depart from the Gospel and present love as if it is some requirement we have to fulfill. Let me remind you this sacrificial love we are speaking about (as well as faith itself) is not something we can do by our own reason and strength. Unexpected challenges do a particularly good job of reminding us of this. When we anticipate the challenge, we can ready ourselves and set our minds on doing the right thing. In unexpected challenges, we are forced to confront the reluctance in our own flesh. To wrestle with the words of Jesus, "Father, if You are willing, remove this cup from Me. Nevertheless, not My will, but Yours be done" (Luke 22:42). Certainly, there is not a sacrificial bone in my body. When the emergency call came at two in the morning, I did not wake up thinking, "Now's my chance to strengthen someone's faith; now is my chance to show sacrificial love."

Rather, my thought was, "What now!?" But as God's people, we do get up, we do use God's Word to strengthen people's faith, we do make sacrifices and do so, in a sense, despite ourselves. In unexpected challenges, God puts us in a place where we have no choice but to love with sacrifice. And you respond to those challenges not out of your own will but out of the faith that knows the greater love of Christ.

Handling the challenges of dual-parish ministry is not so different than handling the challenges of a sole parish, except since you have two churches, you have twice the chances for challenges to arise. Actually, it would be three times the chances, for you not only have the challenges of two parishes but the additional challenge of getting both parishes to work together. In every challenge, it's not always a matter of finding the best solution. It is a matter of finding a solution that reflects faith and love. In fact, maybe it's not a matter of finding a solution at all. Maybe the challenge is God's gift that will strengthen your faith and give you opportunity to show the greater love of Jesus.

CHAPTER 3

THE PASTOR AND SCHOOL MINISTRY

Rev. Robert Riggert

Fresh out of seminary, Jeff is excited about his call to Redeemer Lutheran Church and School. Even though he had not attended a Lutheran school as a child, his fieldwork experience in a Lutheran school was positive, and many of his seminary peers shared their faith formation in a Lutheran school. Jeff and fellow pastors privileged to serve in Lutheran school ministries celebrate the joys and opportunities of Lutheran early childhood centers, elementary schools, and high schools. In Lutheran schools,

- → Children and staff gather daily around God's Word. Faculty begin the day together as they are refreshed in Bible study and bonded in prayer, sharing joys and concerns. They worship together at the weekly chapel service, and the weekend Divine Service is emphasized. Each school day, children open the Scriptures.
- → Relationships with children, parents, staff, grandparents, and other partners are deep and rich. School shepherds interact with children in the hallway, greet parents on the parking lot, meet extended family at school programs, and strengthen partnerships with teachers in casual classroom conversations.

→ Opportunities for outreach to the community are numerous and natural. The "mission field" arrives onto the parking lot and walks into the building. Many Lutheran schools enroll children and families who are not members or part of the worshiping fellowship of the hosting congregation. Some are unchurched. There are numerous entrances from the school setting to the sanctuary setting. Through the Spirit's direction, ministry to a hospitalized child or a parent in crisis can lead to the sacramental ministry of the church.

→ The presence of children, whether they are three-year-olds or teens, brings joy and energy. While many church settings are relatively quiet during the week, the Lutheran school is an active ministry. Members love seeing children. The Lutheran school can ignite other opportunities for Bible study, prayer, and fellowship.

Veterans of Lutheran school ministries have seen the Spirit work as the Means of Grace are shared daily and richly in classrooms, hallways, gymnasiums, playgrounds, and especially the church sanctuary. Lutheran schools become Jesus' voice and arms to children.

> "Let the children come to Me; do not hinder them, for to such belongs the kingdom of God. Truly, I say to you, whoever does not receive the kingdom of God like a child shall not enter it." And He took them in His arms and blessed them, laying His hands on them. (Mark 10:14–16)

However, Lutheran school ministry takes place among sinners—sinful pastors, principals, teachers, children, parents, church members, and community patrons. Lutheran school ministry takes place in a sinful world where human theories are proposed as truth and trends erode historical confessions. Because the soil of a Lutheran school is so rich, Satan sows temptations generously. The devil, the world, and our sinful human natures interact to bring challenges that regularly distract and sometimes even destroy ministries.

GOD'S GUIDANCE IN ALL CHALLENGES

St. Paul directs the church of Ephesus to be well-armed for challenges. The concluding words of the admonition are especially applicable, "Take . . . the sword of the Spirit, which is the word of God, praying at all times in the Spirit, with all prayer and supplication" (Ephesians 6:17–18).

This chapter describes seven different challenges. The challenges presented are not the only challenges that the school shepherd will encounter. The challenges in each ministry setting are different. Different times bring different challenges. God's guidance is applicable to all times and places.

CONNECTED TO GOD'S WORD

God's Word proclaims His grace to His Church and guides His people in all contexts and vocations. School shepherds study the Word to preach and teach the Word. School shepherds personally receive the Good News for themselves and are then guided by the Word to lead the celebrations in the Lutheran schools. The Word also brings the Spirit's direction to challenges. God's Word is studied individually, as a church-school staff, in boards and small groups, and in school assemblies.

PRAY PERSISTENTLY

One's own knowledge and experience are always inadequate. In prayer, we humbly seek God's direction in all challenges. Prayers for the school ministry are part of the routine of the Prayers of the Church in the Divine Service. Prayers are part of every meeting. Prayers are offered for and with individuals. God is brought into every challenge through prayer. Prayers of thanksgiving are offered when resolutions take place.

In addition to God's guidance, seek the guidance of trusted individuals, ministry partners, associate pastors, school administrators, and appropriate board members.

Challenges are not the sole personal responsibility of the pastor. The challenges belong to school ministry partners. Unless they involve confidential matters, they should be shared quickly and frequently with ministry partners—"I want you to know what's happening." While the process is often confidential, the conversations among the ministry partners are open and honest.

MINISTRY PEERS:

Others in similar ministries, circuit visitor, confidants

Through seminary connections (professionals and students) and through ministry experiences, the pastor develops relationships that are varied and trustworthy. Ministry peers may have had similar experiences that they can share. The network can bring honest evaluation and direction.

MINISTRY PROFESSIONALS:

District staff, Christian counselors

When a pastor begins ministry in the church-school setting, it is important to be acquainted with the professional support system. What support staff does the district office have to enrich Lutheran school ministry? Does the district or region have a Lutheran counseling service to support church and school ministry workers professionally and spiritually? Are there other resources in the area that offer assistance consistent with the Christian values of the local ministry?

CHALLENGE: TEAM MINISTRY

Pastor Smith and Principal Jones interacted regularly in staff devotions, board meetings, and in casual conversations during the routines of the week. Each got busy in his own ministry area, and communication became less frequent. Pastor Smith sensed some distance between himself and the principal. After a stressful week and in response to a board discussion in which Pastor Smith expressed a strong personal preference, Principal Jones responded to Pastor Smith, "You do your ministry, and I'll do mine."

Whose ministry is the Lutheran school? How do pastor, principal, and teachers serve together?

Two-year-olds playing together often get possessive with their toys. ("That's mine!") Unfortunately, as adults, the conversations get more intense, and our claims of ownership get more vocal.

Ministry of the Lutheran school is solely under the ownership of Jesus. Jesus' suffering and death bought our salvation. We have been bought with the price of His own blood. We stand together under His cross. We seek to serve and glorify Him together.

RESPONSES:

- → Center ministry on the Word and Sacraments. This certainly includes gathering in the Divine Service. It also includes regular Bible study for the leadership and staff. The divisions that Satan would sow and encourage are uprooted when God unites His people around the Word and Sacraments.
- → Acknowledge the Office of the Holy Ministry. The Commissioning and Installation of a Lutheran School Teacher (*LSB Agenda*, p. 210) notes, "This office has been established in love by the Church to support the Office of the Holy Ministry." The Lutheran Confessions affirm and celebrate the office of the pastor. It is important for ministry partners to respect the office in the local setting. At the same time, the Rite of Ordination (pp. 160–69) includes God's Word in 1 Peter 5:2–3, "Shepherd the flock of God that is among you, exercising oversight, . . . not domineering over those in your charge, but being examples to the flock." The Lutheran school pastor is a school shepherd who gently and lovingly shepherds the flock, including those with whom he works closely.
- → Affirm the gifts of others. We have the same Spirit but different gifts. Our gifts are not in competition but are meant to support the ministry and complement the gifts of others. Staff should humbly acknowledge their own spiritual gifts and celebrate the gifts of others. The pastor may have gifts for viewing the big picture while the principal may have gifts for describing details, and the blended gifts bless the ministry.

→ Develop realistic and meaningful ministry position descriptions. It is important to specifically define the responsibilities of the pastor, principal, teacher, and others. While there is always fluidity in those roles, those descriptions provide accountability. The district president or his staff typically have resources on the process of developing position descriptions and sample descriptions.

→ Communicate regularly. It is important to set specific dialogue times. For example, "Let's meet every Thursday morning at 7:30." While emergencies sometimes change the plan, the set schedule makes the meeting more likely. Casual connections in the routine of the week are also important: "How's your day going?" "What do I need to pray for today?"

→ Develop systems of accountability and support. These systems would generally flow out of position descriptions. The size and complexity of the ministry will determine the system of accountability. For example, the pastor is accountable to the board of elders, the principal is accountable to the pastor and school board, the teachers are accountable to the principal, and so on.

→ Develop a team ministry covenant. While the covenant is staff generated, an outside consultant best facilitates the process. The covenant includes pastor(s), principal, teachers, preschool staff, secretary, custodian, cafeteria workers, aides, and anyone else on the paid staff. The covenant is reviewed and revised whenever a staff person leaves and a new staff member arrives. Texts such as Matthew 18:15–22 and Colossians 3:12–17 provide a biblical foundation for the covenant. Everyone receives a copy of the covenant. The document is framed and visually displayed.

→ Seek conflict intervention early. Intervention may be as simple as, "Can we find a time to talk?" It may be the pastor and principal inviting a teacher into a conversation in the office. It may be a call to the district office inviting the school ministry executive assistant into a conversation. Whatever the type of "intervention," it is best to be proactive rather than having tensions and mistrust build.

GUIDANCE FROM GOD'S WORD:

> And He gave the apostles, the prophets, the evangelists, the shepherds and teachers, to equip the saints for the work of ministry, for building up the body of Christ. (Ephesians 4:11–12)

REFLECTIONS:

1. How does the local ministry team build up one another?
2. Do staff members, school families, congregation members, and other ministry partners and observers see a "team ministry" in your setting?
3. Do your church and school have position descriptions? Are they realistic? Are they reviewed periodically?
4. What gifts do you bring to the local ministry setting? How do you affirm the gifts of others?

CHALLENGE: ONE MINISTRY

The agenda at the Bethlehem Lutheran Church council meeting was varied and long. The trustees shared school building maintenance issues that needed to be addressed quickly and were expensive; the school board chairperson discussed the staffing needs for the coming school year; the board of elders representative shared concerns about the pastor's workload and burnout prevention. As the meeting dragged on and on, it seemed like many of the issues and concerns had a connection to Bethlehem Lutheran School. A frustrated board member responded, "If it wouldn't be for 'that' school, these meetings wouldn't run so long."

"That" reflection denies personal responsibility and distances participants from the reality of the challenge. "That" neighbor of mine, "that" supervisor at work, and so forth. "That" comments are effectively addressed with "our." It's "our" concern. It's "our" church and "our" school.

Imagine a large circle representing the entire ministry of the local congregation. Other smaller circles represent areas or types of ministry. There may be a circle for mission support, another circle for youth ministry, care ministry, and so on. The ministry of the Lutheran school is another circle. Due to its history, numbers, and finances, it may be a rather large circle. Is the school circle outside the large circle of the local ministry? Does the school ministry touch the large circle? Does it intersect the circle at some point? Lutheran school ministry is most effective when the school circle is inside the church circle. The ministry of the Lutheran school is not in competition with the congregation. It is part of the total ministry of the congregation.

RESPONSES:

- → Gather around God's Word to reflect on the purpose of His Church. Lutheran schools live out the Great Commission (Matthew 28:19–20) as children and their families are baptized in the name of the triune God. The Lutheran school is an instrument of "teaching them to observe all that I have commanded you." Lutheran schools make disciples and bring nations to the cross.
- → Review the history of your church and school ministry. Many Lutheran schools have a long and deep history of bringing generations to the cross. Reviewing the history brings to remembrance the original vision for the ministry and recounts God's blessings. Forgetting the history can lead to forgetting the mission.
- → Define the core values of the congregation and school. Core values ask, "What's important here?" Sharing and living in God's grace is important. More trivial concerns or distractions are distanced by remaining true to core values.
- → Prepare and share the mission statement. It's important to review why we are here. A clear mission statement builds on

the Great Commission and describes how that Commission is practiced in the local ministry setting.

- → Develop a vision for the ministry. While the past is foundational, and the present typically consumes the day-to-day attention, future goals are energizing. The vision assures that future generations will be blessed by the ministry of the Lutheran schools. While the mission of the church and school is constant, the vision may be reviewed and revised as opportunities and resources change.
- → Educate the members on the blessings and opportunities of a school ministry. "Out of sight, out of mind" is also true of many aspects of the Lutheran school ministry. Pastors, school principals, and others should often and creatively inform the local supporting congregation(s) of Lutheran school outreach (Baptisms, adult confirmations, etc.). Congregation members should be invited to school chapel services and other worship assemblies. Elderly members would be thrilled to be included in activities with children.
- → Emphasize to staff and parents the importance of worshiping and serving in the supporting congregations. Worship together is the primary activity of the church. Staff and parents are not only part of a school; they are part of a church! Congregation members should know and pray for their teachers. School families should thank those who generously support the ministry in which their children are blessed.
- → Gather stories of the blessings of the Lutheran schools. The Spirit works in and through the Lutheran school as children, families, and staff gather around God's Word. While the greatest story is the story of Jesus' love, there are personal and powerful stories of little children learning about Jesus and being welcomed to His family. There are stories where lives continue to be impacted by the Good News of forgiveness and new life in Jesus. With praise and thanksgiving, those stories strengthen and unite the ministry.

GUIDANCE FROM GOD'S WORD:

> There is one body and one Spirit—just as you were called to the one hope that belongs to your call—one Lord, one faith, one baptism, one God and Father of all, who is over all and through all and in all. (Ephesians 4:4–6)

REFLECTIONS:

1. How is "one ministry" evident in your setting? How could that unity be strengthened?
2. Review the history of your church and school ministry. What have been the strengths through the years? What have been the distractions, and how have they been overcome?
3. How is the Lutheran school ministry a blessing to your church and community?
4. How are the stories of your Lutheran school being told (pulpit, social media, parents, and grandparents)?
5. Has a vision statement been discovered, written, shared, or revised? Who has the local responsibility for communicating and carrying out the vision?

CHALLENGE: HEALTHY MINISTRY

Amy, the first-grade teacher, stopped by the pastor's study at the conclusion of the school day. "I wanted you to know, Pastor Smith, that my husband and I have separated, and we are planning to file for divorce."

Sometimes the conversations are brought to the pastor's study by those affected and afflicted. Other times the conversations come indirectly by those concerned about their peers, or sadly, by those wishing to continue the hurts through gossip. Fellow staff members or parents face substance abuse issues. Lutheran school professionals and families experience mental health struggles. Relationships (marriage, friendships, professional) are strained or even fractured. Families face the reality of cancer and other diseases. They mourn the death of loved ones. Teachers are stressed in their concern for their own children or parents.

Personal and professional health is a prerequisite to healthy ministries. Sometimes individuals are blessed to self-determine, "I'm not healthy." Other times, the observations and subsequent interventions of pastor and peers reveal the need to take steps to gain and maintain physical, emotional, social, and spiritual health. Interventions are difficult because they may test relationships. Interventions are necessary for the sake of the personal health of individuals and for the health of the ministry.

RESPONSES:

- → As pastor, you are, first of all, the shepherd of the flock. You are the spiritual leader sharing Law and Gospel. The pastor brings the truth and love of Jesus and a compassionate presence to the situation. He is not the physician, counselor, or mediator. It is important to stay within the boundaries and privileges of the pastoral office.
- → Listen attentively. Everyone brings their own perspectives and even prejudices to situations. You may assume that you know the individual and the details of the challenge; however, it is important to take the time to listen to the dynamics of a situation and the hurts and needs of those affected.
- → Address the situations with both Law and Gospel. Pastors are ministers of the Gospel. Pastors are also students of C. F. W. Walther's *Law and Gospel*. It is one thing to be a student of doctrine and another thing to be a practitioner. Trust the Spirit to determine when to share the Law and when to share the Gospel.
- → Stay personally healthy! Ministry is often physically, emotionally, and spiritually exhausting. It is difficult to tend to an unhealthy marriage of a ministry peer if one's own marriage

is troubled. It is difficult to remain calm and objective when struggling with one's own emotional issues. Pastors should never be too proud to admit they need counseling or other professional support. The support of ministry peers, associations with friends, vacations with family, and regular physical exercise are elements important to maintaining personal health.

→ Avoid the invitation and temptation to immediately choose sides. One teacher comes to the pastor complaining about another teacher. A parent expresses frustrations with the principal. We need to be on the alert for people sinfully seeking to manipulate others to their side. It's easy in a conversation or situation to take the side of the person we are listening to or that we are sympathetic to. Bring everyone to seek the truth and to seek God's will.

→ Protect the ministry. The individual situations and needs of the teachers and other professionals must always be addressed compassionately. Personality disorders, significant mental health diagnoses, substance abuse, and other emotional health factors may compromise effective ministry. For the safety of the children, the health of the worker, or the reputation of the church and school, a fellow worker may be counseled to take a leave of absence or even resign from the ministry. Those conversations and decisions are made with the direction of the district president or other assistants.

→ Explore the resources of Concordia Plans. We are blessed to be part of a church body that values the health of its workers. In addition to support for the physical health of workers, the plans provide support for personal and family counseling.

→ Develop a listing of resources of other Christian agencies. The pastor is the school shepherd, not the school or personal counselor. Most congregations and schools have contacts with Lutheran family and counseling agencies. The pastor's and principal's offices should have a file of professional organizations and contacts. Most communities have other Christian and reputable agencies to which the pastor and others can refer those in need. If possible, it is helpful to have professional conversations with agencies and counselors to assure that they support the Christian values of the church and school.

→ Welcome the assistance of the district president and his staff. *Synod* means "walking together." In the districts of The Lutheran Church—Missouri Synod are those who walk most personally with the pastor and others in school ministry. Districts provide support for Lutheran schools and preschools with full-time or part-time staff who themselves have experience in school ministry and who have a network of resources available. The pastor will want to be acquainted with the district president and his staff.

GUIDANCE FROM GOD'S WORD

> I praise you, for I am fearfully and wonderfully made. Wonderful are your works; my soul knows it very well. . . . Search me, O God, and know my heart! Try me and know my thoughts! And see if there be any grievous way in me, and lead me in the way everlasting! (Psalm 139:14, 23–24)

REFLECTIONS:

1. What actions and activities are supporting the personal health of the pastor and professional staff of the church and school?
2. Are the pastor and fellow professionals perceived as good listeners?
3. What individuals and agencies are part of your "help" listing?
4. How did Jesus, as true man, pursue personal well-being in His mission?

CHALLENGE: STAFFING THE MINISTRY

After forty years in the teaching ministry at St. John Lutheran School, veteran teacher Tom announces his retirement to the principal, pastor, and school board. Two conversations begin among the ministry leaders of St. John. One conversation focuses on a public affirmation and celebration of Tom's ministry.

The other conversation is seeking a replacement for Tom's teaching position. Should the school and congregation seek a candidate with a Lutheran Teacher Diploma? Should they seek an experienced candidate from another school ministry setting? Should they advertise and hire from the local congregation and community? School boards may favor a local candidate because of family or community connections or a negative experience with a previous called teacher.

Staffing the Lutheran school is more than just finding another teacher. Among the texts for the Commissioning and Installation of a Lutheran School Teacher (*LSB Agenda*, p. 211) are the words of Colossians 3:16–17. "Let the word of Christ dwell in you richly, . . . And whatever you do, in word or deed, do everything in the name of the Lord Jesus, giving thanks to God the Father through Him." The teaching staff and other ministry partners are faithful to God's Word and are fellow servants dedicated to sharing Jesus with children. They are positive representatives of the church and school to parents, supporters, and the community.

Ministry staffing is done prayerfully and intentionally. The pastor supports the principal, board, and others who assume the primary staffing responsibility.

RESPONSES:

→ Celebrate the teaching ministry. The roster of The Lutheran Church—Missouri Synod includes "Ministers of Religion—Commissioned." Established to support the Office of the Holy Ministry, those who hold a Lutheran Teacher Diploma or who have been admitted through the colloquy process are celebrated as ministry professionals. They are rightly called to their position. Pastors join congregation members, parents, and others in affirming their important ministry roles. Teachers are called or contracted to minister to children and families.

- → Preserve the Lutheran identity of the school. As ministries of local Lutheran congregations or ministries qualified as Recognized Service Organizations, Lutheran schools subscribe to the Lutheran Confessions. Staffing decisions are made not only to support but also to celebrate the confession of the Lutheran school. While state accrediting agencies may designate schools as "public," "private," or "parochial," our identity in the congregation and community is "Lutheran."
- → Call and contract staff consistent with the core values of the ministry. While over two thousand schools may identify as being Lutheran, each is unique in its history, setting, strengths, and so forth. It is important for a school to clarify who they are and to seek staff members who identify with the values of the school.
- → Support the Lutheran Teacher Diploma and the Synod's university system. Lutheran education goes beyond preschool, elementary, middle, and high school. The Lutheran Church—Missouri Synod is blessed with a university system and seminaries. Historically, the Lutheran teacher colleges focused primarily on preparing teachers to serve in Lutheran schools. Today, those universities graduate students for many Christian vocations. They prepare servants for various ministry careers (family ministry, youth ministry, music ministry). Students graduating with degrees in education (early childhood, elementary, high school) and with a Lutheran Teacher Diploma are ready to share their gifts in a Lutheran school setting. Explorations for filling teaching vacancies might begin with a graduate of one of the Lutheran universities.
- → Encourage the colloquy process. There are not enough Lutheran university graduates to fill all the positions in Lutheran schools. The particular skills needed for a position may not be available through the call process. Teachers who

have come through other education programs are encouraged to become commissioned ministers. Lutheran universities offer a series of courses of biblical study, knowledge of the Lutheran Confessions, Lutheran history, as well as the office of the Lutheran teacher. Valuing the Lutheran foundation for their school and the theological and professional enrichment of their teachers, many supporting congregations and associations encourage and financially support this process.

→ Have a clear job description. All ministry roles include the "by the way" informal and spontaneous expectations. Lutheran educators respond with servant hearts. However, it is important that position descriptions are concise and clearly communicated: "You are being called to teach third grade and direct the children's choir. Your duties begin on August 1 and conclude on June 15. You are expected to be professionally available to the children and parents" (and so on). The worship life of the professional is typically not contracted, but it should also be communicated. The Lutheran school professional continues to grow in Christ with fellow staff, school families, and the church family.

→ Develop a benefits package that honors the ministry and responsibly supports the individual. Districts typically have a suggested salary scale reflective of the economic contexts of the region. In addition, schools and congregations have a salary scale representative of education, years of experience, and responsibilities. It is vital that the benefits are fair and reflective of the importance of the ministry position.

→ Continue to recruit church workers from the local congregation. There are future ministers and teachers in Lutheran school classrooms. Historically, the Holy Spirit has used the Lutheran school to plant the seed for full-time ministry. Pastors and teachers model the joy of ministry, identify gifts for ministry, and thus begin to recruit those who will take future positions in Lutheran churches and schools.

→ Affirm the ministry of the Lutheran teacher so that quality professionals continue their service. Individuals leave Lutheran school ministry for a variety of personal and professional reasons. Some leave because the benefits are not adequate to support themselves or their family; some leave because of conflict or discouragement. It is important to celebrate the ministry and affirm church workers. Perhaps more important than material benefits are the words and deeds of affirmation: "We appreciate what you are doing." "Thanks for making a difference in the lives of children." "You are gifted for this ministry."

REDUCTION IN FORCE

For several years, Trinity Lutheran School has experienced a decline in enrollment. Reluctantly, the board determines that a teaching position needs to be eliminated before the next school year. There don't appear to be any teaching vacancies (retirements, calls to another setting, etc.) among the present staff. Who will be eliminated from the staff? What criteria will be used in making that decision? Who makes the final decision?

Adjustments in school staff (sometimes referred to as "Reduction in Force") are extremely difficult. They are painful for the staff member and for those who make the decision. Those decisions need to be made compassionately, professionally, objectively, and legally.

RESPONSES:

→ Have a Reduction in Force (RIF) policy in effect before this situation arises. Being proactive is always preferred to being reactive. It is important to make an objective rather than subjective decision. Criteria might include years of experience on the staff, professional and ministry credentials, and documented performance evaluations. The district staff may be able to provide models for policy development.

→ Act professionally and fairly in giving notice to the individual whose position will not be renewed. RIF decisions should be made months (hopefully at least a semester) before they go into effect. This allows time for those affected to seek other ministry positions and to consider personal and family transitions.

→ Offer transition benefits. Salary and benefits for several months should be offered to those workers who do not find professional employment. The length and scope of benefits may depend on the personal situations. Again, the district staff can provide models.

→ Respect the office of the Lutheran teacher. Commissioned Lutheran school teachers deserve special consideration in the process. The church respects the call of the commissioned minister. Not handling the process compassionately, respectfully, and professionally may lead to additional challenges involving an appeals process.

GUIDANCE FROM GOD'S WORD:

> Let the word of Christ dwell in you richly, teaching and admonishing one another in all wisdom, singing psalms and hymns and spiritual songs, with thankfulness in your hearts to God. And whatever you do, in word or deed, do everything in the name of the Lord Jesus, giving thanks to God the Father through Him. (Colossians 3:16–17)

REFLECTIONS:

1. How does your ministry setting celebrate the service and accomplishments of the ministry staff?
2. How is the importance of the Lutheran confession and Lutheran heritage demonstrated in staffing decisions and professional development?
3. Are staffing policies regularly reviewed and updated? Are all entities informed of school policies?

CHALLENGE: FUNDING THE MINISTRY

Budgets and balances seemed to dominate the school board and, subsequently, the church council discussions at Holy Cross Lutheran School. As the year's budget was being developed, the treasurer shared the realities: "It looks like we are going to end the year with a significant budget deficit. We have some hard decisions to make for next year." Church and school ministries struggle with funding challenges. Are we going to cut staff? Will we decrease programs or services? Do we increase tuition or conduct more fundraisers? Do we cease the ministry?

Financial discussions are challenging in all contexts: marriage, business, and Lutheran school ministry. How and when those discussions take place and the result of those discussions are critical to the health and future of the Lutheran school ministry.

Lutheran schools are priceless. However, the reality is that they have a price tag. Quality Lutheran schools demand quality staff, facilities, programs, and so forth. All of those areas demand adequate funding. In recent years, the LCMS School Ministry office (an entity of the National Mission department) has been very helpful in providing counsel to congregations exploring the start of a school ministry. An adequate financial plan is crucial to success.

Addressing funding challenges begins with facing realities. Some Lutheran schools minimize situations until they become a crisis. Ongoing budget deficits cannot be ignored. Reducing staff, combining classrooms, or other adjustments have to be considered. As with many challenges, honest evaluations and conversations precede actions.

Funding the school is only one of the aspects of Lutheran school management. Too much focus on the monetary aspects of the ministry can drain energy and distract from the mission of the school.

RESPONSES:

→ **Emphasize Lutheran school ministry as an eternal investment. Dollar signs can also receive too much attention and take away** from the importance of the ministry. Lutheran schools do more than provide a quality temporal education. As the Word of God is taught, as children and families are brought to the baptismal font, as families gather for worship, the kingdom of God grows and is strengthened. "Can we afford not to do this?" is an important question. Pastors, administrators, and boards can continue to tell the story of the Spirit's work in and through the Lutheran school. Those stories might be shared in worship announcements, church newsletters, social media, publicity pieces, and so on.

→ Be responsible and realistic stewards of the resources available. Wise stewards in families, businesses, civic entities, and so on have budgets and follow them. The budgeting process in a Lutheran school is important. Whoever develops the budget (administrator, business staff, board) should begin the process early and responsibly. The process should involve the participation of all who are affected by the budget and should be open to conversation. Clear and honest communication to those who give final approval (board, voters assembly) is important.

→ Teach stewardship to families enrolling children in the school and the congregation members who support the ministry. The vast majority of Lutheran schools receive tuition support from the families enrolling their children. If the school is supported by the local congregation, many of those families may also be members of the congregation. Stewardship education is important for all church members, including those families blessed by the school ministry. The tuition payment is not the church ministry donation. The mission and ministry of the congregation go well beyond the school to other ministry staff, maintenance of facilities, local and international mission activity, and more. The stewardship education extends to children in the school. All that they have is God's gift to them, and as stewards, they manage His resources.

→ Build relationships with donors. Progressive Lutheran school ministry is funded beyond tuition payments and congregation support. School ministry needs the additional support of donors. Donations may include a one-time gift from an individual or family. Ideally, it includes the annual gifts of many who realize the blessings and needs of the school. Donors may support an annual funding event. Donors may consider a gift in memory of a loved one or in thanksgiving for special blessings. Donor support depends upon clearly communicating the needs of the school and how the gifts will be a blessing to children. Donor support depends upon building and keeping relationships with donors. The presence and involvement of the pastor are very helpful in gaining donor support. Depending on the size of the school, donors may be contacted and affirmed by the administration, volunteers, or perhaps a staff person specializing in public relationships and donor engagement. Regular and genuine expressions of "thank you" are critical.

→ Look at the long-term needs and potential. "What would you do if funding were not an issue?" "If you received a substantial gift, how could it make a difference in the school ministry?" These questions are stimulating for Lutheran school pastors and leaders! Congregations and schools celebrate the Spirit of generosity. God's generous people also seek to invest in Lutheran schools. Schools develop their dream list and plant seeds for fulfillment. Increasingly, congregations and schools set up endowment funds and other avenues to receive and manage estate and other larger gifts. The Lutheran Foundation is one of the agencies that can be a helpful resource for congregations and schools.

GUIDANCE FROM GOD'S WORD:

He who supplies seed to the sower and bread for food will supply and multiply your seed for sowing and increase the harvest of your righteousness. You will be enriched in every way to be generous in every way, which through us will produce thanksgiving to God. (2 Corinthians 9:10–11)

REFLECTIONS:

1. How would you rate the financial health of your school ministry?
2. What stewardship education processes or programs engage the congregation, school families, and children? Explore the stewardship education resources of the district and Synod. Stewardship education should include time, talent, and treasure.
3. How are donors identified, contacted, encouraged, and thanked?
4. Does the school have an endowment fund or other means of encouraging, accepting, and managing gifts for long-term support?
5. Have the congregation and school enlisted the services of a planned giving counselor?

CHALLENGE: LEADING THE MINISTRY

Zion Lutheran School was conducting interviews for the role of school principal. When the interview committee invited questions from the candidate, he asked, "What is the vision for the school?" The candidate was curious about the board's desires to connect the school ministry to the community, update the facilities, or strengthen ministry to families.

The committee chairman hesitated in his response. While the school board had entertained an evaluation and planning process, it had never been completed. It seemed like the day-to-day and year-to-year routine of the school had demanded the attention of the school staff and board.

There are always immediate concerns that need the attention of the pastor, principal, board, and others. However, attention to only the immediate concerns leads to stagnation or worse. Professional staffing, first-rate facilities and programs, sustained funding, church/school partnerships, and other challenges can be avoided or lessened through effective long-term planning.

Pastors have different leadership gifts and skills. Not every pastor can or should be a visionary leader. The pastor is the spiritual leader of the Lutheran school. The pastor provides the Word and Sacrament foundation for the ministry. However, in many settings, the pastor influences the leadership of many ministry areas. Oftentimes, the pastor's most significant leadership task is identifying leaders who support the mission of the school and who can be trusted to carry out their roles effectively. The pastor asks the question and joins in developing the answer, "What is the vision for our Lutheran school?"

Leading the ministry also involves administering the wide variety of tasks in a Lutheran school—managing staff, developing and fulfilling curriculum, supervising children and activities, and so forth. In most cases, the pastor participates in finding, equipping, and encouraging those who take on the day-to-day administrative tasks. The pastor should not be a school micromanager.

RESPONSES:

- → Lead with the core values. The importance of this response was emphasized earlier.
- → Have clear and familiar mission and vision statements for the church and school. Leadership supports the mission and seeks to fulfill the vision. Leadership is purpose-driven. If the mission and vision statements are antiquated, unclear, or in other ways not familiar or engaging, encourage the staff, board, patrons, and other partners to engage in the process of writing (or rewriting) the mission and vision statements. Periodically review the vision statement and evaluate the progress in accomplishing the vision.
- → Equip the principal and other administrators for their leadership tasks. Trusting others to effectively carry out their responsibilities is important. Develop appropriate position

descriptions and have accountability systems for those positions.

→ Provide training for new board members and an annual orientation for the board. Lutheran school boards are tempted to micromanage the ministry. Sometimes parents who are board members focus on areas of interest to them or their children. Others may become board members focusing on one area of interest—finances, staffing, and so on. School boards focus on the big picture and developing and following school policies. The day-to-day aspects of school life are the responsibility of the administrators. Board members prayerfully and carefully choose administrators and support them in their endeavors. Board members need to be informed as to what is and isn't their responsibility. Board and school policies are regularly reviewed and consistently followed.

→ Evaluate the governance system: church and school ministry governance systems vary greatly. Some settings have very traditional school board and church council systems. Others have governance teams that oversee all ministry areas. No one system is right or wrong. Leaders ask, "Is the present system working? Is it serving the present and future needs of the ministry?" Decisions to change the governance system should be made with careful evaluation and planning. This should not be a short-term decision based on the preference of a single individual. While the school ministry is an important entity, the whole of the mission and ministry of the congregation must be considered.

→ Teach and live servant leadership. True leadership is not position leadership. When the mother of the sons of Zebedee requested honorable positions for her sons (Matthew 20:20–21), Jesus taught the disciples, "Whoever would be great among you must be your servant, and whoever would be first among you must be your slave, even as the Son of Man came not to be served but to serve, and to give His life as a ransom for many" (Matthew 20:26–28).

GUIDANCE FROM GOD'S WORD:

> **Of Issachar, men who had understanding of the times, to know what Israel ought to do.** (1 Chronicles 12:32)

(Following the death of King Saul, the tribe of Judah made David its king, while the other tribes at first followed Saul's son Ish-bosheth. But in time, God moved the leaders of those tribes, including Issachar, to give their loyalty to David.)

REFLECTIONS:

1. Is leadership a strength of the school ministry? What could be done to strengthen the leadership component?
2. How are board members chosen? Are they equipped for their important role?
3. Is your governance system effective and efficient?
4. Do the pastor and principal have leadership development plans? Does the budget reflect the importance of leadership development?
5. How are policies developed and reviewed?

CHALLENGE: MANAGING THE EMOTIONS OF THE MINISTRY

Pastor Jones casually glanced at the social media posts of the day. He was startled to read the post of a parent:

> Yesterday my child was inappropriately disciplined by the second-grade teacher at Trinity Lutheran School. Not only were my concerns not addressed by the teacher, but neither the principal nor the pastor has contacted me regarding the incident. This isn't the first time I've been ignored. I am

seriously considering enrolling my child in the local public school. Maybe other parents should do the same.

No parent is ever perfectly objective when it comes to the actions of his or her child. While parents should always seek a safe and effective education for their children, they sometimes do not have all the information or have false information about matters affecting their children. Parents who enroll their children in a Lutheran school have just as much investment in their children as parents in other school systems. Sometimes, because of their tuition payments or other "investments," they assume they have more influence in decisions regarding their children.

Quick access to social media forums becomes problematic. Opinions that typically should be shared privately in a school classroom or office are quickly open to debate in a public forum. The effect can be damaging to the reputation of the pastor or other staff and the ministry of the school.

Lutheran school pastors and educators have experienced more than social media assaults. They have been face-to-face with angry, and sometimes irrational, constituents who have threatened to hurt them or their family physically or to damage their reputations. While discipleship certainly involves "taking up the cross," ministry must be physically and emotionally safe for everyone, including pastors and staff.

RESPONSES:

- → **Always serve "above reproach" (1 Timothy 3:2). The pastoral office is held by sinful men who fail God and others. While the perceptions and prejudices of others cannot be avoided, the pastor and other ministry professionals should avoid situations that open the door to misperceptions and cause gossip.**
- → **Ensure that school policies and procedures protect the physical and emotional safety of all individuals connected with the school ministry. Never compromise the safety of children, staff, families, and visitors. Various state, church, and insurance entities are available to help develop policies. Policies on the use and abuse of social media should be included.**

- School and church facilities should adhere to all state and local standards of building security for the safety of children and staff. Tragedies in school settings have generated protective measures (surveillance cameras, locked buildings, access codes, etc.). School safety measures are sometimes challenging for the church and school settings as other ministry groups seeking access to the facility are inconvenienced. Conversations with ministry partners are important.
- Trust the Spirit and stay calm. Pastors find themselves in a variety of situations that can be stressful, inconvenient, and perhaps even frightening. Remembering God's presence and power through His Word and dialoguing with Him in prayer will often relay a sense of calm and control to others. The spiritual calm and control do not replace caution.
- Inform other trusted ministry partners of emotionally charged situations. Don't face aggressive or uncertain situations alone. Accusations, threats, and other strong emotional responses should be shared. The pastor might inform associate pastors, the principal, or an elder. The principal might inform the pastor, an administrative assistant, or board chairperson. If a situation gets escalated, others are informed of the dynamic and can provide immediate support.
- Protect your family. Families of professional church workers make many sacrifices. Professional church workers rightly want to protect their loved ones from some of the problems and pains of day-to-day ministry. Healthy marriages and family relations allow the worker to also share the trials and challenges. If a situation may affect the safety or the reputation of the family, it should be shared early and openly.
- If the situation has any legal implications, contact local authorities. Build relationships with local law enforcement and legal partners in a response to "what if" scenarios. Lutheran school leaders have faced situations when the local police force is involved or when legal counsel is needed. Names of those professional and protective partners should be on file so they can be readily accessed.

GUIDANCE FROM GOD'S WORD:

> Jesus said to them again, "Peace be with you. As the Father has sent Me, even so I am sending you." And when He had said this, He breathed on them and said to them, "Receive the Holy Spirit." (John 20:21–22)

REFLECTIONS:

1. Do you and others feel safe in your ministry setting? Do policies and procedures protect your professional and emotional safety?
2. Who would you turn to in an emotionally charged situation?
3. What helps you stay calm, focused, and compassionate in stressful situations?

SUMMARY CONSIDERATIONS:

The challenges of Lutheran school ministry go beyond those listed in this chapter. The responses given to the challenges are the result of real-life situations and actions to challenges. Other Lutheran school ministry veterans can offer additional responses. No listing will ever be complete, and no response will ever be perfect. Readers may not remember specific responses. However, pastors and other Lutheran school ministry partners are invited to remember four summations:

→ CHRIST

→ CHILDREN

→ CONTEXT

→ CLARIFICATION AND COMMUNICATION

CHRIST

> **Jesus Christ is the same yesterday and today and forever.**
> (Hebrews 13:8)

Lutheran schools are always experiencing change. There are changes in the curriculum, changes in school leadership, changes in pastoral staff, changes in facilities, and many more. Jesus Christ as Lord and Savior does not change. Jesus Christ as the means and message of salvation for children, staff, and families does not change.

Every challenge begins and ends with a focus on Jesus. When we fail to see and address challenges, we find forgiveness in Jesus. Broken relationships that lead to challenges and follow challenges find peace and restoration in Jesus. If Christ is not the focus of our Lutheran school and church ministry, challenges cannot be addressed in God-pleasing and God-glorifying ways.

The ministry of Ambassadors of Reconciliation derives some of its principles from Peacemaker Ministries. Peacemakers begins its response to conflict with "Glorify God." Rather than focusing on our own sinful desires to feed our egos or to maintain a position of power, a helpful response to conflicts and challenges is to ask, "How can I glorify God?" in this situation. In Christ, we celebrate that we are "justified by His grace as a gift, through the redemption that is in Christ Jesus" (Romans 3:24).

> **O God, our help in ages past, Our hope for years to come,**
> **Our shelter from the stormy blast, And our eternal home:**
> **Under the shadow of Thy throne Thy saints have dwelt secure;**
> **Sufficient is Thine arm alone, And our defense is sure.**
> (*LSB* 733:1, 2)

CHILDREN

Lutheran schools are for children of all ages (early childhood centers, elementary, secondary). While that statement seems obvious, it is sometimes forgotten. Challenges arise when the staff considers their priorities before those of children, when parents fail to seek what is best for their children, when elderly members want to return to their childhood rather than the present needs of children.

Jesus' defense of His children is strong and clear, "Whoever causes one of these little ones who believe in Me to sin, it would be better for him if a great millstone were hung around his neck and he were thrown into the sea" (Mark 9:42). Jesus welcomes children into His kingdom, and through the Church and its Lutheran schools, He still takes them in His arms and blesses them (Mark 10:13–16).

When physical and emotional challenges endanger children, they must be addressed. When challenges distract from bringing children to faith and nurturing them in that faith, they must be addressed. Appropriate questions to ask in all aspects of Lutheran school ministry are, "What's best for the children?" and "How will this decision affect children?"

> **Let children hear the mighty deeds**
> **Which God performed of old,**
> **Which in our younger days we saw,**
> **And which our parents told.**
>
> **O teach them with all diligence**
> **The truths of God's own Word,**
> **To place in Him their confidence**
> **To fear and trust their Lord.** (*LSB* 867:1, 4)

CONTEXT

The district president welcomed new pastors with the advice, "Learn their history before you write your own." Pastors were encouraged to learn the history of the congregation and school—when it was founded and by whom. What were some of the high points of the ministry? What were some of the challenges of the past, and how had they been addressed? Who were some of the pastors and principals? How long was their ministry tenure? Similarly, the history of the community was reviewed.

In addition to history, new (to ministry or a ministry setting) workers were encouraged to learn the culture of the congregation and community. Learning and appreciating the context of ministry is important. Demographics of a community (population, income, age levels, etc.) give a picture of who is being served.

Every church and school has its ministry context. Some challenges could be avoided or more easily addressed by an understanding of and appreciation for the context of the ministry. While leadership should never be stymied by "we've never done it that way before," understanding how and why something was done previously can be helpful.

Pastors and school ministry leaders not only learn the context of ministry, they also celebrate that context. God is at work in the places where He places us. In His grace, He gives us the privilege and responsibility of serving in His context.

A Lutheran school principal was retiring after forty years in the teaching ministry. He reflected on his time of serving and noted, "God gave me the privilege of doing what He could have sent angels to do." To serve in a Lutheran school ministry is a high and holy calling. We give thanks to God for the privilege of serving in the contexts to which He calls us.

> **You, O Lord, Yourself have called him For Your precious lambs to care;**
> **But to prosper in his calling, He the Spirit's gifts must share.**
> **Give him wisdom from above, Fill his heart with holy love;**
> **In his weakness, Lord, be near him, In his prayers, Good Shepherd, hear him.** (*LSB* 681:2)

CLARIFICATION AND COMMUNICATION

Surprise! Surprises are appropriate and fun for birthdays and anniversaries and other occasions. Children in an early childhood classroom love a surprise activity. Elementary children love a surprise field trip. Surprise situations or obligations are not fun in ministry. The pastor may be surprised to learn that he is expected to teach a daily religion lesson to the eighth grade. The principal may be surprised to learn that he is also to serve as youth ministry advisor.

Servant leaders are always willing to do and be more than the minimum. Unexpected tasks come up that are energetically and joyfully addressed. However, unexpected surprises drain energy and cause unnecessary challenges.

While God's Word and the message of salvation are always clear, ministry responsibilities and relationships are clouded by sin. While not every situation and dynamic can be easily anticipated in advance, clarification and communication in as many realms as possible are helpful.

Some areas for clarification and communication:

- → The core values and principles of the ministry.
- → The mission statement of the ministry.
- → The vision for the ministry.
- → Position descriptions for the pastor, principal, teachers, and other staff.
- → Policies and handbooks for board members, teachers, and families.

Seeing Jesus as the way and living in His truth, we describe the ways and truths of day-to-day Lutheran school ministry.

> You are the way; through You alone
>   Can we the Father find;
> In You, O Christ, has God revealed
>   His heart and will and mind.

You are the truth; Your Word alone
True wisdom can impart;
You only can inform the mind
And purify the heart. (*LSB* 526:1–2)

APPLICATIONS:

New Life Lutheran School represents Lutheran schools from early childhood to secondary contexts. New Life Lutheran School can be of any size in any setting. New Life Lutheran School is guided by the Word and blessed by the Spirit. Contextually, the school may be supported by a single congregation, be part of an association, or even be an independent Recognized Service Organization ministry. Administratively, the school might be under a traditional school board, or it may be governed more corporately. The staff may be large or small. The following situations have happened in a variety of Lutheran school ministries.

MINISTRY TEAMWORK AT NEW LIFE LUTHERAN SCHOOL

Lutheran schools have teams. Much more complicated than the game of any school athletic team is the teamwork among staff members.

Principal Mary had served the school for a decade before Pastor Mike was called to serve the congregation and school. In retrospect, Principal Mary or a school board member should have been invited to serve on the call committee to provide input on the pastoral gifts that could enhance the mission and ministry of the school.

New Life Lutheran School was Pastor Mike's first experience as pastor of a Lutheran school ministry. He was quickly surprised by the expectations of Principal Mary and the school board. Principal Mary and Pastor Mike had different styles of administration. Principal Mary was very organized. Pastor Mike was more random.

A variety of other matters soon led to a distance between the pastor and principal. Both valued ministry teamwork. How could God be glorified?

How could their relationship be strengthened? How could the ministry of the church and school not only survive but thrive?

Together, Principal Mary and Pastor Mike contacted their district school representative, who shared the dynamic with the district president. A district reconciliation team visited with the principal and pastor.

Prayerfully, each looked at his or her own role in the conflict. They confessed their sins and took personal and professional steps to grow as servants of Christ and as professionals in the setting. They were blessed to work together at New Life Lutheran School for many years.

Another scenario: The conversations with the reconciliation team revealed to Principal Mary that her style and gifts were vastly different than Pastor Mike's. While she felt no resentment toward Pastor Mike and no pressure from the pastor or board, she felt that perhaps it was time for her to seek another ministry setting. She had been at the school for a number of years and was even excited about starting over. She contacted the district office to have her availability shared with other ministry settings. Blessed by the Spirit's guidance, she began the next school year at a different Lutheran school.

PROTECTING THE MINISTRY OF NEW LIFE LUTHERAN SCHOOL

Immoral and sometimes illegal activities are a challenge to Lutheran school pastors and leaders.

Teacher Bill has been a member of the staff of New Life Lutheran School for three years. One day, Bill's computer revealed visits to immoral websites. The principal was informed of the discovery. (As this situation has developed in several Lutheran schools, the discovery of the impropriety varies.) The principal made immediate contact with Bill and invited him into the office. The pastor was invited to be part of the conversation. In preparation for the dialogue, the principal had reviewed all the school policies regarding this behavior. The church and school insurance carrier was also contacted.

Bill admitted to the immoral behavior. Local authorities were immediately contacted to make sure that no children were violated or threatened by the discoveries. The school board chairman was also contacted and informed of the discovery and admission. Bill's teaching ministry was immediately suspended. After further investigation and consideration, Bill resigned as a teacher. The district president and his representatives were contacted to consider roster implications.

The devil tempts Lutheran school teachers and leaders. Those who serve in Lutheran schools also succumb to sins of the flesh. While all sins are taken to the cross and upon Confession, Absolution and personal new life in Christ are offered, the ministry must be protected.

Children need to be protected. While state laws and accreditation agencies regulate the safety of children, Lutheran schools additionally see each child as a child of God. Each little lamb is to be safe with the Shepherd and in the flock of the Church.

The witness of the church school needs to be protected. New Life Lutheran School shares and lives new life in Jesus. All things are done to the glory of God.

The reputation of the workers is to be protected. Illegal activities are handled by local authorities. Schools cannot divert from or minimize the justice system. At the same time, every effort is given to protect the reputation of those who violate laws and policies (and the reputation of family members). If there are any questions about legal procedures, always seek the advice of the school and church lawyer. If there are questions about ministry procedures, always consult the local district president's office.

NURTURING THE STAFF AT NEW LIFE LUTHERAN SCHOOL

Some challenges are personal. Amy graduated from Concordia University and began her first year of teaching at New Life Lutheran School. Amy was well prepared and excited.

Just a couple of weeks into the school year, Amy felt overwhelmed. She was lonely, as this was her first experience living away from family and college friends. Amy struggled to have enough time to prepare for the demands of each school day.

Pastor Collins had the routine of often walking down the school hallway at the conclusion of the school day. Pastor Collins greeted the children, "How was your day?" "Great job at the game yesterday." Pastor Collins also glanced into the classrooms and conversed with the teachers. "How was your day, Amy?" Pastor Collins valued Amy's ministry and had seen her growth from a tentative first-year teacher to a staff veteran. Pastor Collins was also aware of Amy's family situation and recent struggles. Amy's joy seemed to be waning. Sensing Pastor Collins's genuine concern and trusting his confidentiality, Amy responded to the casual question, "How was your day?" with her personal needs: "I'm really struggling."

Many personal challenges in the lives of staff members can be addressed with personal and pastoral care. Pastor Collins can pray with Amy. He can direct her to God's Word and His encouragement for her. Pastor Collins might direct Amy to other resources that will provide support for her. With Amy's permission, he might request special prayers at the staff meeting and offer the support and shared experiences of fellow teachers. He might suggest individuals or families in the church who can provide some social and emotional support.

It is important to spiritually and emotionally nurture those who lovingly minister to children and families.

VOCATIONAL AFFIRMATION AT NEW LIFE LUTHERAN SCHOOL

Finding the right vocation can be a challenge. Lutheran school pastors and teachers are privileged and challenged to examine their own calling and to assist others in discerning their vocational call.

Kellie spent three years teaching at another Lutheran school. Her years at the school were not particularly fulfilling. Perhaps it was a setting too far from her family. Perhaps it was not a grade level that matched her skills. Kellie was excited about accepting the call and teaching first grade at New Life Lutheran School.

After the first semester, some of the same feelings of uncertainty in her vocation came to Kellie. Was she really gifted to be a teacher? Was this the vocation best suited for her? Kellie shared her questions with Pastor

Tim. Pastor Tim listened attentively. He also contacted a local career counseling agency. Kellie met with a career counselor and completed an evaluation of gifts, personality, and so forth to see the best match.

Kellie shared her journey, reflections, and explorations with her principal. After much prayer and reflection, Kellie resigned as a teacher at New Life Lutheran School. She received additional training to pursue a career as a nurse. She finds great joy in working with the elderly in a care center.

Not every student that begins in teacher education at a college or university will find fulfillment in a classroom. While a calling to the teaching ministry is certainly a godly calling, it does not fit the God-given gifts of every individual.

FACING FUNDING REALITIES AT NEW LIFE LUTHERAN SCHOOL

New Life Lutheran School was facing its annual budget crisis. Pastor Chris acknowledged the deficits and the implications: Would staff get paid? Would raises be given? Would a special appeal again take place? Would a memorial or special gifts rescue the ministry again? Pastor Chris observed that there was no action plan to avoid the crisis next year or the years to follow.

At the suggestion of Pastor Chris, a financial task force was established. Among the recommendations of the task force were a stewardship education process for all church members, a capital campaign to fund some of the facility improvements and to establish a ministry enhancement fund, an annual funding effort inviting school alumni and ministry friends to join in supporting New Life Lutheran School, educating families of the true cost and value of the school ministry, and raising the tuition rates.

Three years later, the church and school ministry finds itself financially stable. The church members, staff, and school families find joy in the generosity and confidence in financial security.

Another scenario: Three years later, the church and school ministry is still financially unstable. Accompanying the budget deficit is a declining enrollment due to the church and community demographics and other factors. In late fall, the school board came to the conclusion that the school ministry was no longer financially viable. At the January voters assembly, the congregation voted to close New Life Lutheran School at the end of the school year. As the school year concluded, a special service of thanksgiving was held celebrating eighty years of the blessings of the congregation's Lutheran school.

Sometimes Lutheran schools and the congregations or other affiliates that support them have to make the difficult decision to conclude a ministry. Such decisions are made prayerfully considering all the information available. Such decisions are also made in a timely manner for staff and families to make adjustments. While such decisions are difficult and will cause grief, they can also include a time of thanksgiving. Give thanks for children and families who perhaps for generations were blessed by the school ministry. Give thanks for the staff who served faithfully. Give thanks for new ministries that may continue to make a Kingdom impact in the congregation and community.

CONCLUSION:

As the chapter began, Candidate Jeff was about to begin his pastoral ministry at Redeemer Lutheran Church and School. By God's grace, Pastor Jeff is still serving Redeemer Lutheran Church and School twenty years later. Imagine the conversation at that twenty-year anniversary: "What have been some of the challenges, Pastor Jeff?" Most likely, some of the challenges addressed in the chapter would be mentioned.

"How did you survive (and perhaps even thrive) during those challenges?" "Why do you continue to serve this church and school ministry?" Pastor Jeff reflects on the ministry of the apostle Paul and celebrates with him, "I can do all things through Him [Christ] who strengthens me" (Philippians 4:13).

Lutheran school ministry is challenging. Lutheran school ministry is exciting. Christ is the message. Christ is the strength. To Christ be the glory!

CHAPTER 4

THE PASTOR AND STRATEGIC PLANNING

Rev. Todd Kollbaum

THE VALUE OF STRATEGIC PLANNING

Growing up in northwest Iowa, I can vividly remember my dad and my grandpa having conversations about the farm. These weren't just casual visits about the price of corn or where the fences needed to be fixed. These were in-depth conversations that were often well researched and thought out. While these two earnest men weren't sitting in a boardroom or at a conference center, they were engaging in planning for the farm. They weren't just planning for the day's work either, even though that was certainly important. No, these informal meetings over the hood of a pickup or at the kitchen table with a cup of coffee were big-picture, future-of-the-business planning meetings. What would be planted in which fields the next year, when we'd buy, when we'd sell, how many hogs, how many cattle—the conversations would flow.

At the time, I didn't realize the full impact of these sessions or even what they were actually doing. But in hindsight now, I have come to understand and appreciate that they were truly engaged in the process of strategic planning. They certainly didn't call it that and, at the time, didn't give it much thought, as they were just doing what needed to be done to most efficiently and successfully engage in the work they had before them. But as simple as that may have seemed, this is the very essence of strategic planning—researching, discussing, formulating, and executing their plan.

Fast-forward a decade or two. As a nursing home administrator, as a healthcare consultant, as a husband, a father, a pastor, and as the director of Rural and Small Town Mission for The Lutheran Church—Missouri Synod, I have had numerous opportunities to engage in this same process. Sometimes it was quite formal, and other times it was more informal; regardless, we were engaging in strategic planning. Over and over again, whether in healthcare, in the family, or in the church, strategic planning has proven to be an invaluable tool to navigate through the waters of this crazy, sin-fallen world in which we live and operate from day-to-day.

THE MINISTERIAL USE OF STRATEGIC PLANNING

It has often been my experience that the mere idea of engaging in strategic planning is met with a certain skepticism or, worse, downright fear of the idea. While most would agree that it is fine to plan ahead for home or work, why would we do that for the church? That's God's work, right? He is in control of the whole process, and far be it from us to get in His way.

I'm told to consider the parable of the rich fool from Luke chapter 12. Here, the rich landowner has such an abundant crop that he makes a plan to build bigger storehouses for all the grain so that he can sit back, "relax, eat, drink, be merry" (v. 19). The fear of this kind of planning among congregations and even some pastors comes from God's response when He says, "Fool! This night your soul is required of you, and the things you have prepared, whose will they be?" (v. 20). It seems the farmer engaged in strategic planning, and look what it got him! However, what is often left out of this argument against strategic planning is the fact that this parable is taught by Jesus as a warning against covetousness and the mindset that life is all about an abundance of wealth.

In fact, the parable isn't warning the crowd about the evils of planning, but it is an admonition concerning the inclinations of the heart. This is why the parable ends with, "So is the one who lays up treasure for himself and is not rich toward God" (v. 21). The issue isn't at all about strategic planning, as if that is evidence of not trusting in the Lord, but it is about the obsession our hearts often have with the acquisition of much wealth. Quite the opposite of this is what we are talking about in the realm of strategic planning.

That doesn't mean that planning can't be used as a tool for covetousness and evil, but it doesn't have to serve as that. In fact, for the Christian and the Church, at the very heart of this process is the faith we have in the Lord to provide for His Church and His mission. Using our First Article gifts of reason and sense in service of the mission of our local congregation is, in fact, an act of great faith, trusting that the Lord will guide and direct our decisions and actions.

Consider, if you will, Psalm 20:4: "May He grant you your heart's desire and fulfill all your plans!" and Ephesians 1:7–10: "In Him we have redemption through His blood, the forgiveness of our trespasses, according to the riches of His grace, which He lavished upon us, in all wisdom and insight making known to us the mystery of His will, according to His purpose, which He set forth in Christ as a plan for the fullness of time, to unite all things in Him, things in heaven and things on earth."

When strategic planning is utilized in ministerial service to the Word of God, serving the church rather than ruling her, this is a great blessing. That is to say, strategic planning certainly isn't to be held in priority over worship, prayer, and study of God's Word. But when it is seen in the proper light as a tool to serve the Gospel, it is of immense value to the church.

Acts 16:6–10 provides an excellent example of this Spirit-led planning. Paul, Silas, and Timothy plan to travel to Bithynia to proclaim the Gospel, having been forbidden to preach in Asia by the Holy Spirit. Yet even though this was their plan, they remained open to the Lord's guidance, and when the Spirit again refused them entry, they waited for direction. Then, in a vision, Paul was made aware that God's plan was for them to move on to Macedonia to preach the Gospel.

PLANNING FOR STEWARDSHIP

When we carefully and prayerfully engage in our strategic planning efforts, we remain open to the Spirit's guidance in the process. As God directs the plan, adjustments and modifications can be made. We then are able to continually pray for God's guidance throughout the process, which opens us up for God's direction, as opposed to rigidly adhering to man's plan.

An apt example of this is a congregation that is considering establishing a Lutheran day school in their community. They mulled over this idea for a number of years but simply couldn't decide how they should proceed. This issue was causing some dissension among the members, especially among those who were pushing firmly to open the school and those who were opposed to the idea.

When they finally approached the situation through a strategic planning process, having carefully looked at their community's demographics, the resources and assets of the congregation, and prayerfully considering the Lord's will, the whole picture took on a different light. The congregation realized that the community would be far better served, and the congregation far better equipped, to open a Lutheran early childhood center with a preschool and daycare component. Since this was done in a structured and strategic manner, all sides were able to be brought on board because the necessity and the benefits could be communicated objectively to those concerned.

Since we really want nothing more than to conform to God's will as we carry out the work of the Church, we want to be good stewards of the resources that He grants to us. While we are neither commanded nor forbidden to engage in strategic planning, I would say that it is quite difficult to be the best stewards of God's riches if we don't engage in at least a minimal amount of strategic planning. Again, as Luther says in his Small Catechism, in the explanation of the First Article of the Apostles' Creed, God gives us "our reason and all our senses." Then it is indeed good, right, and salutary to use these good gifts in service to our various ministries.

We needn't fear this process nor be overwhelmed by it but engage in it earnestly for the good of our work in Christ. As I stated before, we improve our stewardship of those resources God grants to us when we focus our attention on what it is that God has equipped and called us to do. We waste a lot of effort and precious resources when we leave our work to chance or take a haphazard, helter-skelter approach. Yet when we engage in strategic planning, we are able to focus our attention on what is truly important. We can allocate resources to those endeavors that are in line with what we perceive as that which God has enabled us to accomplish.

Strategic planning doesn't just allow us to best use resources but also equips us to most efficiently utilize the time and talents of our members. This is well illustrated by the congregation who desires to provide some type of outreach event so that they can create a higher profile in the community and provide a service for them. Some members came up with the great idea of providing a parent's night out event where parents could drop off their young children for a few hours on a Friday night so they could go out without having to find and pay for a babysitter.

Since this sounded like a good idea and maybe even some fun for the workers, they decided to go ahead with the plan. The plan was carried out by a few key players who were most interested, and most of the congregation had no idea that it was even happening. On the night of the event, nobody showed up, and all of the preparation and work they had done seemed to be for naught.

Several months later, the congregation embarked upon a strategic planning process. In the course of the process, the failure of the parent's night out event was brought up. Rather than dismiss it out of hand because it failed, the group found that the concept did truly fit into their plan. However, what they realized is that as part of the strategic plan, they could involve several different groups in the planning and implementation. Rather than a small group of individuals, the youth were involved for games, the Ladies Aid was involved for snacks, and the Sunday School was involved for devotional content.

They also uncovered the fact that a parent's night out event was already being regularly offered in their community; they just hadn't done their research to find that out. Their planning then led them to realize that a better and more impactful concept would be an after-school ministry once a week. They researched, planned, allocated resources, and publicized the event extremely well, and while it took some time for the ministry to catch on, they weren't deterred and they worked their plan so that today, this congregation has a robust after-school ministry that continues to flourish.

PLANNING FOR STRUCTURE

When congregations have plans and people are educated on expectations and requirements, they are far more apt to agree to serve and will likely do a far better job. In a great number of congregations, this simply isn't the case. We tend to operate with governance and structure that is decades old and doesn't reflect the current ministry scenarios that are present today.

Take, for example, the congregation that has a parochial school they have operated in an association partnership for thirty years. Upon review of their forty-year-old constitution, they realized that document didn't reflect much of anything as it currently was being done. In fact, the constitution stated that they could only issue a divine call to male teachers. At that point in time, they only had one male teacher. They also found that specific days and times were delineated for all meetings and voters assemblies. They hadn't met on those days or times for years. This doesn't seem like a big problem since they just did what they wanted to do anyway. However, the constitution and bylaws are important documents that serve to direct and protect the congregation. When the only time it is referred to is when someone has a problem, this isn't how things are done in good and proper order.

Another big issue is congregations that lack job descriptions for various boards, organizations, offices, and servants in our congregations. These congregations are setting themselves up for failure. That is to say, when people don't understand clearly what their duties are or where the organization is going and how they fit into that organization, very little that is positive or constructive is able to be accomplished.

Under these circumstances, people will generally do whatever it is they are accustomed to (i.e. "we've always done it this way" or "we've never done it that way before"). While things that have been done in the past might be perfectly ideal for what is going on in and around the congregation, it just might not be either. Often we see this when a particular leader decides to take their particular board in whatever direction they desire, and there really is no mechanism to keep them in their own lane.

I have seen the destruction this can cause firsthand. A most egregious example was when a board of elders concerned themselves primarily with the work that ought to be assigned to the trustees. They busied themselves with repairs and building issues, while spiritual care of members, oversight of worship activities, and support of their pastor went by the wayside.

Not only did this leave a void in what needed to be accomplished by the elders but it also caused a great deal of conflict with the trustees because they often found themselves at loggerheads with each other because of differing views. This also caused much consternation for their pastor, as he wasn't supported and found that he had to make all the decisions regarding worship and Bible study, which often left him criticized and unsupported when people didn't care for his choices or decisions. Good job descriptions could have prevented all of that pain and heartache.

Without direction and a method for evaluating these activities, congregations often just flounder. The other side of that coin is that without direction, servants in the congregation will simply do nothing. They are afraid to reach out in faith and try because they fear failure or, even worse, stepping on others' toes.

However, with a carefully and prayerfully developed plan and expectations for all, the congregation can evaluate the what, where, and how of all of their activities in light of what they believe is the direction the Lord is guiding them. In this way, strategic planning not only serves the mission and ministry of the congregation but also frees up our servants to reach out in faith and do those things that the Lord of the Church is equipping and calling them to do in service to Him and the Gospel.

PLANNING FOR COHESIVE MISSION

The value of strategic planning doesn't end with just the best stewardship of resources and service to the church, but it aligns the congregation's membership and leadership so that there is an intentional methodology in order to carry the "business" of the church. When consensus is built, every board, team, and task force, and the servants who make them up, will more likely be united in purpose in support of the congregation's mission and ministry.

Strategic planning will shine the light on the mission and vision of the individual congregation in light of the Church's overall mission. With the congregation's mission and vision concretely communicated through mission and vision statements, members can more clearly focus their efforts on what fits within that stated framework. This clear plan will foster ownership of the congregation's mission among its leaders, which will then assist the membership at large to embrace that vision as well.

This also positions a congregation to be proactive, as opposed to reactive, to those forces of change that affect the Body of Christ gathered there. This will also foster a mentality of willingness to adapt ministry to the vision, as opposed to forcing the vision to match ministry activities, whether or not they should be continued or are fruitful efforts of the congregation.

Consider, if you will, Emmaus Lutheran Church. Emmaus has a long and faithful history of serving the people of their small community, proclaiming the Good News of Jesus Christ, and being a beacon of hope in this death-shadowed world. Today, though, they find themselves struggling with budgets, attendance, outreach, and a general sense of foreboding with regard to the future.

Their pastor, who has served them faithfully for a short time, recognizes that something must be done, but no one seems to have a sense of what direction they should go or what they should do. Couple that with the fact that the last several outreach efforts they have attempted haven't produced the results they desire, and Emmaus finds itself plodding down the road without direction or hope.

We would often say that Emmaus and congregations like it have found themselves in survival mode. When forces and pressures both internal and external push in upon a congregation, they can either proactively meet these changes or reactively bend to them. Too often, congregations without a plan will find themselves in a reactionary frame of action, which forces them into survival mode. By this I mean a congregation will hunker down, trying to weather the storm and survive.

However, in an ever-changing, decaying world, these forces never cease, so the congregation will find itself trapped. This survival mentality is unproductive and exists in an atmosphere of scarcity, which doesn't recognize that the blessings of God are always present for His people. Ultimately, this congregation will simply try to "keep the lights on" until they no longer can.

Breaking out of this survival mentality is excessively difficult. Yet Jesus reminds us that believers can live according to God's provision, not their fear of scarcity, when He says, "Give, and it will be given to you. Good measure, pressed down, shaken together, running over, will be put into your lap. For with the measure you use it will be measured back to you" (Luke 6:38). That is to say that God freely bestows His grace upon His people. In so doing, He calls His people through the Church to do likewise in the making of disciples. It is His will that must be done, which is what we pray will happen "on earth as it is in Heaven." The Lord of the Church will provide and equip His Church to do the work that He calls them to do.

Here, Emmaus could have given up, decided they could just exist until the last person turns out the lights. This would have been the path of least resistance, the path of great pain but the "easy" road nonetheless. However, they sat down together and prayed and prayed, studied the Scriptures, and, not unlike the disciples on that Emmaus road who were all but lost, they heard the Word of the Lord and their hearts burned within them. They determined that if it be the Lord's will, they could keep on fighting "the good fight of the faith" (1 Timothy 6:12), venture on without fear and trepidation, roll up their sleeves, and begin digging in and working on a planning process.

But after coming to the conclusion that the Lord's work wasn't done there, they struggled with where to start. Unlike the common misconception that we should figure out where we want to be, then plan on how we get there, the strategic planning process needs to start with a healthy understanding of who we are as a congregation, the gathering of the varied body of Christ.

A thorough process of self-evaluation is an absolute prerequisite to formulating a productive plan. Most districts have some type of self-evaluation tool that congregations can use, especially when they are entering the call process. These are helpful but tend to focus only on the specific goal of calling a pastor, which is a bit too narrow.

One assessment tool which is available to all LCMS congregations is very thorough and produced specifically for congregations to use independent of needing a facilitator. This is the Congregational Assessment of Development/Decline Status available through LCMS re:Vitality. It is an online assessment tool that can also be made available in printed form for those who don't have online accessibility.

According to their website,

> The Congregational Assessment of Development/Decline Status (CADDS) is a survey-based self-assessment tool designed to provide your congregation with a consistent and objective way of answering the question "Where are we . . . really?" CADDS is simple, straightforward and nonintrusive—it does not require anyone from outside the congregation to assist in the assessment. Instead, CADDS relies on input from the people who know your congregation and context better than anyone else: you.[1]

Congregations should also consult with their district to find out if they have a tool available such as in the Mid-South District, which offers

1 "Church Revitalization," Church Revitalization—The Lutheran Church—Missouri Synod, accessed October 30, 2020, https://www.lcms.org/church-revitalization.

the COMPASS, which helps congregations find new direction in their ministry, and C.A.R. (Congregational Assessment Resource).

PLANNING FOR IDENTITY

Too often we assume that since we are all members of a congregation of the LCMS, we should inherently have a proper understanding of who we are and why we exist. Unfortunately, this is simply not the reality. As a gathering of individuals, we all bring to the table our own ideas and biases. History also plays a huge role in our understanding of who and what we are.

Consider Emmaus's history of membership, which is common for many congregations. For decade upon decade, Emmaus found itself thriving because its members and their subsequent generations stayed in the area and were loyal to Emmaus because that was their families' church.

However, as time moved on and major demographic shifts began to happen in their community, they felt somewhat insulated from these changes because they were still bustling with internal growth. However, as members became more mobile and moved away from the area, things began to be a bit stark. Demographics of the community also became less and less homogenous, and Emmaus found that they were neither equipped nor ready to reach out to these new demographic realities. This left them in a position where they felt as if their future was bleak, and they had no idea how to move into the future.

Strategic planning allows our congregation's leaders and members to build consensus around who we are, where we should be going, and how we can (and should) get there. There are several self-assessment tools available to assist congregations in this process. Regardless of the tool used, though, Emmaus recognized they should seek to answer and build consensus around these fundamental questions:

- → What does the church do?
- → What should the church do?
- → What does this congregation do?
- → What should it be doing?
- → What are our limitations?

→ What are our strengths?

→ Where should we focus our efforts?

While this list certainly isn't exhaustive, it is a good place to start, as well as return to regularly, in order to consider where we are and where we are headed. If this task alone seems daunting, that isn't particularly surprising as it is a substantial undertaking. More often than not, congregations find themselves operating for decades without really taking stock of where they are and what they have. Identifying why a particular congregation exists in a particular place for a particular time is a question that is seldom asked. Engaging in a substantive self-evaluation will help you to take an objective look at what resources you currently have, the ministry opportunities and activities you are currently engaging in, as well as the ministry opportunities that are available.

PLANNING FOR EVALUATION

So Emmaus formed a strategic planning team to engage in the evaluation and questioning process. They asked themselves what they as the church were doing. Their realization was that they were primarily engaged in what might be described as palliative care. They were keeping themselves comfortable by gathering once a week, which I must emphasize, isn't a bad thing. They were continuing their calling of proclaiming both Law and Gospel week in and week out.

However, they recognized that they were doing little "to equip the saints for the work of ministry, for building up the body of Christ" (Ephesians 4:12). The question of what the church should be doing—reaching out to the lost and the wandering, serving the community with acts of mercy connected to their Word and Sacrament ministry, and supporting the proclamation of the Gospel in places outside their own walls—was at best being overlooked or, at worst, deliberately ignored.

With this in mind, Emmaus leadership undertook the task of listing out all of the activities they were engaged in, attempting to determine if these were related to mission and ministry or simply to maintenance. As part of the self-assessment process, this is a difficult move. Often, there are items on this list that have been done for so long that they would be sorely lost if discontinued. Events such as annual mission festivals, Easter breakfasts, and community festival booths are fine events in and of themselves but often lose their mission and ministry focus.

Through planning, these types of events can be retained with a renewed focus on why they are carried out. On the other hand, though, there are many activities that could be discontinued or modified to better fit the mission of the congregation. Events such as those that are completely inwardly focused or that wear the moniker of missions but do nothing to fund, promote, or even encourage missions, but instead are self-serving, would be examples of the types of activities that should at least be revisited and perhaps even done away with (more on that later).

This also gave them the opportunity to ask what they *should* be doing. That is to say, they allowed themselves the freedom to look at where there were gaps in their mission and ministry that were forcing them to lose sight of or make them unable to accomplish the work the Lord had set before them in their particular location at that particular point in time.

Emmaus had to take a hard look at the demographics of their community in order to determine what portions of their community they were leaving unreached and how or if they were equipped to reach out to them. They also had to look at their own membership to see where there were missing mission and ministry opportunities, such as to those who had wandered away from the church or who were, at best, tacitly connected.

PLANNING FOR RESOURCES

The congregation then had to take a hard look at what their limitations were as a congregation. This is a point in the process where it is easy to slip back into scarcity mode and lament all of the things we used to have that we don't currently have at our disposal. Hurdles such as a lack of money, dwindling attendance, aging membership, and people who lack a desire to serve are common to all and were certainly a reality for Emmaus as well. But they resolved not to focus on doom and gloom and, instead, remember that God would provide everything they needed to accomplish the mission and ministry they were called to accomplish.

Congregations who find themselves in this scenario do well to remember the Gospel of Luke, where we are reminded, "Give, and it will be given to you. Good measure, pressed down, shaken together, running over, will be put into your lap. For with the measure you use it will be measured back to you" (Luke 6:38). Along with Emmaus, we can come to the realization that we are not a people of scarcity, but in the Lord, we are a people overflowing with blessings and resources for the days to come.

However, taking a sanctified look at where we are realistically positioned with regard to resources is helpful. Emmaus recognized that God had indeed blessed them with many physical, financial, and human resources through which they could carry out the ministry there. Rather than seeing their building as a financial strain, they saw it as a resource for mission and ministry that they were underutilizing.

They realized that their building was equipped with great access for people with limited mobility, so they developed a ministry to seniors, which was a way to facilitate fellowship for some folks who were otherwise somewhat isolated. This involved the group bringing in snacks to share, card playing, and devotions led by either group leaders or the pastor. This way, their pastor was also able to meet a demographic of people he would have otherwise been unable to meet.

Another great move was to utilize their kitchen facilities for cooking classes that were hosted by a ladies group but put on by friends of theirs who were of differing cultural backgrounds. Again, people of all ages would gather to cook together, eat together, and also have fellowship and devotions together.

PLANNING FOR SERVICE

As it stood, without a plan, Emmaus realized that people were reticent to get involved. The members sincerely wanted to do something, anything, but were afraid that their work would be in vain and that everything would come to nothing in the end. However, with a plan and direction, they were more than willing to engage in the work of the congregation. In fact, this optimism became contagious, and the planning team continued to communicate these positive findings to the larger body of members.

They determined that their constitution and bylaws put them in a position where they were limited in the number and ways that people might be able to serve the congregation. Not that the structure was bad in and of itself, but it was put together in a way that made sense for the ministry situation forty years prior and wasn't good for their current reality.

This could be clearly seen in the number of boards and elected positions that the constitution demanded. Because of their decline in membership, it just didn't make sense to have so many boards, and they certainly struggled to get people willing to volunteer (or not say no) to a leadership position. This created great tension among the members who repeatedly had to hold the same job term after term, even when their term limits were up. It also forced people into jobs for which they had no passion, desire, or ability. This sets up these servants, who have their hearts in the right place, for failure. However, because it is what the constitution said, this is what must be done.

PLANNING FOR CORE VALUES

Emmaus found that, over the course of the last couple of decades, attendance, service, and giving attitudes and practices had changed in such a way that they needed to undergo some very serious and deliberate stewardship training so that they would all be on a similar page with regard to whole-life stewardship. But they also found that the Lord had still blessed them with many strengths and gifts, which they could focus into their mission and ministry efforts as they better prepared themselves through their planning processes. This gave them a much better direction for how they could focus their discussion on future efforts rather than shooting their shotguns into the dark without any direction.

Having undergone this thorough evaluation of the congregation and having begun to answer the necessary questions, Emmaus was at a point where they could determine their core values and begin to develop their overall purpose and mission. Again, this is often a scary topic.

We know Jesus and His Gospel message are at the very heart and core of our congregations, so why would we need to determine our core values? Also, why wouldn't we want to just use Matthew 28, the Great Commission, or another mission text in Scripture as our mission statement? It would seem as if we were failing to be faithful if we would do otherwise.

However, without a doubt, these texts definitely determine and shape the work of mission and ministry of the Church at large and in our congregations. But what we are looking for in these items focuses specifically on what God is calling us to do in our individual congregations. The self-assessment and answering the questions help to identify this key concept: What is God calling us to do and accomplish here in this specific place for this specific time?

Emmaus definitely struggled with this as well. They wondered how you could boil decades of ministry and the unknown future into a few simple yet worthwhile words. However, once they gained sight of what was truly at stake and how the Lord could continue to use this congregation for the good of His kingdom, they began to start to see how this might all come together.

It became apparent to them that they weren't a congregation of scarcity and survival but one of *abundance* and *life*. Instead of being motivated by fear of loss and death, they were *motivated by the truth and the Gospel*. Rather than just being a ministry of convenience and safety, they were challenged to *focus on equipping the saints and reaching the lost and wandering*. These factors began to emerge as the core values for Emmaus Lutheran Church and would serve to guide them in all of their discussion and determinations.

PLANNING AND PURPOSE

Having determined these core values, Emmaus was then poised to make a statement that would encapsulate the original "why" questions. Why does our congregation exist? This is a big, long-term purpose that will guide the mission of the congregation into the future. Emmaus came to the agreement that this was their purpose: "To make and equip disciples of Jesus Christ." This statement is broad enough to guide discussions and decisions without being overly restrictive, while providing direction to the congregation in its work.

One issue that Emmaus struggled with in this process was to ensure that any guiding statements or core values they determined weren't those of just one person or group or simply that of the pastor. It is very easy to slip into those ruts when engaging in strategic planning, as stronger personalities or leaders put forth their ideas. However, a good reminder is that people will come and go, but the mission of the congregation is what will remain for the duration.

Now, equipped with the purpose statement, Emmaus was ready to develop their mission statement, which would more narrowly guide their work of mission and ministry in the nearer term while maintaining a focus on their core values. This statement will be used to evaluate decisions regarding what the congregation will do and how they will do it.

To guide them, Emmaus developed this mission statement: "Motivated by the Gospel and equipped by God's grace, Emmaus Lutheran Church will equip the saints and reach out to the lost in word and deed." While this statement is more descriptive than prescriptive, it helps to assure that as decisions are made, they can be weighed against the mission statement to make sure the ministry is remaining on track. If something is going to be considered, it must fit into the parameters of the mission of the congregation. If it doesn't, then the congregation has to determine whether or not it is good stewardship to engage in that particular activity.

PLANNING FOR GOALS

At this stage of the process, members might think that they could sit back and relax and just let the plan run its course. However, this would be a grave mistake. In fact, engaging in a strategic planning process will indeed create more work for those involved. Yet this shouldn't scare you away from strategic planning. Remaining faithful to God and the work He has placed in front of a congregation shouldn't be frightening but exciting as we faithfully carry out our mission.

So once a framework has been developed, the nuts and bolts of the plan can begin to be put in place. This is where we get into the realm of goals and objectives. As stated earlier, each group, team, task force, or organization within the congregation must develop their own job or ministry descriptions that determine their function within the greater entity.

This also allows congregations to be more streamlined and eliminate overlap and waste as mission duties are carried out. Understanding the relationship between the established boards, the staff, and other auxiliary organizations is paramount so that all know what they are expected to accomplish and who is supposed to do what work.

Once that is established, each entity can start to develop its own goals and objectives in order to carry out its work. In the case of Emmaus, they developed a simple structure to facilitate communication and promote unity as they moved forward. This way, as goals and objectives were being established, everyone was aware of their responsibilities and could "stay in their lane" so that redundancy or conflict could be avoided.

These goals and objectives were developed as a concrete way to describe the ministry functions of all the servants in the congregation. They were constructed using the SMART goals method, which means the goals were Specific, Measurable, Attainable, Relevant, and Timely (Time-bound). In following this structure, the goals developed by the various groups at Emmaus would be understandable not only by other groups but, as leadership and servants changed, they could be continued and carried out without a break in the action. Some examples of the work Emmaus did to achieve this are as follows:

Board of Christian Education Goal: We will offer weekly biblical instruction outside of our regularly scheduled worship times for adults throughout the coming year.

Stewardship Board Goal: In the next eight months, we will engage in purposeful stewardship education efforts utilizing Stewardship Basics, available from LCMS Stewardship Ministry.

Board for Finance: For the coming fiscal year, the board for finance will develop a comprehensive budget, reviewing how to best fund the mission and ministry of the congregation. This will be done with input from all the various boards and organizations of the congregation so that the best stewardship of resources will be attained.

Emmaus took great care to ensure that the goals they developed were not only SMART but were also developed by those who were stakeholders in the various boards and organizations who had the responsibility to carry them out. This accommodated the elders, the budget and finance board, the stewardship board, the evangelism board, and the trustees, along with the LWML and LLL groups and the youth group, to develop their own plans and goals so that they would have ownership of them. This placed them in a position where they would be more apt to succeed and modify their plans as they needed to, based on need. This also allowed them to more accurately determine how much funding they would need to carry out their portion of the congregation's mission (more to follow on that later).

Too often, top-down leadership develops in congregations, where a select few determine the work for the whole. In the case of Emmaus and congregations who do likewise, it is imperative to involve those who will be carrying out the work to determine the work that they need to carry out the mission. In turn, they set themselves up for a greater chance of successful completion because ownership in the process can be attained.

There are some important issues to note regarding these goals that Emmaus has developed. Unlike a secular organization, which would formulate measurable goals that are often numeric in nature, those of the church should avoid that in many, if not most, occasions. It is a bit foolhardy to assign numeric value to goals such as worship service attendance or offering receipts. These are simply not appropriate to measure numerically because we would then be placing our goals above our reliance on faith in the Lord's provision.

It would be appropriate to say that a congregation might desire to increase attendance at a particular event by a specific percentage but certainly not appropriate to measure the success of worship by attendance. A classic example of this way of thinking is the oft-asked question, "How many people showed up to the adult Bible study?" We naturally, as sin-fallen humans, want to measure success in this way. However, an appropriate, SMART way to measure success is with the answer, "The number isn't particularly important because our goal was to ensure that we are gathering to study God's Word on a weekly basis, and we did just that. It was a great study, and we enjoyed some good fellowship as well." Here, Emmaus has done well to steer clear of this sort of thinking, and they have established for themselves a more faithful measurement of their mission and ministry goals.

PLANNING FOR EVALUATION

Now that this has been established, it is imperative to set up a system by which the mission and ministry goals will be evaluated. One of the biggest downfalls to a sustained and successful strategic plan is the failure to evaluate. When evaluation of goals and the work of the congregation and its workers are neglected, it won't take long for the whole plan to fall apart and the congregation devolve back into survival mode or even worse.

Emmaus employed a structured method by which each group and organization could evaluate their own work based upon their goals and job descriptions. This also allowed them to objectively report to the congregation at large how well they were employing the plan or where things needed to be reevaluated or the plan reworked.

Another key factor to planning success is the evaluation of key leaders and staff, including the pastor. This doesn't necessarily mean that the congregation will conduct "employment" reviews in every case. However, at minimum, an informal yet objective evaluation, which reviews key job description factors and goals and objectives, improves communication and opens the door to avoiding adversarial relationships.

Too often, when some type of evaluation isn't undertaken, communication becomes stifled, and interested parties begin to make judgments based solely upon personal preferences, which inevitably devolves into congregational, leadership, and pastoral conflict. While this isn't always preventable, the easiest way to avoid conflict is to maintain open and honest communication regarding expectations and outcomes.

PLANNING FOR UNITY

Prior to their engaging in strategic planning, Emmaus often found itself in conflictual situations. Their pastor often felt as if he sat on pins and needles because he was unsure of what to do, fearful of the future of the congregation, and bore the primary burden for planning as well as action. Once they had a plan, opened the lines of communication, and developed a system of evaluation and adjustment, they had far less conflict. Instead, the leaders, members, and pastor felt more comfortable with expectations, the sharing of ideas, and, ultimately, felt more like a team together in ministry as opposed to a group of individuals vying for their own positions or desires. This also allowed them to better share one another's burdens and pick one another up when they were down or struggling.

PLANNING FOR FUNDING THE MISSION

Another major benefit of a well-executed strategic planning process is what I like to refer to as funding the mission. Much more regarding this topic will be attended to in another chapter of this book, but I will note a couple of important points.

Note what I said—funding the mission. Most budgeting in congregations is done in a backward fashion if they even budget at all, which some congregations don't. We take a look at what we have received in the past and then fill in the blanks on the budget so that we allow our congregation to "spend" the offerings to keep our church going. I say this is backward not because this isn't how most budgeting is done; most people use this method for their own personal finances. They determine income and then based on that, they determine expenditures.

When we are in mission in the church, though, this sets unhealthy limits on our mission and, I dare say, doesn't reflect a positive stewardship of God's good gifts. When we have a plan and stick to that plan, we can determine what it will take to fund that plan and carry it out.

Consider Emmaus again. Prior to strategic planning, they employed a budgeting process much like I described above. Because there was not a plan, the members subjectively decided whether the budget was accurate or reasonable or not based solely upon past giving and expenditures. Rather than funding the mission, they were giving to the budget. This takes stewardship, prayerful consideration, tithing, and faithful giving right off of the table.

Prior to strategic planning, Emmaus had all but ended their support of district and synodical missions. They had cut budgets for youth and children's ministries, such as youth group, VBS, and Sunday School, down to virtually nothing. They were also in fear of whether or not they would be able to continue with a full-time pastor. Now, strategic planning wasn't a panacea, to be sure. But with their focus on mission and ministry, people saw the value in giving to fund the mission and they were able to re-fund those mission activities that had been earlier decimated. No longer were they concerned about maintaining full-time ministry and, in fact, were looking at ways to further enhance their current ministry and mission to be able to reach out and impact a larger portion of their community.

Contrast that with their experience after strategic planning. Emmaus sat down and carefully planned out how the mission should be funded in order to carry out the work that they believed God intended for them to accomplish. The congregation was then informed thoroughly regarding the mission and ministry goals and objectives so that all were on the same page. The members were much better informed and trusted that the budget accurately reflected that which needed to be spent. While Emmaus still wasn't always ahead of budget, they were able to better serve with confidence because they were employing sound fiscal management practices and good stewardship of God's resources.

As you can see, strategic planning isn't an easy process, but it is of great value! It is important to take note of some hints and helpful points that can assist congregations in being more successful in their planning processes. Once again, we'll return to Emmaus, as they learned some interesting things while they struggled to make their process successful.

PLANNING FOR BIBLE STUDY

First, Emmaus realized that while they were faithfully carrying out Word and Sacrament ministry on Sundays, they were spending precious little time studying God's Word together. As noted earlier, strategic planning must be ministerial to the Word of God. It seems that it should be self-evident, but because we tend to compartmentalize our work, we tend to put strategic planning, even in the church, on the business shelf. When we move that thinking into the realm of faithfulness to Christ, it becomes evident that everything has to be couched in God's Word.

The more a congregation studies God's Word together, the closer they become, and not unlike the disciples themselves, they become more of one mind and heart. This also includes intentionally praying for one another, with one another, for the planning process itself, and for God's guidance. The old adage "the family that prays together, stays together" certainly holds true in this respect. As Emmaus intentionally and in a winsome way began praying and studying together, their efforts at strategic planning and simply doing ministry together became far easier and much less contentious.

PLANNING FOR RELATIONSHIPS

To this same end, Emmaus realized that even though their congregation was relatively small and many of their members were even related, they were operating without any real cohesion when it came to matters of the church. Individuals were more concerned with their personal preferences and desires than what was good for the Kingdom. This is a historical issue. Think of all the congregational wars that have been fought over the color of the carpet, which, as we all know, has no effect on one's salvation or the proclamation of the Gospel. Even though congregations are united as the body of Christ, they often fail to act that way.

Leaders at Emmaus quickly realized they needed to be intentional about building relationships within the congregation that centered on the Gospel. With strong, faithful interpersonal relationships, the process of planning and carrying out ministry became more directed toward the cross and found its identity in Christ instead of being individualistic in nature.

No longer were the members at Emmaus worried about the color of the carpet, but instead, they wanted to ensure that the church building was an asset to the proclamation of the Gospel—not a deterrent. Gone were the days of arguments over which brand of water heater should be purchased, and in their place were people united in a passion to make sure the visitors to church would have warm water to wash their hands. This lowered greatly the hurdles of personal preferences and differences so that they were easily managed and maneuvered for the good of the Kingdom and the community surrounding the congregation.

This focus on relationship building increased the levels of trust among members so that they realized they could rely on one another as brothers and sisters in Christ. No longer were meetings and activities colored by distrust of one another's motives, but instead, they reflected the love of Christ for our neighbor.

Emmaus began to emerge from nervous fear of those who would endeavor to push their own agenda to mutual trust, respect, and support for one another. That isn't to say that they didn't have their differences; even the disciples ran into that. But they were equipped to deal with them in a respectful, loving manner instead of letting them devolve into deep-seated wounds that heal very slowly. This also positioned the congregation to continue mission and ministry, even while settling differences, instead of just shutting down until resolution could be attained.

PLANNING FOR A CULTURE OF RESPECT

Similar in nature to trust and relationship building is the fact that Emmaus leaders had to develop a culture of respect for one another's opinions. Even though one of the objectives of strategic planning is to move beyond personal preference, every one of us still has our ideas and opinions.

This is a good thing (remember that "reason and all my senses" business Luther talked about). We don't want to squash one another's creativity.

In the past, Emmaus found that ideas and their implementation were coming from a small group of people. In fact, that group often complained that they had to do everything. Yet when others stated their opinions or ideas, they were met with either great resistance or outright rejection.

This was illustrated best in the church's kitchen. The "old guard" at Emmaus was tiring of putting on all the lunches and dinners and attempted to recruit new and younger members to pick up the mantle. Yet as the new servants came in to serve, if they neglected to do everything in the exact manner that it had always been done, they were met with hostility and a general sense they were there to work, not to think.

This "new guard" didn't feel as if their contribution was valued in any way, so they simply quit coming and things continued as they had always been. Yet, as this deficit was attended to and a culture of respect developed and strengthened, people began treating one another with collegiality, and ever-increasing numbers of people were willing to be involved because they felt as if their ideas and opinions would be valued.

PLANNING FOR COMMITMENT

Emmaus's leadership also learned quickly that they had to breed an attitude of commitment to the process. Strategic planning isn't for the faint of heart because it is a lot of hard work. In the past, Emmaus had tried different programs in order to carry out their ministry. However, because there was no consensus building, programs would falter due to a lack of commitment. When the work became difficult and long and few results were seen (even though no objective, measurable standards had been set and no method of evaluation developed), the people grew tired and simply gave up. This led them over and over to do what they had always done.

Because of this, when the leadership at Emmaus began presenting the strategic planning process, most folks just went along with it because they knew eventually it would falter due to lack of interest. The leadership had to continually project their commitment to the hard work of mission and ministry and assure the other members of the value of the process.

Take, for example, youth ministry. This was an aspect of Emmaus's ministry that was all but gone. Interest and support had waned to such a degree that most had written it off altogether. However, after the strategic plan was developed, there was a renewed interest in support of the youth. Still, as time moved on and the numbers didn't seem to be increasing as quickly as they'd like, many thought it was a lost cause. But the leaders stuck with the plan and didn't worry about numbers but focused on ministry and communicated that repeatedly.

Down the road a bit further, through consistency and determination, the youth ministry became far more dynamic. The numbers never returned to their former glory, but the members at Emmaus were able to celebrate what they realized to be successful youth ministry. As others began to see this level of commitment and understood better what was being undertaken, they, too, were willing to put in the hard work because they could tangibly see the value in the undertaking. Certainly, there were ebbs and flows in the action, but when interest faded, a renewed commitment could be called for, and more and more people's interest was piqued.

Through this, Emmaus realized that they needed to focus on loving the Lord, caring for one another, and working the plan. When this priority list was implemented, they found that their lives in the church were much easier and more productive. As Jesus stated, the greatest command is "You shall love the Lord your God with all your heart and with all your soul and with all your mind. . . . And a second is like it: You shall love your neighbor as yourself" (Matthew 22:37, 39). Strategic planning facilitates this focus and gives the congregation and its members the freedom to live out these commands with faithfulness and joy.

PLANNING FOR ROAD BLOCKS

Emmaus found that working the plan wasn't always as easy as it may sound. Several factors regularly and repeatedly threatened to derail this faithful work. First and foremost, the biggest threat is always Satan.

Whenever the Church is doing good for the Kingdom, Satan will always attempt to thwart that activity.

There were several times throughout the initial work of Emmaus's strategic planning process that Satan would rear his ugly head and try to throw up some sort of roadblock. We sin-fallen humans are particularly good at falling prey to his lies, so too often this really becomes an issue. When giving failed to meet expectations or would dip a little, Satan would use this to "show" the members how things weren't working. When there was a debate over how to proceed with a remodeling project, Satan "assisted" members in worrying more about their personal preferences than the Kingdom of God.

Satan is a wily one, and he will use anything, even the seemingly innocuous activities of ministry to lead the plan off track. This is where mutual sharing and caring for one another really do come to the rescue. In that way, congregational members can lift one another up and support one another with mission and ministry focus rather than being overly concerned about money and preferences.

When the group found that they were once again under attack under the guise of a disgruntled member, a lack of results, or just frustration with the process, Emmaus could rally around the Word and prayer, reminding one another that this was Satan trying to thwart their good work and not a reason to stop the process.

PLANNING FOR MISSION, NOT PROGRAMS

Another big sticking point for Emmaus was getting bogged down in programs, rather than keeping their focus on mission and ministry. This primarily manifested itself as policies and procedures were reviewed and job descriptions were being written and revised. It was easy for members to assume that if they just dotted their *i*'s and crossed their *t*'s properly, everything else would just fit into place. This hearkens back to the old three-ring binder method of ministry programming, where if you just followed the steps outlined in the binder (program), everything in your congregation would be fantastically successful. While there was a time and place for binders, they simply do not replace planning and hard work.

PLANNING FOR THE LONG HAUL

Another issue was that of the "quick fix." So much of what was being done was really long-range in nature and provided little in immediate gratification. So it was easy for them to desire a programmatic quick fix in order to gin up some immediate results. Too often they desired flash over substance because the flash promoted immediate gratification. "If we just promote our church better, more people will come and we'll be able to take in more offerings." "If we just make VBS more exciting, more kids will come." Or my personal favorite, "If we could get envelopes to our delinquent members, maybe they'll start contributing their share." The primary issue with this is that quick results are simply that, here today and gone tomorrow. What might seem like a good idea at first has no staying power and will often actually detract from the desired mission and ministry plan.

This leads us to another issue that Emmaus found to be particularly problematic—loss of focus. Because this is a long-range process that requires regular attention and revision, it is easy for the congregation to forget the reason why strategic planning is good in the first place. This is where a return to focus on the key values, mission, and purpose statements, as well as goals and objectives, is imperative.

PLANNING FOR COMMUNICATION

Regular and consistent communication of the work will ensure that all interested (and even uninterested) parties are informed of what is going on, and as things change, they will keep apprised of the developments. Something important to remember is that when people lack information, they will always fill in the blanks with something, and it is rarely positive in nature.

Emmaus discovered this the hard way when they failed to adequately communicate some minor changes, which then led to some serious miscommunication of what was happening. Reviews and revisions to the constitution and bylaws were being considered, which would simply change the structure in order to better reflect how the congregation was operating.

Prior to formal discussions of what was happening and how, rumors began to circulate that these changes were going to alter what was to be believed and taught at the church. While this couldn't have been further from the truth, because there was a gap in communication, the gap was filled—and not in a positive way. This resulted in some very tense times as the record was corrected. While things did ultimately work out fine, there were a lot of hurt feelings and raw emotions that simply could have been avoided if everyone had been able to keep their focus on what was actually happening and the reason why.

PLANNING FOR MEETINGS

Emmaus also found that they had an almost unseen barrier to their success, as well as to their recruitment of leadership. This issue boiled down to one thing—*meetings*! That's not to say that meetings in and of themselves were a problem. In fact, meetings are quite necessary in order to be even remotely productive. However, Emmaus had a long culture of lengthy, somewhat rambling meetings that rarely had any kind of agenda.

While these meetings were often quite congenial, they accomplished very little. The culture had long been established that a meeting wasn't worth having if it didn't last for hours on end. This seemed to have grown out of the days when the church was a primary social center of the community, and people spent a great deal of time catching up at meetings, rather than dealing with the issues at hand.

The other issue with lengthy meetings was that without an agenda prepared ahead of time and disseminated to those involved, no one came to the meetings prepared. This caused most issues to have to be tabled for months when the interested parties finally gathered the information necessary for items to be completed. To put it simply, meetings just weren't productive, and strategic planning requires productive activity.

A side issue to these lengthy, unproductive meetings was that people were well aware of the fact that they consistently had lengthy and unproductive meetings. That is to say, people were simply unwilling to serve in leadership roles because they had no time or desire to be a part of this type of situation.

Emmaus found itself forced to address this issue before they could really move forward with the process of planning in earnest. They found that when they showed they were concerned for people's time and for the people themselves, more were willing to step up and be involved. Agenda-driven meetings focused on study, mission, ministry, and developing necessary relationships became the norm. This attracted people who were no longer concerned about having their time wasted but instead felt a greater desire to engage.

Included in this shift was an opportunity to review the agenda prior to meetings so that all involved could come prepared to work. This focus on mission and ministry, as opposed to meetings, allowed those who served to best utilize their gifts and talents without suffering undue stress and annoyance. Emmaus was also afforded the freedom to meet or not meet based on necessity, as opposed to a forced schedule imposed by the constitution or bylaws.

PLANNING FOR LEADERSHIP

Another related issue was, as noted above, the recruitment of qualified leaders and servants. Emmaus, not unlike many congregations, employed the "who won't say no?" method of filling roles and offices in the congregation. While this may seem expedient as a way to fill all the boxes, it rarely produces leaders who are suited and equipped for the roles in which they are serving.

To remedy this, Emmaus began a process of identifying people's desires and talents and keeping good records of those. This wasn't the old time-and-talent surveys but personal conversations about where people might best fit into ministry roles in the congregation. Once these were identified, people were assured of their fit for various roles based upon a comparison of their passions and skills with the job descriptions that had been developed.

It simply didn't make sense to have the accountant who loved numbers but disliked plumbing to be on the board of trustees, while the local plumber served on the budget and finance board. Making these adjustments allowed people to serve in ways for which they had a passion instead of just out of a sense of duty to the church. These servants were then adequately trained and equipped for the roles in which they were serving. From these workers, leaders were identified and cultivated so that continuity of mission and ministry could be maintained.

Voids in leadership were avoided, as former leaders were literally training and equipping their replacements, who were glad to do it because they were filling a role for which they had a passion to serve.

PLANNING FOR TRAINING

Along with this same concept is to allow those who are willing to serve the opportunity to try things based on their planning and have permission to "fail." Not everything is going to be a resounding success, but sometimes the success is in the trying. If servants are afraid to fail, they will often not try at all. If people are equipped and trained, they should be given the latitude to attempt things that fall within the parameters of their jobs, as long as they are in line with the mission of the congregation. When things don't go as hoped, these leaders have an opportunity for growth that otherwise wouldn't have been available.

A similar issue to this is actually having the manpower to fill all the roles that might seem necessary. This is where Emmaus got very creative. Because they were a relatively small congregation, they had a somewhat limited pool of workers to take up the mantle of leadership. They took the time in their planning process to assess what offices and jobs were actually necessary to fulfill their mission and ministry goals. Instead of having a board for youth and one for Sunday School and one for family ministry, which would have required three chairs and several board members on each board, they were able to merge the three boards into one board of youth and family ministry. This allowed persons who were interested in serving in that type of ministry to actually work and carry out the plan, as opposed to just needing to attend meetings for planning. This allowed for active service versus boards, which were simply mandated by structure but not necessary for the current time and place.

In response, Emmaus leadership determined which roles needed to be filled immediately and which ones could be eliminated or filled down the line at a later time as that portion of their work became necessary.

CLOSING

As you can easily tell, strategic planning is no easy task but is well worth the effort. Consider once again Emmaus: prior to strategic planning, they were existing in survival mode. They were trudging down the road, constantly concerned about finances and numbers. Meetings were long and unproductive, and members were reticent to engage in ministry. They spent precious little time together in the Word but spent most of their time squabbling about things that had little to nothing to do with God's kingdom. After strategic planning, the members of Emmaus were optimistic about their church's future. They were concerned less with money and more with ministry and mission. They weren't hung up on numbers, and more and more people became interested in participating in the mission and holding offices. Most importantly, they were spending ever-increasing amounts of time studying God's Word together and on their own so that each part of the Body of Christ could be built up in faith and strength.

This doesn't mean that strategic planning is a panacea for a congregation's problems. Yet when congregations engage in planning, their outlook and attitude change so that those problems don't seem insurmountable. Throughout all of this, it is vital to remember the wisdom of Proverbs 16:9, which states, "The heart of man plans his way, but the LORD establishes his steps." For Emmaus, strategic planning meant that they were equipped with God's Word to run back out and engage their Jerusalem, Judea, Samaria, and even the ends of the earth!

As you engage in strategic planning yourselves, please know you don't have to go it alone. Don't hesitate to reach out to your district for advice and guidance. There are also myriad resources available to you through the Office of National Mission, especially LCMS Rural and Small Town

Mission, LCMS re:Vitality, LCMS Urban and Inner City Mission, and several others. Finally, remember the Lord's promise to be with you always to the very end of the age. May the Lord of the Church bless you in your planning process and establish your steps as you seek to faithfully serve Him and those to whom He has called you.

CHAPTER 5

THE PASTOR AND WORK AND LIFE BALANCE

Rev. Don Neuendorf

So you want to learn to funambulate? That's the fancy word for tightrope walking, and it's a pretty good image of what it means to strive for a work-life balance.

Funambulism comes from the Latin word *funis*, for "rope" or "line," and *ambulare*, meaning "to walk." So many people are anxiously seeking to achieve the balanced life. They think that if they can only make it to the other side, across the frightening depth, if they can only keep their balance long enough, then they will be able to rest.

Unfortunately, funambulism is not necessarily fun. It's frightening and fraught with danger. And it's not enough to make it to your destination; life continues and you must continue walking the wire, no matter what. In life, as in tightrope walking, the consequences of failure can be catastrophic. Thanks be to God, you don't have to be a Flying Wallenda to be victorious. You've got a Helper who can catch you and put your feet back in place. He is "the God who equipped me with strength and made my way blameless. He made my feet like the feet of a deer and set me secure on the heights" (Psalm 18:32–33).

God does not call you to be a tightrope walker, toeing a straight line from here to there. He calls you to be like the deer and to ascend the heights. He has not called you to a white-knuckled walk across a chasm. He has called you to a journey, following Him, that will lead you to a new place to see your world.

What is a work-life balance? Over the years, I've seen many different schemes for achieving this mystical goal, and I've been given advice from many experienced pastors. Some I like, and some I don't. Some seem too rigid to me, and others too complicated. Here is a sampling:

→ Your day off is your Sabbath; keep it just as strictly as the Sabbath. (Wait! Does that mean I can't golf or mow the lawn then?)

→ Don't publish your personal phone numbers. Let the church secretary or someone else serve as the gatekeeper to your time. (But wouldn't I just be giving my work-life balance decisions into someone else's hands?)

→ Divide your week into twenty-one pieces (morning, afternoon, and evening for each day), and then agree with your elders how many of those pieces you'll work. This pastor suggested twelve was a fair number, allowing you to work five days, plus an evening for meetings and a Sunday morning. If you must work on your day off, then we swap another piece in place of the lost time. (This sounds good in theory, but can I really tell someone that I can't work because I'm out of chunks?)

→ Get a good day planner—there are dozens of types to help organize your life. Or buy a new device, a faster computer, a better cell phone, or a whizbang app that will do the organizing for you! (Hint: the device won't do it, but it feels good to buy new toys.)

→ Or you could just meet the needs as they come up, whether personal or congregational, and let the Lord take care of the balancing. (Otherwise known as "putting out fires" or "chasing your tail.")

Do any of those appeal to you? Any time we are seeking to balance something, we see the weight shift first one way and then another. Like a pendulum, we may see it swing between extremes. Rather than trying to put into place hard and fast rules, perhaps we would be better off thinking of our work-life balance as a series of balancing tasks. I like to think of it in terms of four main areas of balance in your life. At any given time, one of them may be less stable, but those that are in equilibrium will help you to recover.

1. Balance in the Word
2. Balancing two brides
3. Balancing two families
4. Balancing your body

1. BALANCE IN THE WORD

> **This Book of the Law shall not depart from your mouth, but you shall meditate on it day and night, so that you may be careful to do according to all that is written in it.** (Joshua 1:8)

I've heard it said many times at pastoral conferences that the pastor needs to have a meaningful devotional life, "and that doesn't mean your sermon preparation!" The argument is that studying God's Word in order to write a sermon or prepare a Bible study is not the same as *meditating* on Scripture.

I'll confess, I struggled with that for years. Why don't my hours of textual study count as meditation? I spend plenty of time in the Bible! Of course, whenever I read God's Word, my mind drifts to possible sermon themes, ideas I want to be sure to share, excellent points to make in a Bible study, and a passage I should send to someone who needs it right then. Isn't that meditation? Well, yes and no.

A few years ago, I found myself hanging from the tightrope wire. A combination of the loss of my associate pastor, a series of major decisions in the congregation, and some personal health issues brought me to the point where I knew I needed a serious time of rest. My congregation very graciously granted me a couple of months of sabbatical, and I decided to use the time I was given to study the question of spiritual disciplines. I wanted to know what spiritual disciplines are and how they might fit into a Lutheran view of Scripture and life. Making a quick trip to the seminary library, I identified about thirty books tracing ideas of spiritual disciplines and meditation from the desert fathers to the twenty-first century. (If you are interested, I'd especially recommend *Eat This Book* by Eugene Peterson and *Invitation to a Journey* by Robert Mulholland.)

There were many detailed plans for spiritual growth, but out of all those books, I distilled one single idea that has been most helpful. It's this:

READ LESS OF THE BIBLE

That doesn't sound very Lutheran, does it? But I'm not suggesting you surrender your hours of study and preparation. I'm suggesting that you take some time each day—or at least each week—to spend a significant time on a very small part of God's Word.

> **Oh, how I love Your law! It is my meditation all the day.**
> (Psalm 119:97)

The word we translate as "meditation" is the word for chewing. Not gobbling. Not wolfing down. Not devouring a massive dose. But mastication—long, slow, reflective chewing—on the Word of God. My natural tendency is to race through to see what's next. My natural tendency is to find a puzzling verse, search for the answer, check the cross-references, consult a commentary, consider how I might use this in a sermon. But meditation? Long, slow reflection? Not so much.

I need a deliberate approach to make me do what my mother used to tell me, "Chew each bite twenty-one times."

Try this:

- → Take a paragraph, or a chapter at most, and read it silently.
- → Then read it a few more times. (Read it as it applies to yourself. Read it again as it applies to your family, to your congregation, to your community, etc.)

→ Read it out loud. (You'll be surprised at how this changes your view of the text.)

→ Maybe write down on paper the verses that jump out at you most.

→ Pray about each of them.

→ Choose a part of your reading selection to memorize, and write that on a slip of paper that you can keep in your pocket.

→ Next time you're tempted to check your Facebook News Feed, try your memory work instead. You may work with many parts of God's Word in that same week, but this should be the piece that you live with, pray with, and review before you go to sleep.

Meditating on God's Word, taking real time with it, allows time for more fruitful thoughts, for God to point out things that you don't see right away, and for God's word to soak into your spirit.

> **Blessed is the man who walks not in the counsel of the wicked, nor stands in the way of sinners, nor sits in the seat of scoffers; but his delight is in the law of the LORD, and on His law he meditates day and night.** (Psalm 1:1–2)
>
> **Your words were found, and I ate them, and your words became to me a joy and the delight of my heart.** (Jeremiah 15:16)

It is a fine thing for a pastor to be a workman in the Scriptures, bringing forth from his storehouse treasures new and old (Matthew 13:52). But the pastor must not only be one who works with God's Word like a carpenter works with wood; he must also be a disciple who subjects himself to be shaped by God's Word.

Instead of trying to balance your sermon preparation time with your personal devotion time, consider changing the way you approach the Bible. Think of it not as a mine to delve into, furiously digging to get past the dirt and find the gems. Think of it instead as a wonderful world to live in. A bath to soak in. A river to be refreshed in. A balanced life in the Bible is not just a busy pastor plowing through one text after another.

It's taking time to let God's Word speak to you instead of worrying only about how you will speak God's Word.

In his book *Meditating on the Word*, Dietrich Bonhoeffer said that the reason he meditated was because he is a Christian, that every day in which he failed to penetrate more deeply into the Word was a lost day for him. Since the Word is that tool that the Holy Spirit uses to change you, the instrument by which the Spirit gives us God's Sacraments, and the only source of knowledge about your Savior, do you have something more important to do?

2. BALANCING TWO BRIDES

It is an old cliché among pastors' wives that the congregation is "the other woman." And what a demanding mistress she is. When she has an emergency, she expects the pastor to jump! She never seems to stop talking to him, messaging him, demanding all his time. Not content with his workday, she demands his evenings and weekends, and she has opinions about his manner of dress, his hobbies, and his haircut. She is more insistent on controlling the pastor's daily life than the woman he once said was bone of his bone and flesh of his flesh.

That's the most negative way to think of it, and unfortunately, it is all too often the most common way that pastors' wives are forced to think of it. They often see themselves in competition with "the other woman," the congregation. But is this the only way?

What is the congregation, after all? Isn't it the Bride of Christ?

The congregation is the Bride of Christ, but it is not the pastor's bride. You didn't marry the congregation when you were ordained. But you did agree to take care of the one that Jesus loves above all things. In fact, the pastor and his wife ought to *both* love the Bride of Christ, shouldn't they? The congregation is not in competition with your bride. The congregation is Jesus' Bride, whom you both are called to love.

Every pastor feels as if the time he spends on the congregation is time that he steals from his spouse, and the time he spends with his spouse is time he is robbing from the congregation. But if these two precious brides are in competition for your time, you will lose, no matter how you decide to use your time. On the other hand, if you and your spouse are devoted to caring for the precious, wounded, weary Bride of Jesus, then you are allies in the same cause, and all that you do will be done in love.

How can we get to such a place? For starters,

- → **Stop talking about the congregation like it's a business entity or a non-profit. The congregation is Jesus' Bride to be loved, not a problem to be managed.**
- → **Stop thinking of your spouse as a competitor for your time. She is God's gift to you and to your congregation, and she also is a part of the beautiful Bride of Christ.**
- → **Speak to your wife and to your co-workers about the congregation as the Beloved of Jesus, and speak to your congregation about your wife as a great blessing who serves them by keeping the pastor sane.**

Some pastoral couples try to guard family time by setting down hard and fast rules about certain times, certain evenings, or certain family events that are sacrosanct. You must not miss them or change them. In my experience, that approach is doomed to failure because it will inevitably pit your spouse against your congregation.

I believe that God calls you to make your spouse a partner in your work-life balance, not by giving her veto power over your schedule, but by planning together how the two of you will care for Jesus' Bride this week. Try this:

- → **Whatever your weekly day off is, and I assume you have one, reserve some time with your spouse to look at your calendar for the week.**
- → **Discuss together how Jesus' Bride needs you this week. Not just you (singular), but both of you. In order for you to be free to serve God's people, your spouse must be preparing, strengthening, and enabling you. And don't just talk about this in terms of events or meetings you must attend, but rather how you are called to care for God's people in those events.**

→ **Discuss together how you will nurture your marriage this week. What time will you reserve? How do you need to serve one another? Answer frankly the question, "What do I need from the life partner God gave to me this week?"**

→ **Finally, take turns praying together for the needs of Jesus' Bride and for your own marriage. Then hold one another accountable, listening to your spouse when she reminds you that you are neglecting your bride or Jesus' Bride.**

Your wife is not your co-pastor or your associate. She is something far greater than that. She is bone of your bone and flesh of your flesh. You may be the one who attended seminary and received ordination, but she has been called by God Himself to be your life partner, to care for your body and spirit as you also care for hers. Surely, she is a critical part of your ministry to the Bride of Christ. If you leave her out of your ministry, if you segregate your marriage from your ministry, then you are asking them to be in competition with one another.

Let me be clear on this; I'm not speaking about your wife's choice to lead some part of the congregation's work. She may or may not be called to chair the Ladies Aid. She may or may not be called to teach Sunday School or sing in the choir. Just because you are called to be the pastor does not mean that she is required to serve as extra part-time labor for the church. But because you are married, she certainly is called to be your partner. And she can help you to balance your life, to arrange your time to care for both your own bride and Jesus' Bride.

If you include your wife in the time-balancing decisions of your ministry, then you will also recognize that you and she both need time to care for one another. Ask her opinion about where you ought to delegate more, about which family times you really should not miss. My wife and I try to look at our calendars together at the beginning of each week, not just so that we're both informed (although that's critical!) but also in order that she can suggest changes. Sometimes she reminds me to reserve more time for my work! "Where are you going to work on your sermon?" she has asked me when she sees every block of time filled. "When will you exercise?" And very gently but firmly, "Do you have time to come with me to do this?"

I may think that I am making time for my wife because I graciously planned to take her out to dinner, but she may value other things more. In particular, she values my listening to her as we make those decisions together.

Consider what God's Word says about the Bride. The Church, and your congregation, are portrayed metaphorically in Revelation 12. She brings the Savior into the world. Just as Mary gave birth to Jesus, so your humble members bring Jesus into their communities. And what is the result? Satan pursues them to destroy them. The Bride flees into the desert. So also your members go through times of spiritual drought and weariness. She is nearly captured by the enemy, Satan, and your members are targeted by him too. But, just as all seems lost, she finds a refuge in the wilderness, a hiding place where she may dwell secure.

Your members, and you yourself, are living through this time of tribulation. You and they both require the water of life, the fountain of life that springs forth from the Word and Sacraments. Your wife is your partner in caring for them as the two of you care for one another.

The congregation is not an enemy, no matter what the difficulty may be this week, no matter whether there are "alligators" who oppose your ministry, and no matter whether she does what the pastor says or not. The congregation is exactly what we would expect of the Bride of Christ who has been chased by Satan into the wilderness (Revelation 12:6). She is weary. She is afraid. She is weak. She is wounded. But she is beautiful in the eyes of Jesus, and you and your spouse need to see her through Jesus' eyes.

3. BALANCING TWO FAMILIES

My wife and I have four children, all grown up now. As I look back on our busiest child-raising years, I often wonder where we found the energy and time. I also feel some guilt about the many times I was away in the evenings and the family times that I missed. The funny thing is, when I ask my children about it, they tell me that they didn't think I was gone too much at all. We did fun things together, and they have many great memories. How did that work?

Maybe you've been warned about the "PK problem." The pastor's children often suffer from their father being an authority figure. The children of the congregation see him preaching and pontificating in front of all the adults. They see others defer to him. No matter how kindly he may be during the children's sermon, he still seems like the boss. That puts the pastor's children in a strange place. To their classmates, your children may seem to carry some of your authority. They may be treated differently by other adults. They may be expected to be holier or better people.

What a heavy burden to carry! If they live up to the role and they try to be obedient and devout, then other children may feel guilty by the comparison and try to belittle them. If they rebel against the role imposed on them and try to show that they are more than just the pastor's kids, then their friends may use them to justify their own poor decisions. If you are primarily an authority figure in the eyes of your members, and especially the children of your congregation, then your children will be caught in an impossible situation.

What is the answer? Your mileage may vary, but I will suggest three rules to follow:

- → **Pay attention to which hat you're wearing. Be a "father" to your members, but never forget to be even more than that for your children. They need you as parent more than as pastor.**
- → **Be there! Think less about contact time and more about consistent connection.**
- → **Make the most of the PK problem. Help your children to help their friends.**

WATCH WHICH HAT YOU WEAR

There's a reason people sometimes call you "Father" when you are wearing a black clerical shirt, and it's not just because you look Roman Catholic. It's because a pastor really does have a fatherly role in the congregation. You are not the provider in the way you may be at home, but you are the teacher and leader, you are also a loving listener, and you are sometimes the disciplinarian. As a father to the congregation, you may become extremely close to some members at critical times. Just as you carried a sleepless child around the living room at 2 a.m., you may also sit beside the hospital bed of your sister in Christ or listen to a brother pouring out his griefs.

You have a fatherlike role as pastor, but you are not literally the parent of the congregation. One day you will leave them, and another will take your place. But you are called for life to be the parent to your children.

When your own family is in church, you don't stop being father to your children. Instead, you are father to them in two ways, as pastor and as parent. But this can be confusing. Pastors who confuse their parenting roles make things difficult for their members and for their children.

Sometimes a pastor is extra hard on his children if they disobey in church because he fears that their behavior has an impact on his ministry. Sometimes the pastor (and the congregation) expect that the minister's children ought to know the Bible better, do their memory work more faithfully, and be more sanctified than their peers. When you do this, you are asking your children to take some responsibility for your pastoral ministry, but your children are not miniature assistant pastors. You need to be their parent first and their pastor second. You need to be their parent because other people will tend to make them surrogates for the pastor.

If you must use an illustration from your family life in your preaching (a temptation to which we all succumb), then make sure that you are the one who is the fool in the story, not your spouse or child. Their job is not to be the punch line of your jokes. But if you are self-deprecating in your illustration, then you allow others to see that you also need a Savior.

You also need to humble yourself and learn. And you are not the master who sits over them but the disciple who learns beside them.

Sometimes your family will be present with you while you are wearing your pastor/father hat. Be ready to change hats. If your child misbehaves, do not discipline him because he has embarrassed you in front of the congregation. Use only the discipline that would be appropriate for any other father and child. Most of the time, that will take the form of helping your child to participate in worship with you. Remember that the way you treat your child will have a profound impact on all the families present. Let that weight of responsibility fall on you, not on your child.

BE PRESENT, CONSISTENTLY

There will be many times that you have to miss a family event. Birthdays may have to be scheduled around church responsibilities (heaven help you if you have children born in December). You may be called away from the dinner table, and you may have evening meetings that infringe on the time that you hoped to spend with your children. There is only so much you can do to avoid these things. However, it is possible to arrange your work to find regular times for you to participate in your children's lives.

Each pastor's day is different, depending on the circumstances of his congregation. But you can find, or make, time that will work every day. For several of the years when our children were young, we had all four in school at the same time, and the school was just across the soccer field from home. Instead of eating with their classmates, our children walked home for lunch. We tried (and sometimes failed) to have breakfast together (getting ready for school is hectic). We often, but not always, had supper together. But we always, always, always had lunch together. Better still, since their classes were dismissed at different times, we had lunch with each one of our children in succession. I made sure to keep my calendar clear. (I have to eat lunch, right?) And we used that time to talk with our children about their day. God blessed it so that we were often able to help them deal with challenges during the day.

Perhaps that won't work for you. It worked for us for several years, and when that season ended, we looked for other opportunities.

Another time we took advantage of was bedtime. I often missed the evening hours because of meetings, but I was normally home in time for bedtime. (Try to discipline your lay leaders so that they follow an agenda and keep meetings to a reasonable length. Trust me—everyone in the meeting will gladly vote to keep it short.) We made it a practice to read a book with Dad at bedtime. Long books. We read all the Narnia books with me laying on the hallway floor between bedrooms and the children listening in bed. We read *The Lord of the Rings*, and we read *The Count of Monte Cristo*, though they took months. But these were not only quiet reading times; they were opportunities for conversation about the challenging things happening in those stories (and, may I say, my children have excellent vocabularies as a result).

Some pastors try to balance work time and family time by measuring the amount of time each receives. But you will never ever have enough time. They deserve more time than you can give, and your church family also needs you. But you can be there regularly and faithfully for your children so that they know they can daily have time to talk and pray with you about what's happening in their lives.

Some of you may be blessed to have much more time than I was able to have, but even then, consistency is comforting for your children. That's true for your children at home and your "children" at church.

MAKE THE MOST OF THE PK PROBLEM

We described the "PK problem" above and the special burden that children of pastors can sometimes carry. But there is an upside to it. Your children, whether you plan it or not, will have a window into the lives and problems of others more than most people.

You may not talk about it openly, but children hear more than you realize, and they pick up on tension in the congregation, on tension in mom and dad, and on the concerns for people who are sick, dying, getting divorced, dealing with grief. The proper place to deal with all of these things is in your family prayer.

Of course, you should never share confidential information with your children or burden them with the heaviest parts of people's problems.

But since they already know that something is wrong, then this is the perfect time to teach them what we do when something is wrong—even if we don't quite know what it is. We pray!

In your family prayers, include some bits of those things that are on your hearts. Pray for those who are sick. Pray for those who are grieving. Your children are not mini-pastors, but they are mini-Christians, and as such, they are entitled to come to their heavenly Father as dear children come to their dear father. In fact, don't their angels behold God's face at all times? Leading your children in prayer will allow them to release the tension that they have picked up from your concerns and put it back where it belongs, in the hands of their heavenly Father.

Better still, as you lead your children to deal with their own problems with prayer, you will teach them to pray for their enemies, for those who are making them unhappy at school, for broken friendships, and for academic struggles. They will always be preacher's kids, no matter how you try to shield them, so why not let them join you in prayer, grow in faith, and serve their childhood friends in prayer as you serve your members?

4. BALANCING YOUR BODY

Those who know me best would laugh to think of me writing about fitness. I am not an athlete of any kind, and I've never been a big fitness buff. And yet, as I have gotten older, I've come to appreciate the value of physical exertion to help balance my life. In the other sections, we had a few bullet points to summarize how to balance that aspect of your life, so it's only fitting that we do the same here.

GET UP!

Personally, I like nothing better than sitting in a comfortable chair with a good book and a glass of bourbon. That's my escape time (especially when I'm reading junk fiction). For you, that might be binging on Netflix, sitting with a hook in the water, or sleeping in. Those are all good things, and you need them from time to time. But whether you are an athlete or not, the best medicine for stress is sweat.

Pastoral ministry doesn't always seem stressful. Hopefully, the times that you are in actual conflict with others are rare. But you participate in the conflict of others all the time. One of your members reflects that this has been a very hard year because of the serious illness of a loved one. You were alongside that loved one and several others who were going through similar life-threatening events. Your own marriage is healthy, but you have been counseling and praying with couples whose marriages are a battleground. You have soaked up some of their stress. Other members of the congregation, or even of your staff, are in conflict with one another. It's not your problem, but you are called into the middle to be the one to help them communicate. You get the anxiety from both sides.

The insidious thing about stress is that it leaks into your life slowly. It's not just the big crisis that causes stress; it's the long-term exposure to toxic situations. The recent COVID-19 crisis has been an excellent lesson in stress. Friends who have had no financial setback from the epidemic, who have not been sick, and, in fact, who say that their lives are going really well, nevertheless tell me that they're exhausted. They are stressed out. They're sick of all the conflict around them. It's as if they have absorbed the stress of the conflicted world around them.

It's important to have restful meditation time in God's Word that renews your sense of who you are with your heavenly Father. It's critical to have the haven of a loving marriage that provides healing for your spirit. It's vital to have a healthy family life where you can escape your much larger congregational family for a time. But you also need to have a way to deal directly with the physical effects of stress.

Dr. Archibald Hart, in his book *The Hidden Link Between Adrenaline and Stress,* actually uses the example of a pastor to illustrate how we sometimes generate extra adrenaline from our own conflict, from the conflict of others, and even just from public performance (like preaching). We love that adrenaline. It's that feeling you get when you are leading your congregation in worship, you're boldly sharing the Word, you're engaged with all your members, and then you come home and crash. You are totally wiped out after a morning of high engagement.

Hart explains that what you are experiencing is not just fatigue, the kind of weariness that comes from carrying a heavy pack for a twenty-mile hike; you are experiencing adrenaline exhaustion. You can come to count on that adrenaline surge to get you through a tough task, but eventually, your body cannot keep up. When you can no longer produce enough adrenaline, then your crash will be truly severe.

Adrenaline is great! It helps us do things we'd otherwise be unable to do. It gives us extra sharpness and strength and focus when we need it. But it is like high-octane fuel; it wears our engine down more quickly. There is a physical cost to psyching yourself up to lead worship, to confront a discipline situation, to enter the room of a dying friend. The physical toll must be paid by physical recovery. Sleep, exercise, and diet are essential parts of balancing your life.

In order to deal with this adrenaline and stress, you need sleep, quiet time, and exertion. You need to take care of this amazing and delicate instrument God has given you in order to be able to take care of others. You don't need to prepare to run an Ironman Triathlon, although that would be wonderful. You don't need to be a champion athlete. But you do need to find an activity that burns off stress. You do need to arrange your life to provide regular hours of sleep. You may break that routine out of necessity, but it's far better to break a routine from time to time than to have no routine at all. And you need regular exertion of some kind that fits into your life so that you can continue it week after week.

AN ELLIPTICAL ORBIT

My third-grade classroom had an orrery, a small 3D model of the solar system. Each planet was suspended on a thin rod of the proper length to represent its distance from the sun. The earth and moon even had tiny gear-driven chains that caused them to rotate as they orbited the sun. Unfortunately, there was one big mistake. All the orbits were circular. The planets were always the same distance from the sun.

In real life, most orbits are elliptical. Sometimes they are closer to the sun and sometimes further away, but the most important feature of an orbit is this: the sun is always at the center.

This is true for your life as well.

We like to talk about a work-life balance as if it were possible to keep anything in our lives in balance. It is not. Here is something that it would be well for you to acknowledge right from the beginning of your ministry: your life will never be in balance.

There will be no month, no week, not even a single day that will be perfectly balanced, that will keep all the plates spinning, that will work in all the essential elements, that will meet all the needs. Like Peter, walking for just a few moments on the water of the Sea of Galilee, you will quickly be overcome by the wind and the waves.

That's okay.

Peter cried out, "Lord, save me" (Matthew 14:30). And although the Scripture does not record him ever repeating that phrase, I am confident that he said it again and again and again in his life and ministry. Peter was not capable of keeping everything in balance, as we see with his failure to balance his relationships with the Jewish and Gentile believers (Galatians 2:11–21). Paul says that Peter was privileged to bring his family with him in his ministry (1 Corinthians 9:5), but I wonder if Peter always considered it a privilege. Imagine the complexities of traveling with a family to the various points of ministry in the first century, during a time of intermittent persecution! I have no doubt that Peter struggled, just as Paul struggled with his fractious congregations.

An object in elliptical orbit does not always move at the same speed. Earth, when it is close to the sun in January, moves faster than it does in July when it is further away. Similarly, your ministry may seem to be flying sometimes and dragging by at other times. You will fly through showers of meteors some days and through clear skies on others. But always, always and every day, you will orbit the center of gravity. Your ministry and your life, your work and your family, your church and your home will be centered on Jesus, your Savior.

The motto of my alma mater, Concordia in Ann Arbor, is drawn from Colossians 1:18: "And He is the head of the body, the church. He is the beginning, the firstborn from the dead, that in everything He might be preeminent." I used to think that "Christ first in everything" meant that He was at the top of the list, the number one. And after I was done with the first item on the list, then I could get on with the rest. But Jesus is not just first. Jesus is the center of all the things on my list. All of the other things revolve around Him. They are about Him. They all serve Him.

Jesus is the balancing force in your life.

When you worry that your work-life balance is out of whack, it will not be because of too many church meetings or too many family responsibilities. It will not be because you need more hours in your day. It will be because you are forgetting to look to the center, to orient yourself on the Star of the Morning.

What a wonderful thing, then, to realize that Jesus is the grounding force that will pull steadily on you, no matter what. You will constantly pull away, like any body in motion, but Jesus will never let you go.

> **And I, when I am lifted up from the earth, will draw all people to Myself.** (John 12:32)

RECOMMENDED READING:

Eat This Book: A Conversation in the Art of Spiritual Reading, Eugene H. Peterson, Eerdmans, 2009

Invitation to a Journey: A Road Map for Spiritual Formation, M. Robert Mulholland Jr., IVP Books, 1993

The Hidden Link Between Adrenaline and Stress, Dr. Archibald D. Hart, Thomas Nelson, 1985

CHAPTER 6

THE PASTOR AND MANAGING HIS SPIRITUAL AND PHYSICAL HEALTH

Rev. Ron Garwood

My hobby is mountaineering, and when I was younger, I did a lot of mountain climbing—ascending most of the high peaks in Wyoming, including Wyoming's highest, Gannett Peak in the Wind River Mountains, and the Grand Teton near Jackson, Wyoming, which is the second-highest peak in the state. The Grand Teton is one of the most well-known and often-viewed mountains in the United States and is a wonderful challenge to climb. I also did some climbing in Canada, Alaska, and Scotland.

Mountaineering, and specifically mountain climbing, is highly exhilarating and greatly rewarding. However, serious mountain climbing is inherently dangerous and requires physical and emotional training, preparation, and discipline. Without serious attention to these areas, bad things happen. Several men I climbed with in the past are now buried in the ice on some very high mountains because they failed to be attentive to some very important things.

However, I have lost many more friends and associates to death due to their failure to give attention to their lives in much less dramatic situations than climbing mountains. Many of us take this life for granted and move through it without giving attention to basic but very important things—like eating, drinking, resting, physical exercise, and emotional and spiritual health.

Please consider for a moment, how often do you give real, deliberate attention to how you live your life in general? How often do you remember your Baptism and that you are a very valuable person because of whose you are? And how often do you consider that as a pastor, you are a very important person because of your call into the Office of the Ministry of the Word?

As a pastor, you serve in the highest office in the Church, the preaching and teaching office, and your responsibilities are important. So important, in fact, that no man can properly and effectively carry out this critically important ministry except by the grace and mercy of God.

Now, though you serve as a pastor only by His call and serve faithfully only by His grace and mercy, you nonetheless have a responsibility to take care of yourself both physically and spiritually. Part of our obligation as children of God is to be good stewards of our physical life. As the Bible teaches, "You are not your own, for you were bought with a price. So glorify God in your body" (1 Corinthians 6:19–20). And as a Christian man, you also have an obligation to care for your spiritual life. St. Paul wrote to the Colossians, "Therefore, as you received Christ Jesus the Lord, so walk in Him, rooted and built up in Him and established in the faith, just as you were taught, abounding in thanksgiving" (Colossians 2:6–7). So taking care of yourself physically and spiritually is good, godly, and very important to your ministry.

In this chapter, we will discuss some ways to practice self-care of both our physical and spiritual life. The information shared here is neither exhaustive nor the last word in physical and spiritual self-care, but the points made are based upon good factual information and the experience of seasoned pastors.

CARE FOR PHYSICAL LIFE

Let's begin by considering our physical life. Whenever we consider our physical body, we can and should say to God, as did David, "I praise You, for I am fearfully and wonderfully made. Wonderful are Your works; my soul knows it very well" (Psalm 139:14). Our physical body is, indeed, a masterpiece of the Lord's work and worthy of excellent care and stewardship.

And one very real danger for a faithful pastor is to feel guilty about giving time and attention to your physical being. As a faithful pastor, you love Christ and His people, and you truly want to serve the Church in all ways that you can. And so taking time to care for yourself may seem selfish, and you may feel like you are neglecting your work and the people placed into your care. But that is not true and can be a ploy of Satan to do you and your ministry great damage. If you are not physically healthy, rested, fed, and strong, you can't serve properly or well. So you must not feel guilty about taking time to care for yourself and keep your body fit and strong.

We should watch our weight, be aware of our blood pressure, address any health conditions or problems we have with proper attention and medical advice, have physical checkups with our physician, visit our dentist regularly, and a host of other things we could list here.

Consider Jesus' many healing miracles as recorded in the Gospels. Jesus, God in the flesh, had regard for the physical lives of the people to whom He ministered. When people were in severe need of help in their physical lives and begged Jesus for His assistance, He responded with great love and care. If our physical life is important to Jesus, it should also be important to us.

And by the way, do not be hesitant to ask for help when you need it. Sometimes men are too proud to seek help and, therefore, suffer needlessly or miss great opportunities to receive some great blessings.

There was an incident in one of my climbing expeditions when I needed help badly but in pride neglected to ask for it as quickly as I should have.

My two sons and I were coming down a very steep glacier from a summit ridge right at thirteen thousand feet at about 1:00 p.m. The sun was very warm, and the snow on the surface of the glacier was getting soft, which made foot purchase very difficult, even with inch-and-a-half spikes on our crampons. So I roped myself to a rock spur and belayed my boys (I say "boys," but they were both young men in their thirties) down the steep slope to an ice shelf, where they could anchor themselves with snow pickets.

While they were engaged in that, I unroped and began a descent down the glacier very, very carefully. But I lost my footing and very quickly was sliding down the steep glacier. I rolled onto my stomach and tried to arrest my fall by burying the spike on my ice axe into the surface of the glacier. However, I could not get my axe to hold and finally yelled very loudly, "Falling!" which is the urgent distress call for a mountaineer.

My son nearest to me, and to whom I was roped, quickly stopped what he was doing, clipped himself into his snow anchor, and began to take the slack out of the rope to which I was attached. He pulled me to a stop about twenty feet from a fifteen-hundred-foot drop. When my heart stopped racing, I was able to use the rope to gain the safety of the ice shelf with my boys.

Once there, I gave them a good talking-to about being sure to seek help quickly when they needed it and not to arrogantly think that they did not need it. They received my lecture with big smiles on their faces and some knowing nods. And whenever it is opportune for them, they remind me of the incident with great glee.

So ask for help when you need it, seek good counsel and advice when it is available, and use what you can learn to take good care of yourself. And you must be wisely open to that, or you probably wouldn't be reading this book.

All that being said, let's get to some details for wisely caring for our physical lives.

TAKE CARE TO FUEL YOUR BODY

We need to eat regularly and well to maintain the health and well-being of the body God created for us. To help us do that, our gracious God provided many different kinds of food for us in His creation. And eating good food is enjoyable and a pleasure in this life.

However, eating regularly and well does not come naturally to us and requires good discipline on our part. You serve as a pastor twenty-four hours a day, seven days a week, and so the demands on your time can be severe, interfering with your personal life in many ways, including your meals. But it is important that you take time to eat regularly and properly.

My dear wife is a great blessing to me in this regard. I do not like to cook or prepare food, mainly because I don't do it well, and so if I had to care for myself in this department, I would be in trouble. But my wife does a great job of making sure our family meals are served regularly, and she also takes the time and trouble to make sure our meals are properly balanced and nutritious. I pray the same is true for you. But whether you have a wife who cares for you in this department or not, eating properly and at regular times is a very important discipline.

Good food is a gift from God and one that I enjoy very much. I do eat to live, but I also love to eat. There are also certain foods that I enjoy a great deal, and I suspect that this is true for you too. That being the case, it is necessary to exercise good discipline in how much we eat. As you know, gluttony is noted in the Scriptures as a sin. Proverbs 23:20 states, "Be not among drunkards or among gluttonous eaters of meat." And gluttony is considered so serious that Proverbs 23:2 states, "Put a knife to your throat if you are given to appetite."

We must remember that our food is a gift from God, for which we constantly give thanks, but we must enjoy our food in a disciplined manner, and food and eating must not become a god or a passion. Obesity is a problem for many Americans in our day, and we pastors should be good examples in maintaining a healthy weight. A healthy weight will enable us to better enjoy our life and family and be better equipped to carry out a robust ministry, both of which are God-pleasing. As we are encouraged by St. Paul in his First Letter to the Corinthians, "Whether you eat or drink, or whatever you do, do all to the glory of God" (1 Corinthians 10:31).

There are many good books and resources available on eating properly, for good health and nutrition. There are also a number of good websites that offer helpful information in this regard. One example of these is concordiaplans.org, which has articles and resources on wellness and health. And the site also provides the opportunity to phone or email them with specific questions. I would recommend that you do some reading and research in regard to eating properly and see what appeals to your tastes and interest. We are not all the same, and what works well for one person may not work well for another. Our age, metabolism, likes, dislikes, experiences, and so on are all different. And so good and proper eating may be different for one than it is for another. What's important is to eat properly and regularly in whatever way works well for you.

REMEMBER TO DRINK WATER

> **And when he drank, his spirit returned and he revived.**
> (Judges 15:19)

After Samson slew a thousand of Israel's enemies with the jawbone of a donkey, he was very thirsty, but there was no water to drink. So he prayed to the Lord, "You have granted this great salvation by the hand of Your servant, and shall I now die of thirst?" (Judges 15:18). The mighty Samson, who was invincible among men by the grace and power of God, was brought to the point of death for lack of water.

Just as eating properly and regularly is important, please remember that we all need to drink water to maintain good physical health. The body is reportedly about 60 percent water. And our bodies are constantly losing water, primarily via urine, sweat, and evaporation through the lungs. And this is problematic because water is necessary to our bodies for regulating body temperature, protecting body tissues and joints, ridding the body of waste, aiding digestion, boosting energy, helping the body fight illnesses, and aiding in cognitive function, to name some of the main benefits. So, to prevent dehydration, fatigue, and other health issues, we need to drink enough water. Health authorities encourage us to drink eight 8-oz. glasses each day. If you remember to drink eight times eight, you'll do fine.

Remember that feeling thirsty, or wanting a drink, isn't necessarily a helpful indicator of your need for hydration. In fact, by the time you're thirsty, you could already be in the first stages of dehydration. And it is also said that it is easy to mistake thirst for hunger so that when we feel the need for a snack, we might be smarter to take a drink of water first.

With our busy lives, it is easy not to drink enough water. I notice as I get older, I find it is even more necessary to remind myself to drink enough water. A discipline I have developed is to drink a full glass of water as soon as I get up in the morning because if we sleep from six to eight hours during the night, that's a long period of time for our body not to have had water. And I also put a large mug of water on my desk during the day when I am in my office working, and I make sure that mug is empty by noon and ready for a refill. You can develop your own routines for drinking enough water, but the important thing is to do it!

GET GOOD PHYSICAL EXERCISE

St. Paul wrote to Pastor Timothy that a pastor must keep the faith, teach true doctrine, and resist false teaching, but he also wrote to Timothy that "bodily training is of some value" (1 Timothy 4:8), which brings us to the point that another very important feature of caring for our body is getting enough exercise. Sometimes a pastor's duties require that he be at his desk for several hours at a time during the day, but it is important that we not sit too long. It is now being said that sitting is the new smoking because too much inactivity results in a lot of negative things for our body.

So as you work at your desk, discipline yourself to get up and move around at regular intervals. This was difficult for me in that I would become very focused on a project or be concentrating intently on what I was doing and would forget to get up and move about now and then. So I bought an activity tracker to wear on my wrist, and I set it to vibrate every twenty minutes so that I am reminded it is time to get up. How often you get up from sitting is up to you, but it is recommended that a person get up and move about at least every hour.

At some times of the day, it is easy for a person to become drowsy after sitting for a period of time, and if that happens to you, that is a great time to get up and move about. The movement is good for our bodies, and it will also help us to be more alert, which makes us more productive as we get back to our desk for work.

When you do get up, just move your body in whatever way is available to you. Take a short walk, swing your arms, do some stretches, or the like. Your period of movement need not be long, as just a few minutes will be helpful for your body.

In addition to these short periods of moving and exercising a bit, we also need to have longer periods of sustained exercise in our routine. Expert after expert tells us that regular exercise is critically important for each of us. Exercise has been called a regenerative medicine. Exercise proponents tell us that there is not an organ system in our body that is not positively affected by good exercise. Medical researchers have linked inactivity with a higher risk of heart disease, a higher risk of developing type 2 diabetes, as well as having high blood pressure and dementia. It is also being reported that a lack of regular activity in our lives may result in developing lung and colon cancers. In short, it is quite clear that being active benefits a person greatly in maintaining good health and being energetic and productive.

Exercise has also been shown to improve our mood and attitude and also decrease our feelings of anxiety and stress, which can lead to depression. It is reported by some researchers that exercise increases the production of endorphins in our body, which are hormones secreted within the brain that have a number of physiological functions. Endorphins are peptides that activate the body's opiate receptors, causing an analgesic effect. In short, these hormones make us feel good and give us a sense of well-being, which is a part of our being fearfully and wonderfully made. So exercise is helpful in maintaining a good attitude.

Regular exercise can also help us with weight loss or in maintaining a body weight that is good for us. And regular exercise helps us build and maintain our muscles and bone structure. The benefits of being strong of muscle and bone are many.

In regard to weight loss or maintaining a proper weight, muscles burn calories even when we are not active. Strong muscles and bone mass protect us when we fall and also enable us to maintain good balance and get around properly. As we age, we lose muscle mass and bone strength, so it is important as we get older to keep moving and have a good exercise regime.

And believe it or not, a good exercise routine can actually increase our energy level. As we exercise, our body becomes more toned, and we grow in physical conditioning, which enables us to be more efficient in our regular life functions. And exercise can also help us relax and enjoy resting after a period of physical activity. In addition, a good exercise routine can improve our sleep quality. And in some cases, exercise can help reduce pain in areas of our body.

Now, before we get into specific disciplines for exercise and activity, it should be noted that we should all have a primary care physician who sees us regularly, which may be at least once a year if we are generally healthy. And we should seek our doctor's advice in regard to what kinds of exercise are beneficial to us, given our state of health and age, and how intense our exercise routine should be. I would also note that as a pastor, having regular checkups with a physician is being a good example to the members of your congregation to do the same and take care of their own bodies.

And in regard to your healthcare visits, Concordia Health Plans provides good advice and funding in regard to having wellness checks with your doctor. The Plans also have good resources for being active and developing good self-care plans and routines.

Once we know that we are healthy and fit and able to engage in physical activity, exercise pundits recommend that we get at least 150 minutes a week of physical activity that works our heart and lungs to a good degree. There are a number of excellent exercise resources available in the form of books, websites, magazines, and the like, which can help us determine the number of hours of exercise each week that is optimal and what the target heart rate should be for our exercise. Amazon has a variety of books on exercise and fitness material. You can also do an internet search for exercise and fitness and be led to numerous resources that are helpful. And YouTube has videos available on exercise, weightlifting, and fitness in general for people of all ages.

An important feature of exercise is to choose an activity or activities that you enjoy and find fulfilling. Engaging in an exercise activity you do not enjoy makes it drudgery and something you will tend to avoid. So if you don't already have exercise activities that you enjoy, try a number of different kinds to see which you enjoy most and even look forward to.

Some exercise activities a pastor or church worker can consider, depending on your age, interest, and condition, are brisk walking (about two to two and a half miles an hour), swimming, biking, light running, jumping rope, weight lifting, stationary bicycling, or hiking. One can join a gym where there are a number of exercise options, including elliptical machines, weight machines, treadmills, and the like. The professionals at a gym can be helpful in giving advice on form, cadence, duration, and so on, in regard to exercise options.

Another good practice is to have a hobby that offers a diversion and mental rest. Sports hobbies like golf or tennis not only offer diversion but are also good sources of physical exercise. A side benefit of having a hobby or joining a gym or physical fitness group is that it often provides the opportunity to develop contacts and friendships outside our church family, which can be good for us personally and also good for our ministry.

A great example of the benefits regular exercise can work in a person's life is an incident that occurred in my pastoral ministry. My entire parish ministry has been carried out in the state of Wyoming. In the first parish I served, I had an elder who had been born and raised in Wyoming and had spent a good deal of his working life as a cowboy. He had married a schoolteacher who was an LCMS Lutheran, and by the grace of God, he not only became a Lutheran Christian but was a very committed and faithful Lutheran. At the time of the incident I relate here, he was seventy-two years old and in generally good health. His son owned a physical fitness business in town that had a good assortment of exercise and weight machines. Even though he was seventy-two years old, his son had talked him into coming to his business at least three times a week and working out with various machines.

One spring day, he was out on an area ranch helping work some cattle. He was roping some steers to be cut out of the herd that was being worked. As he worked, he roped a good-sized steer that suddenly bolted away from him after he put the loop over its head, and as my elderly friend went to dally the rope around the saddle horn, he missed the horn, and the rope whipped around his wrist. The steer came to the end of the rope and jerked him out of the saddle and dragged him a good distance across the corral, slamming him into a wooden snubbing post.

A few hours later, I received a phone call that he was in the hospital being treated for his injuries. When I entered his room, I was shocked at the sight of him, for there did not seem to be a spot on his body that was not black and blue with bruises. However, he was in good spirits and said that other than being very sore, he was feeling okay.

After a devotion and prayer, his son and I left the room to go visit with the doctor. The doctor said that he was amazed that a man his age was not hurt worse than he was. He had no broken bones and seemed sound internally. The doctor went on to say that his remarkable strength and good physical condition had enabled him to come through this accident fairly well when it should have seriously injured or even killed him at his age. His regular exercise and weight training had served him extremely well.

As he and I talked later, we knew that he had not been hurt more badly than he was due to the grace and mercy of God, but also due to his excellent physical condition, which resulted from his exercise and weight training routine. And that, of course, was also a part of God's grace and mercy. Being healthy and fit through good and regular physical exercise is a way that God can bless us and extend our ministry to others for many years.

So regular exercise is extremely good, even critical, for us for a number of reasons. But having a disciplined program of activity and exercise is not easy for a busy pastor, and therefore, we must be disciplined and intentional about it.

REST YOUR BODY

In Mark 6:31, Jesus spoke to the apostles after they reported to Him on some of their ministry activities. He told them, "Come away by yourselves to a desolate place and rest a while." From the Word of God, it is obvious that Jesus knew the need and value of rest for His disciples and also for Himself as a true man. There are several verses in Scripture that report Jesus sleeping or resting.

So as important as activity and regular exercise are, getting adequate rest is an absolute necessity. And rest includes taking breaks from work during the day, regularly getting a good night's sleep, and taking your day off, as well as using your vacation days.

Unfortunately, our vocation as pastor or church worker is often a great impediment to resting as we should. Pastors are on call twenty-four hours a day, seven days a week. In addition, since there is always something important to do, a pastor can feel guilty for taking a break, going to bed early, using his day off, or being gone on vacation. And feeling guilty can interfere with really getting the rest we need.

But to be able to continue being a good pastor, husband, and father, a man must rest. So rest is not an option or luxury but a necessity. And therefore, one must be disciplined and intentional in getting proper rest and do so without guilt or reluctance, recognizing that it is good stewardship of our life to rest.

To properly manage your day off, a good practice is to let the congregation know when that day(s) off is and ask their help in protecting it. Your board of elders should be aware of when your day off is and help you protect your time on that day.

You may also need to get away from home now and then on your day off so that you can have some quality time away. If you are home and available, people may stop by and engage with you without realizing it's your day off. And being a kind and loving pastor, you will probably make yourself available to them. So being away from home and office can help you have time for yourself and your family. In any event, your day off, as well as your exercise time and vacation time, are very important in order to properly care for yourself, which makes your time away good for your parish and your family.

A pastor must also be careful of the expectations people in his congregation have of him, and also those that he has of himself. The vast majority of the people in a pastor's congregation have no idea of the heavy schedule he maintains. Most parishioners see their pastor on Sunday morning for worship and Bible class and have little contact with him during the week, which results in the old and incorrect comment that pastors only work one day a week. The average members do not see the pastor at his desk studying, writing sermons, or preparing for Bible study. They do not know of his many visits to the hospital, nursing home, shut-in members, and calls made on visitors. Most do not know of the counseling sessions he has with troubled members, the couples with marriage issues that he cares for, or of the member struggling with alcohol abuse or some other addiction that he serves.

And so expectations of the pastor by his parish may not be realistic or fair, making the pastor feel uncomfortable if he is not working and serving the parish. The faithful and conscientious pastor may feel guilty for taking time to exercise or rest when he feels those expectations. He may feel that it is wrong for him to take any time away from his work for any reason, especially to care for or serve himself.

However, the pastor does actually care for and serve his parish when he cares for himself in a proper way. The pastor who does not care for himself can become tired and lose efficiency. He may become distracted and not able to focus on the proper things. He may become angry with, or resentful of, his congregation for seemingly pushing him so hard or having unrealistic expectations of him. The overextended and tired pastor may become ill or burn out, or in many other ways fail to serve his people as God intends.

Therefore, a pastor must rest and care for himself to be a good servant of the Lord and His people. The Lord Jesus rested and took time away from His earthly ministry to care for Himself. At times, Jesus left His disciples and went up on a mountain to pray and rest. He was resting by a well in Samaria while His disciples went into town to buy food when a woman from the town encountered Him there. He was sleeping in a boat when a storm came up and frightened His disciples.

Jesus is truly and fully God, God in all ways that the Father is God. But He is also fully and truly man. He is a man in all ways that we are, yet without sin. And if the Lord needed rest and cared for Himself in His earthly ministry of working out salvation for all sinners, then the pastor who represents and ministers to people in the stead of Jesus should not feel guilty in taking time to rest, exercise, eat, sleep, and care for himself and his family.

ADDRESS YOUR FIRST MINISTRY RESPONSIBILITY

Now, in regard to his wife and family, if he is married, a pastor may feel guilty in taking time from his parish to be with his family and be a godly husband and father. That is a big mistake. A pastor's first ministry responsibility is to his family. A husband and father has great God-given responsibilities in caring for his family both physically and spiritually. Nowhere in Scripture is it revealed that a disciple of the Lord need sacrifice his family in service to the Lord. The Lord clearly teaches that love of family must be not be greater than love of God (Luke 14:25–27). But a husband and father is to love his wife and family and care for them as Christ cares for the Church (John 15:12, Ephesians 5:25).

So it is important to properly balance our time between our duties as pastor and our duties as husband and father. Likewise, we need to balance our care for ourselves with our care for our families. And just as we may feel guilty for taking time from our congregations to rest or exercise, we may also feel guilty for taking that same time from our families. But for all the good reasons that we must care for ourselves in order to properly serve our congregations, we must also take care of ourselves to properly serve our families.

Many pastors find it helpful to schedule time in their day and week for various ministry responsibilities. It is also wise to deliberately schedule activities for and with our wife and children. Not only is that good for our marriages and our families, but it is a great example to the men of our congregations as they exercise their responsibilities for their wife and children.

In summary, a pastor needs to take good physical care of himself so that he can take good care of his family and his parish. Good care of self includes eating properly and regularly, drinking plenty of water, and getting good and regular exercise, including just getting up and moving around after sitting for a time. Good care of self also means getting rest in the form of regular breaks in the day, a good night's sleep, taking our days off, and taking our vacation. We need to do all that without feeling guilt for our self-care because, as noted above, taking proper care of ourselves is good for our congregation and our family.

SPIRITUAL HEALTH AND WELL-BEING

Now, as important as it is to care for our physical health and well-being, it is even more important to be attentive to our spiritual life and well-being. When I served as a district president, it was my very unpleasant task to remove several men from the pastoral office. All of the men I was forced to remove were physically healthy and well. In fact, all of them but one were very gifted and physically well equipped for the work of pastor. In each instance, their problem was not physical, in a strict sense, but spiritual.

GROW SPIRITUALLY THROUGH THE WORD

In his First Letter to the Corinthians, St. Paul admonished all Christians to be careful of their spiritual lives, saying, "Let anyone who thinks that he stands take heed lest he fall" (1 Corinthians 10:12). And this admonishment is especially important and necessary for pastors. As noted earlier in this chapter, pastors are in the highest office in the Church, the preaching and teaching office. Pastors shepherd the flock of God, tending, guiding, and caring for the people of the Church in many important ways.

Pastors are therefore very special targets for Satan. If he can distort a pastor's faith, distract him from his ministry, tempt him to focus on himself and away from Christ, or bring him down in any way, he can do great damage to the Church of Christ. So a pastor can expect strong and frequent attacks from the devil and his agents. And that being the case, a pastor must indeed "take heed lest he fall."

St. Paul not only offers the admonishment to take heed but in his Letter to the Ephesians, he lays out explicit advice on how we should do that, saying,

> Finally, be strong in the Lord and in the strength of His might. Put on the whole armor of God, that you may be able to stand against the schemes of the devil. For we do not wrestle against flesh and blood, but against the rulers, against the authorities, against the cosmic powers over this present darkness, against the spiritual forces of evil in the heavenly places. Therefore take up the whole armor of God, that you may be able to withstand in the evil day, and having done all, to stand firm. Stand therefore, having fastened on the belt of truth, and having put on the breastplate of righteousness, and, as shoes for your feet, having put on the readiness given by the gospel of peace. In all circumstances take up the shield of faith, with which you can extinguish all the flaming darts of the evil one; and take the helmet of salvation, and the sword of the Spirit, which is the word of God, praying at all times in the Spirit, with all prayer and supplication. To that end, keep alert with all perseverance, making supplication for all the saints. (Ephesians 6:10–18)

As a pastor, you know these words well and have probably preached and taught on these verses. But I encourage you to read and study them intently for your own spiritual edification and equipping.

You know that no man can "be strong in the Lord and in the strength of His might" by his own power and will. The Lord equips a man for the Office of the Ministry and sustains him in the ministry with His Holy Spirit. And the Holy Spirit comes to us through the Means of Grace, the Word of God, and His Sacraments. It is therefore critical to every pastor's spiritual health and welfare that he be a student of the Word of God, reading and studying it regularly.

Now it is a given that a pastor will read and study the Word of God in order to prepare to preach and teach according to his call. And yet, is that a given? I remember taking a homiletics class at the seminary from the sainted Dr. Henry Eggold, and in one of our early class sessions, he said that the first thing a man needs to do in preparing to preach or teach on a text from the Scripture is to read that text.

I thought that this was so obvious that he was kidding with his remark. But he was not kidding and pointed out that sometimes a pastor thinks that he knows a particular text so well that he prepares to preach or teach on the text based on what is in his heart and mind, rather than what is in the text. Dr. Eggold also pointed out that a pastor can read and study a text that he has been reading for years and suddenly see something there that he has not seen before. The Word of God is very deep and can be mined for a lifetime without exhausting it. And all this being true, it is critical for a pastor to really read and study the Word of God intently and with purpose each time he does so.

And it is important that the pastor read and study the Word of God this way in his own devotional life, as well as in his preparation for the ministry of the Word. A pastor must be spiritually well-fed and strengthened in order to be able to properly care for the spiritual lives of others. When we are flying in an airliner and the crew is giving the safety demonstration, they make the point that in the case of a loss of air pressure in the cabin, an oxygen mask will drop from the overhead. They then urge that you make sure that your own mask is securely in place before you try to help another passenger, such as a child traveling with you. A pastor must be secure in his own spiritual life before he can truly help others with their spiritual lives.

And, as already noted, our faith and spiritual strength are not self-generated but worked in us by the Holy Spirit. And as you know quite well, the Holy Spirit comes to us through the hearing and reading of the Word of God. So reading and studying the Bible for your personal spiritual feeding is a must. Set aside a specific time each day for self-feeding in and with the Word of God. There are some excellent tools available to assist a pastor in maintaining a disciplined and orderly reading of the Bible.

Our *Lutheran Service Book* includes a "Daily Lectionary" which provides an excellent daily reading of the Scriptures. There are also some very good devotional books for pastors that include a structured reading of the Bible. One of my favorites is *A Year with the Church Fathers* by Dr. Scott R. Murray. In his book, Dr. Murray directs the reader to a reading from the Psalms, followed by a reading from the Old Testament, and then a reading from the New Testament. There are then some devotional thoughts both from himself and from one of the Church Fathers. I use this book often and recommend it. It is available from Concordia Publishing House.

The *Treasury of Daily Prayer* is another excellent devotional book for pastors available at Concordia Publishing House. CPH also has several editions of *Day by Day*, which are daily devotions taken from the writings of Martin Luther. And of course, Luther's Small Catechism is a staple for a structured study of the Bible and the basic Christian doctrines. And a great aid for a structured daily study of the catechism is *The Lord Will Answer*, which is also available at CPH.

These are only a few examples of many good devotional books and guides for reading the Bible that are available. And using a variety of such resources is a good way to keep your devotional reading fresh and new each year. However it is managed, maintaining a disciplined reading of the Bible is of great spiritual benefit for any pastor.

Another way to be engaged with the Word of God is to use an audio version of the Bible. Years ago, we used to use "The Bible on Tape," but there are now a number of ways to listen to an excellent recorded version of the Bible. And such a tool is an excellent way to hear the Word of God while driving, while walking or running, or as a soothing and comforting way to go to sleep at night.

The bottom line is a pastor should read and study the Bible regularly for his own devotional life and spiritual growth. He should do what he encourages others to do.

BE WELL-GROUNDED SPIRITUALLY

As a pastor, you will hear lots of first and secondhand comments about you and your ministry. Some of these things will be very positive and good, which is always encouraging. But be careful to keep the positive things you hear in a proper spiritual perspective. If good things are being said about you and your work, then give thanks and praise to the Lord, for He is your enabler and strength, and without Him, we can do nothing good. Accolades and praise can be pleasant and encouraging for a pastor, but they can also be a distraction and a satanic trap.

When I served as a district president, other district presidents and I would often talk of the men we had to remove from the pastoral office and discuss the nature of these men, looking for traits that seemed to be common among them. One of the traits often evident in these men was that they were talented and gifted pastors with pleasant and engaging personalities, who therefore received lots of praise and kudos from their congregations. Sadly, the positive attention seemed to feed their egos, and they developed a very high opinion of themselves, which then led them into a variety of sins that Satan used to bring them down hard.

A pastor must take the office of pastor very seriously, but he must not take himself too seriously. A pastor does indeed represent Christ in the congregation, and he speaks the Word of God and ministers to God's people with God's Word in the stead of, and by the command of, the Lord Jesus. But he is a servant of the Word and a servant of the congregation with Christ's Word and must remember that he is a sinner just like any other member of the congregation. The Law and Gospel that he preaches and teaches to others is for himself too.

Pride and arrogance are some of the ugliest traits in a man serving in the pastoral office and can really get in the way of the ministry. And these traits can also be very dangerous to the man serving as pastor. As the Bible teaches, "Pride goes before destruction, and a haughty spirit before a fall" (Proverbs 16:18). So the pastor must apply to himself the Law and Gospel he preaches and teaches to others. The pastor is in the highest office in the church, not by his own merits and worth, but by the grace, power, and Spirit of God, and therefore he must pray for a godly perspective on himself and the ministry.

As a pastor reads and studies the Word of God, by the power of the Holy Spirit, he will be humbled to be serving in this high office in the church. And as words of appreciation and praise come to him, he should immediately give thanks and praise to God for blessing his ministry, and for equipping him for the task. He should also pray that God will protect him from Satan, the world, and himself and keep him from falling into the sin of pride.

Now as important as it is for the pastor to be cautious about words of praise and positive comments about him, being cautious about complaints and negative words is also important. If you are serving faithfully as a pastor, you will receive words of complaint and criticism simply because you are serving faithfully. Consider Scripture and the record of the many men of God who suffered greatly because they were faithful to the call and ministry of God.

Consider the Lord Jesus Himself. He left the glories of heaven and became a man, conceived by the Holy Spirit and born of the Virgin Mary. He is God as well as man, and He is love, and He did all things well. He healed the blind, lifted up the lame, gave hearing and voice to the deaf and dumb, fed the hungry, and even raised the dead. And in spite of all His good and loving service, He was arrested, beaten, spit upon, humiliated, and finally crucified and suffered death and hell. So we should not be surprised when we who bear His name and serve Him receive criticism or are spoken against or treated poorly.

When that happens, try to immediately speak with those who are bringing the criticism and seem to be hurt or offended by the ministry. If possible, determine what the problem is, and address it if you can. Pray for those bringing the criticism and complaints, asking that their hearts will be open to you and the Word of the Lord. And pray for yourself, that you may have an open mind and be able to honestly examine yourself and be objective about your work and service. And then correct what you can, ask for forgiveness when appropriate, and seek the counsel of God in His Word.

Work hard at serving the people that God has placed in your care with love and gentleness but also faithfully with Law and Gospel. Work hard not to get in the way of the ministry, but also be careful not to compromise the Word of God or fail to be faithful in your service to Him and His Word. And as you deal with criticism and negative comments about you and your work, read and study the Word of God often, and by His Holy Spirit, remain firm in the joy of your salvation in spite of criticism and attacks upon you.

My father was a soldier in World War II and served in the Twelfth Armored Division of General George Patton's Seventh Army. He didn't talk much about the horrific things he saw and went through, but there was one incident that he related to me years after the war that was humorous and instructive in several ways. On the day of the incident, he said it was cool and misting rain and that he and about eight other soldiers were riding on a tank as they entered a village in western Germany. The town was heavily damaged after being bombed and shelled earlier. As the tank slowly negotiated its way through the debris and shell craters in the street, a machine gun opened fire on them from the second story of a building to the right of the tank. All the men on the tank leaped off, away from the incoming fire. But as my dad made his jump, his combat webbing caught on an antenna sticking up on the back of the turret as it was swinging around to bring its big gun to bear on the building from which the enemy was firing. This left my dad hanging out in midair off the side of the tank. Dad said that bullets were going past him like angry bees. One round knocked his helmet off, another knocked the rifle out of his hand, and another caught him in the shoulder. He told me that he knew for sure that he was a dead man. But then one of the incoming bullets clipped off the antenna that was hanging him up, and he fell from the tank into a shell crater beside the tank. He landed on his back with a splash in mud and water in the crater. And at that point, he said that he just burst out laughing because though he was wounded, wet, and cold, and people were still trying to kill him, he was alive when just a few seconds ago, he was a dead man.

We, too, can have that spiritual blessing of joy, even in the midst of circumstances in our life that are difficult and painful. In John 15, Jesus taught His disciples how to live the Christian life. In verse 11, He said, "These things I have spoken to you, that My joy may be in you, and that your joy may be full." Jesus is not speaking here of a joy in which Christians are always happy and free of difficulties and hardship. Rather, He is speaking of the deep joy of being loved by God and having the full forgiveness of our sin and the gift of everlasting life, which we have even though we may not be happy or enjoying this life at the moment. Though we may be hurting badly and have pain and sadness, by the Holy Spirit and through the Word of God and His grace and mercy, we may still have peace and joy. We may not burst out laughing in the midst of pain and suffering as my father did in the incident noted in his life, but we can still have true and deep joy on account of Jesus if we are spiritually well-fed and grounded.

MANAGE YOUR EMOTIONS

As a part of our spiritual health and well-being, it is important to manage our emotions well. All human beings, including pastors, have feelings and emotional ups and downs. And managing our emotions, especially the negative ones, is very important.

Pastors experience anger, fear, hurt, jealousy, resentment, sadness, and the like, just like everyone else. And the first step in managing our feelings is to acknowledge them. When a pastor experiences negative feelings, he may think that he should not feel these things and therefore refuses to deal with them. But feelings simply occur, and when they do, it is wise to acknowledge how you are feeling and then try to understand why you are feeling as you are and then manage the emotion spiritually.

And the most important way to manage feelings of any kind is with prayer. Prayer gives us the time to pause and consider our feelings and then to ask the Lord for His help in dealing with them. We can pray for a forgiving heart. We can pray for understanding and discernment. We can pray for strength to deal with the feelings and to manage them in a positive way. So to manage our emotions in a spiritually successful manner, prayer is the first and best step. Prayer is a great help, tool, practice, and blessing in many ways in our life, and this great privilege is covered in the next section.

PRAY

Prayer has already been mentioned numerous times in this chapter as a proper way in which to deal with various issues and matters in our life. And we should indeed pray often and regularly, or as the Scripture states, "without ceasing" (1 Thessalonians 5:17). A pastor will indeed pray for his parish, for specific needs of specific people, for his community and local and national leaders, for many needs of many people in all the world. But a wise and spiritually strong pastor will pray for himself often.

A pastor should pray regularly for a huge measure of the Holy Spirit so that he can remain steadfast in saving faith and be a true Christian, a sinner with saving faith. He should pray without ceasing for protection from Satan, this world, and even his old sinful nature. He should pray for wisdom and understanding through the Word of the Lord. He should pray for discernment and the ability to serve, truly understanding the needs of the people God has put in his care.

A pastor should pray regularly that God will work in him true repentance and a will and ability to amend his sinful life. He should also pray for faith to receive the forgiveness of his sins in Christ Jesus and that his faith will not weaken but be firm all the way through death into everlasting life.

A pastor, like all Christians, should pray thanksgiving to God for all His blessings and do so with true joy, considering all the wonderful things the Lord has poured into our lives, and also all the deliverances He has provided for us. Paul wrote, "Rejoice always, pray without ceasing, give thanks in all circumstances; for this is the will of God in Christ Jesus for you" (1 Thessalonians 5:16–18).

Now it might seem a given that pastors do pray often, regularly, even without ceasing. But in my own experience as a pastor, many things got in the way of my praying, and I would neglect prayer more often than I liked to admit. And when I was going through a difficult time or situation, I often failed to pray but rather spent my time trying to manage the situation or circumstance on my own.

An incident in my life that I recall often in regard to prayer involved my son, David, who was ten years old at the time. He needed some money to register for a soccer camp at the YMCA, but he did not know the exact amount required. We were in my office at church, and I did not have any cash on me. So I gave him a signed check with no payee or amount noted since we did not have that information. I gave him strict instructions to be very careful of the check because I told him that anyone who had it could fill in any payee's name and any amount. I asked him several times if he understood and charged him each time to be very careful and responsible. He then took the check and got on his bike to ride to the YMCA.

About forty minutes later, he came back to my office and, with tears, told me that he had somehow lost the check and that he had searched the route he had taken to the YMCA several times and had not been able to find it. It was too late in the day to contact the bank and cancel the check, so I told David that we had to find it. I told him that we would walk the route he had taken, with him on one side of the street and me on the other, and make another search for the check. I had a prayer with him before we left that we could find the check and told him to keep praying as we made our search, and then we began the search.

As we walked along, scouring the ground, the gutters, the bushes, and so on, I was thinking how impossible this effort was but that it would be a good lesson for my son as to how important it is to be careful and responsible. I was also thinking that I needed to contact the bank immediately the next morning to cancel the check, and I was hoping that I would be in time to avoid a big financial hit. We had walked about ten minutes when I heard my son yelling, and as I looked across the street, he was running to me waving the check in his hand.

I was pleasantly surprised and asked him how he found it. He told me that he was praying with all his might, asking for God to please let him find it, and suddenly there it was in the gutter with some leaves. As we rejoiced together, I gave thanks to God that He enabled him to find the check and also for the great lesson in prayer he had provided for my son and for *me*! I was humbled by my son's faith and his trust in prayer, and

I was embarrassed that my exercise of prayer in the matter with the lost check was so weak.

The Word of God promises that "The prayer of a righteous person has great power as it is working" (James 5:16). And the Word of the Lord is always true. Prayer is a great privilege and does indeed accomplish much. And prayer should be a constant in the life of a pastor. He should pray regularly for many, many things as he carries out his ministry, but he must not neglect prayer for himself and his life. He should pray for his personal spiritual life, that he be kept in saving faith, that he be enabled to live a Christian life, that he may be a great pastor for the sake of the people that God has given into his care. He should also pray for his wife and children and for his marriage. In short, a pastor must remember to pray regularly and often, and he should never underestimate the power of prayer.

CONSIDER HAVING A FATHER CONFESSOR

Another good idea for a pastor in maintaining good spiritual health and well-being is to have a father confessor. A father confessor is a trusted colleague with whom you can speak about personal and professional matters and receive advice, guidance, and even absolution. He is a man with whom you can speak candidly and know that the conversation will not be repeated or shared with anyone.

The district president and circuit visitor are hopefully men the pastor can reach out to for advice and guidance in a variety of matters. But these men are in leadership positions over the pastor, and the district president is the pastor's ecclesiastical supervisor, which can make it difficult for the pastor to share some things of a personal and spiritual nature. A father confessor, on the other hand, is a trusted colleague who is your brother and friend.

A father confessor may be an older, well-experienced pastor, or he may simply be any brother pastor with whom you have a good relationship and whom you trust and esteem. Hopefully he is a man who is close by and easily accessible. But he can be some distance away if he is quickly available for private and secure conversations.

I know of some pastors who are each other's father confessor. They have developed a great friendship and fellowship in the Lord and are able to share personal and professional matters with each other safely and securely. Such a relationship can be a wonderful spiritual blessing to both pastors.

The bottom line is that having a father confessor is worth considering if you can find or develop one.

TAKE TIME TO REFRESH

We have already discussed the importance of maintaining a good personal devotional life, and the extreme importance of studying the Word of God for your personal growth. But there are some other, less regular opportunities for spiritual growth that a pastor should not neglect.

Hopefully the pastor has a good Winkel or circuit pastors conference that he can attend each month, where he can have good theological discussions and study with the pastors in his circuit. And hopefully his district pastors conference will also provide opportunity for good spiritual growth with fine speakers and theological presentations, as well as providing opportunities for helpful theological and ministry discussions with a larger number of pastors, district leaders, and resources from outside the district.

The busy pastor may find it difficult to work these pastors conferences into his schedule, but he will be very wise to do so. If the conferences are meaty, substantive, and well managed, he will be refreshed and spiritually strengthened by attending. And that will make his service to his congregation better and stronger. It is good for his congregation that he takes the time and effort to attend the conferences of pastors available in his circuit and district.

If the available pastors conferences tend not to be theologically meaty and substantive, the pastor should speak with the circuit visitor or the district president in this regard and make positive suggestions as to how the conferences could be strengthened and made more worthwhile. A pastor is wise to do his part in faithfully attending conferences and in making them as positive and helpful for the brothers as possible.

After a pastor has been serving in the pastoral ministry for a number of years, another good exercise to consider for spiritual strengthening and growth is to take a sabbatical. Hopefully a pastor's congregation, working in concert with the district president, can make a sabbatical available to the pastor. The congregation should understand that the sabbatical is not a vacation but a time for him to study, do research, write, or in other ways pursue educational and academic exercise and spiritual and professional growth. Most professions encourage or even require the professional to take time at certain increments of his work to study, refresh, and update his education. That is not required for pastors, but it is a great blessing when it can be available.

A sabbatical could be as short as two or three weeks or as long as several months. The pastor should approach his congregation with a specific plan and proposal and should enlist his district president in assisting him and his congregation in making the plan a reality. A successful sabbatical can be a great blessing to a pastor and to his congregation.

However it is done, a pastor should take time to be refreshed in his education and spiritual life. And he should understand that this is not only good for him but is also good for his congregation and the ministry in general.

CONCLUSION

God bless you and keep you physically and spiritually strong and healthy as you serve in the pastoral ministry. That will be good for you, good for your family, and good for your congregation and the ministry of Christ in general. Be intentional about taking care of yourself, and do not feel guilty for expending the time and effort to do so.

> **Now to Him who is able to keep you from stumbling and to present you blameless before the presence of His glory with great joy, to the only God, our Savior, through Jesus Christ our Lord, be glory, majesty, dominion, and authority, before all time and now and forever. Amen.** (Jude 1: 24–25)

CHAPTER 7

THE PASTOR AND GENERAL MINISTRY CHALLENGES

Rev. Michael Walther

INTRODUCTION

Pastors have always been faced with unusual challenges and problems. The scope of the ministry, dealing with people from infancy to old age and everything in between, exposes pastors to all sorts of situations. In this chapter, my task is to address some of the unusual challenges facing pastors that don't fit easily into the other categories outlined in this book.

I have always enjoyed talking with other pastors and have learned much from their experiences, especially older pastors. In our circuit meetings, we often discuss *cases of casuistry*. These are the unusual problems that come up from time to time. We do well to listen and to learn from one another, even from those who served decades and centuries before us.

Pastor Charles Schliepsick was one of the first pastors to serve in the Collinsville area where I serve today. He wrote of many unusual challenges as a pastor, one of which still encourages me today. Back in the 1800s, some people in the community became really angry with him—so angry, in fact, one of them decided to scare him off. In the dark of the night, a ne'er-do-well approached the parsonage on a horse. He drew a rifle and fired a bullet that went through a front window and exited a back window. His plan for a quick getaway failed, however, when the horse reared, and he fell and broke his leg. The pastor's daughter nearly missed getting killed, and she suffered lifelong trauma from the experience. But Pastor Schliepsick went out to investigate the situation. He helped the man with the broken leg into his house and called for a doctor. The doctor came and set the man's leg. He then convalesced in the parsonage for several days until he could go home. I don't know if he was ever punished for his crime. I think not because Pastor Schliepsick probably didn't ask for any charges. The matter was solved with repentance and forgiveness.

As this book has shown in other chapters, pastors face many different challenges. Sirach ben Jesus wrote in the second chapter of his apocryphal book, "Son, if you come to serve the Lord, prepare your soul for testing" (2:1). As a pastor, you will be tested in many, many different ways. Some of these challenges are predictable and fully expected. But some can be very unusual. I will try to address some of those in this chapter. I have chosen these areas: working with your fellow pastors and area churches, ministry to transients, your church and politics, the problem of active shooters, weddings, funerals, and ministry to inactives. There are many more, and it might be nice to consider a future book that explores the different and unusual challenges that pastors face.

MINISTERIAL ASSOCIATIONS

My first congregation in Nebraska was in the small town of Beemer. We didn't have a ministerial association, but I wish we had. One day, the high school principal called me into his office because apparently, the Lutheran kids and the Catholic kids had had some kind of spat that involved egg throwing. He said he had talked with the priest and was asking both of us to speak to our youth to quell this little uprising. Although we didn't have a formal association, I was thankful that I did get to know some of the area pastors of other denominations. As I moved to other towns with ministerial associations, I learned their value.

In this case, familiarity does not breed contempt. Getting to know the other pastors and churches in your community is important. There will always be some interactions with them, whether they involve people leaving their churches to join yours or vice versa, weddings, funerals, or other semipublic events that always bring people together from other churches. Unfamiliarity with these other pastors *does* often contribute to bad feelings and problems. Gossip and rumors that spill out from other churches will inevitably find their way into yours. Sometimes the gossip will also flow from your church to theirs. I've had more than one person go off on another local pastor, and it has been very helpful for me to say that I know him personally and that I can check on it.

Participation in a local ministerial association also gives us the opportunity to engage in confessional Lutheran ecumenism. I have served as the president and secretary of our association here in Collinsville over the years. Early on, I was pressed to participate in ecumenical services, and it came as a bit of shock to the other pastors that I wouldn't do this. But I had the great opportunity to explain why. Joint worship services are difficult, I told them, because in a worship service there is an assumed kind of unity. Yet we all know that we come from different theological perspectives. It would be inappropriate for me to say, in the middle of a service, that I don't quite agree with everything that was said in a sermon or a prayer. They did recognize that this could be a problem. In fact, the ecumenical services were actually shut down for a while after one pastor took an overly aggressive approach to the problem of abortion. I just sat back with a big "I told you so" grin!

One problem that Lutherans often have is the problem of quietism. We are conservative, which usually means we are cautious. There can be wisdom in being cautious. No one should rush in where angels fear to tread, and so on. Yet our caution can also put us in a bad position. If we always lay back, we give the floor to any number of heretics and kooks who are more than eager to present their nonsense. Now we are in the unenviable position of having to take the negative side of the debate. It tends to make us look overly critical. Criticism is important. But sometimes it's better to let others criticize us. Let them be the negative ones while we are positive with our bold confession of the Gospel.

This happened beautifully when, as president of our association, I asked all the pastors to bring to the meetings "the one distinctive thing about your church/denomination." When it was my turn, I shared the three solas: grace alone, faith alone, Scripture alone. I'll never forget one of the pastors' immediate comments: "That will preach!" I have had and have taken many opportunities to confess our faith at association meetings, and I have gained a lot of respect for doing so. I have also listened respectfully to the other pastors, and I have learned important things from them as well.

Another great benefit to ministerial associations is that they often provide an important opportunity to engage with community leaders. In some communities, there is tension between the churches and the political leaders. Not so in our city. We still open every city council meeting with prayer. We have had discussions with the police, council members, and the mayor. One of the big debates we have had in the past was in regard to the Italian Fest, a large community celebration that always involves a lot of adult beverages. I'll never forget the look on the faces of the Italian Fest leaders when the Methodist pastor said, "I'm tired of everyone peeing in the bushes next to my church!" Those discussions have helped keep things from getting out of hand. When the COVID-19 quarantine crisis hit in the spring of 2020, we immediately planned to conduct drive-in worship services, despite the objections of state politicians. But I wrote a letter to the mayor, whom I knew personally and with whom I sat at association meetings. I told him I just wanted to preempt any complaints that he might get about our services. He responded that he thought it was a good idea!

Ministerial associations give pastors the opportunity to talk to one another so that they can better understand one another's teaching and practice. This provides an important opportunity to influence one another toward the truth. They also give churches a united front as they engage with the community and city government in order to provide a healthy influence of Christian values.

MINISTRY TO TRANSIENTS

Our church is located less than a mile from two major interstate highways. It is not unusual for the state police or the local gas stations to send people to us when they need help. We also have many other people from our own community who fall on hard times and come calling to us for help paying their bills or getting groceries or clothing. Poverty and homelessness are growing problems in our community for many reasons. We discuss this often at our ministerial meetings, and all the pastors are agreed that God calls us to help the poor but not to enable people who continually make bad decisions. Our ministerial association has a large food pantry, and we have a paid person who helps coordinate donations, as well as government programs, to help people in need. However, we still have many people that come to us at odd hours needing immediate help, so our congregation started our own food pantry. This is an important part of our ministry of mercy.

In his Letter to the Galatians, Paul referred to the ministry of mercy to the poor in this way: "Only, they [the Jerusalem Council] asked us to remember the poor, the very thing I was eager to do" (Galatians 2:10). There is a temptation *not* to be eager to help the poor. They almost always show up unexpectedly when we are busy with other things. Sometimes they lie and concoct stories that we've heard many times before: "I just got hired, and I need steel-toed boots. I get paid in two weeks. I promise I'll come back and repay you if you give me one hundred dollars right now." Sometimes they get pushy and demanding. Sometimes they pull out an expensive cell phone and a pack of cigarettes, and you wonder how they can afford that but can't afford ten dollars worth of gas to get home. In addition to being eager to help the poor, Paul also said, "Admonish the idle [disorderly, undisciplined]" (1 Thessalonians 5:14). How do we help and, on the other hand, "admonish"?

One of the best ways I've found to help without enabling is to remember the Golden Rule from Matthew 7:12: "So whatever you wish that others would do to you, do also to them, for this is the Law and the Prophets." If I were coming to a church and asking for food or fuel, would I cooperate with a few guidelines that they might have? Here are a few guidelines that we have found helpful:

1. Talk to the pastor or someone who knows how to work with people in need. It's not a good idea for individual church members to be handing out fifty dollars on the parking lot without really evaluating the situation.
2. Ask them to wait. Some people know they can manipulate a church to give them money when they show up on Sunday morning right before the worship service starts. Asking a person to wait will often separate those who are in real need of basic necessities from those who are just scamming you so they can go buy a six-pack or drugs.
3. Avoid giving cash. Talk to your local police. In our area, heroin is available for as little as ten dollars. We will put ten dollars worth of fuel in their gas tank or give them a couple of bags of groceries. Occasionally, we might buy a train ticket, rent a hotel room, or get some medicine for them. But we don't give cash. No matter how clever their story might be, we just don't budge on this guideline, even though it often takes more time and effort on our part.
4. Keep records. We started making an online document (Google Docs, Dropbox, etc.) for every person we help. We get their name and at least a physical description. Asking for more ID than that can be a problem because a lot of people just don't have proper ID. We keep track of all the help that we give them. Sometimes we catch people coming repeatedly with the same stories.
5. Witness. We never give physical help without trying to give them spiritual help. Sometimes this is well received and sometimes not. But we hope that we are always planting seeds of the Gospel.

6. Microloans. Sometimes our own members come to us with special physical needs that might involve several hundred dollars (rent or utility payments, car repair, etc.). In this case, we have used microloans. These are small, no-interest loans that have no time limit. We write up the terms and have them sign it. This offers them needed help. But we also let them know that they have to pay back the loan before we can give any more help.
7. Mentoring and Financial Counseling. Sometimes we are able to find a member who can sit down with people having financial problems to give them the guidance and motivation that they need to improve their situation.

Guidelines like these are helpful so that our ministry of mercy is actually helpful and not enabling. Your own guidelines will certainly be affected by the community in which you live and the particular needs that you find there.

CHURCH AND POLITICS

I was once invited to a dinner party for campus pastors. The wife of another pastor sat across from me, and after exchanging polite conversation for a while, she sneeringly asked, "How can you be a Christian and a Republican?" I responded by saying, "Politics is always the lesser of evils." I don't consider any political party or politician to be perfect or even very good in many cases. They are all human, and most of them do not share the same worldview with me. However, we all have been given the vocation of citizen, and it is important that we use the rights that we have for the good of God's kingdom. I once shared the dinner party story in one of my sermons, and I immediately lost a member who apparently was equally appalled as the lady at the party. I went to visit him to understand his concerns. I told him that I had voted for people of different political parties over the years and that I always try to focus on the issues first and foremost. Sadly, he informed me that he was staunchly pro-choice, and he thought the Church had no business saying anything about abortion. I realized that our parting of ways was going to come sooner or later.

Every four years or so, important elections take place. What is the pastor's role or the Church's role in politics? We could certainly devote large books to these questions. On the other hand, we could try to take a very indifferent and uninvolved approach. After all, we believe in the two kingdoms, and pastors and churches are certainly called to serve the kingdom of the Gospel. Neither Jesus nor His disciples showed much interest in politics. But was that because they had no interest or because they had no opportunity?

We need to remember that the Early Church functioned in the Roman Empire. There was no freedom of speech in the Roman Empire or the right to vote for leaders. We do have these freedoms, at least for now. Paul also used his rights as a Roman citizen on several occasions for the sake of God's kingdom. He threatened the magistrates of Philippi for beating and imprisoning him and Silas as Roman citizens. In Jerusalem, as he was being bound for scourging, he asked the centurion, "Is it lawful for you to flog a man who is a Roman citizen and uncondemned?" (Acts 22:25). Paul used the rights he had, and Christians should use the rights they have been given. But we must certainly take great care with this as we should in all aspects of our ministry.

I have participated in several political protests against the legality and practice of abortion. One of the most dramatic political and moral messages our church delivered to our community was the display of thousands of white crosses near the busy road where we are located to urge everyone to recognize the rights of the unborn. I attended a large rally at our state capitol when our leaders were considering legalizing same-sex marriage. So far none of this protesting has changed any laws, as far as I know. However, I do believe that such protests send strong messages to the world around us and to our own church members.

There can be minuses. One of the minuses we have to avoid is the association or the appearance of association with individuals and groups that go too far in their moral or political ideology. Pro-life protesters often run into the problem of certain individuals or groups that use rude methods or possibly even violence in their efforts to overcome the problem of abortion. Some political decisions have clear moral guidance from the Scriptures (abortion, marriage, human trafficking, freedom of speech, etc.). Pastors and churches have the wherewithal to speak confidently to these. In other issues (taxes, immigration, military spending, etc.), we are guided mostly by the principles of natural law. Here pastors and churches should be more cautious, especially if the issues are more complex and beyond their expertise.

From time to time, members want me to pass out voter guides before elections. I have used some of them if they accurately summarize the political positions of the candidates. However, I think that voter guides sometimes venture into issues that aren't so easy to summarize. For that reason, I've moved to creating my own voter guides that stick closely to the issues that can be identified and documented. The best voter guide that I have come up with is simply to urge Christians to vote for whatever gives free course to the Gospel and encourages obedience to the Ten Commandments.

Should pastors preach on controversial issues that have political implications, such as abortion? If so, how? I know there are some church leaders and boards of elders who strongly urge pastors to avoid controversial issues in the pulpit. They usually say that such issues are better handled in Bible studies or in one-to-one meetings. But Jesus clearly said that the Church must make disciples, "teaching them to observe all that I have commanded you" (Matthew 28:20). Paul also said that he "did not shrink from declaring to you the whole counsel of God" (Acts 20:27).

What is the Christian to think when a controversial topic is only handled quietly or under the radar and not openly and from the most public place of the pulpit? Yet a sermon is usually not very long. How can we adequately cover controversial topics in such a short time? Won't this overcloud the main message of Law and Gospel? We can carefully and accurately summarize controversial issues. One way to overcome the problem of time is to publish longer explanations in handouts that members can pick up or read on the church website. They can also be referred to other publications and resources, depending on their interest.

At the very least, we should encourage good citizenship through voter participation, being informed, and using the freedom we have to contact political leaders in the hopes of influencing them according to God's will. We should promote respectful discussion and debate about politics. We should certainly pray for all our leaders, as Paul commanded (1 Timothy 2:1–2), and submit to them unless they command us to disobey God (Romans 13:1; Acts 5:29). It is also very wise and helpful to get to know your local authorities.

ACTIVE SHOOTERS

In 2015, just four miles from our church, a well-known pastor was shot and killed during his sermon in the Sunday service. We have seen a number of headlines of even more bloodshed caused by hateful or deranged individuals who have attacked Christians in worship. Churches and schools are preparing for the worst by listening to presentations from law enforcement officials. Having participated in a few of these, there are three things that we are now strongly emphasizing in our church.

1. Greet all who come to worship. Most of the active shooters have not been members of the churches they attack. One of the most important things we can do to prevent such a tragedy is to meet them at the door. I think it is very important for the pastor(s), greeters, and ushers to greet all who come to worship. Hopefully, you can recognize the visitors and especially speak to them. If they seem out of place or nervous, take them aside and engage them in a longer conversation. The more we take away their anonymity, the less courage they will have to carry out their destructive plans. Perhaps they will be dissuaded at this point. If not, at least the ushers can keep an eye on them.
2. Train church leaders to be aggressive. Many members, especially women and children, should try to flee. But if this is the only response to an active shooter, I'm afraid the results will not be good. Some members should be trained and

encouraged to rush and restrain an active shooter. This has been the only way shooters have been suppressed, aside from running out of ammunition. Should we encourage members to bring concealed weapons to worship? Active shooters have been stopped by armed church members. However, in one of our training meetings, a former FBI agent reminded everyone that conceal and carry training is far different from tactical training. The last thing we need is members being shot by fellow members who don't have the skill to handle lethal force in a large group of people.

3. Have an evacuation plan. I make sure to inform all new members where the exits of the sanctuary are, and I periodically remind the members to be prepared for this.

It is tragic that we even have to speak of these things, but it is certainly a sign of the times in which we are living. As Jesus said, "Because lawlessness will be increased, the love of many will grow cold" (Matthew 24:12).

WEDDINGS

Many pastors will tell you that they would be glad to conduct three funerals for every wedding. Lay people are sometimes surprised by such a statement. Without diving too deep into the theology of marriage, I will try to touch on one of the most difficult problems that pastors are facing today when it comes to weddings: living together before marriage.

This once was a common pattern in our culture: friendship, courtship, marriage, and sexual relations. Today the pattern is often: hookup (sexual relations), friendship, living together, and finally marriage. How does a pastor rehabilitate such a messed-up approach to marriage? Some pastors choose to ignore everything, talk about what marriage is and how sex is for marriage only and hope that the couple will somehow make the leap from the messed-up past to the better future. This might work in some ways; however, there are a lot of statistics to show that cohabitation before marriage doesn't bode well for a successful marriage. But we really don't need statistics to tell us this. Living together before marriage usually does not involve any serious promises. It really isn't a test run for the commitment of marriage—it is the test run for living without commitment to each other. When the going gets tough in your marriage, will you have the commitment to push through it with God's help? Or let the mentality of living together lead you to the seemingly simpler, but much more harmful, decision to divorce?

Second, by saying nothing about living together before marriage, we are completely contradicting our teaching of the Sixth Commandment. Are we actually going to tell our youth that it's okay to have sexual relations when you're not married as long as you really love each other and if you are planning to get married? Are we saying that planning to get married is the same as being married? We know that God has given us a very definite boundary for sexual relations, and that boundary is marriage. Adam and Eve did not hook up first for a while and then schmooze into marriage when they had enough money to put on an awesome reception.

I have struggled very much with this over the years. Only a few other experiences in my ministry have given me more of a stomachache than talking to a couple about why living together before marriage is wrong and how that can be fixed. Here is a typical conversation that I have with couples who are living together and want to get married some significant time in the future (six months to a year):

> I'm glad that God brought you together, that you love each other, and that you want to get married! God bless you in all of this! I see that you are already living together, and that's something we need to talk about.
>
> Most people in our culture today think that casual sexual relations are okay. But the Bible is very clear that sexual relations should only be for people who are married. When I teach our youth about sexual relations, I stress that they should wait until marriage, even though the culture thinks this is crazy. My guess is that you believe that your commitment of engagement is basically the same as marriage and that you would agree that casual sex is wrong. There is some truth to that. If you were all alone

on an uninhabited island, this would be all that you could do—make a serious promise to each other to be husband and wife. That would be your marriage. But we're not on an island.

Casual sex is not good. Sex in marriage is good. By living together before marriage, you're kinda married but not really married. If you were really married, you wouldn't be coming to me to perform a marriage ceremony. That's why we have marriage ceremonies—to show everyone that you really are married and that you're not just having casual sex or that engagement is kinda like being married.

So, the best way I found to handle this is just to get married as soon as possible, rather than extend this "we're sorta married but not really married yet" situation—a situation that undermines what we believe and teach about marriage.

You love each other. You want to be husband and wife. You're living as husband and wife. Just put those things together. Rather than wait, get married. What I would like to do is give you some time to think and pray about this. Then, I hope I could convince you to come to church and allow me to perform your marriage ceremony in a small but wholesome way—maybe just the two of you, maybe you and your parents or closest friends. This would be your way of saying, "We want to live together and honor God's Word at the same time." Then, a year from now, or whenever you have the big celebration of the marriage planned, we can continue to celebrate your love and your marriage in another more public ceremony.

Some couples think that this would spoil that special day. I really think (and I've seen it many times) it really blesses that special day. There is nothing more beautiful than a couple who not only loves each other but also loves God. You may not have started in quite the right way. But there's no reason why you can't quickly bring it back to the blessing that God wants it to be.

Some couples work with me on this. Some walk away. But it's the best way I've found to bring the true blessings of marriage to couples that might be torn between the ways of God and the ways of the world.

FUNERALS

As I said earlier, most pastors would take several funerals for every wedding. But there are some funerals that can be very difficult. Those would at least include funerals for those whose faith is sketchy or unknown, funerals for a known unbeliever, and funerals for suicides.

Sketchy or Unknown Faith

Christians are either believers or not. There is no middle ground. But Christians can drift very far from Christ and still be Christians. In one of His messages, Jesus quoted the prophet Isaiah saying that the Messiah would not break a "bruised reed" or quench a "smoldering wick" (Matthew 12:20). He also told a parable about going out to find the one sheep that had lost its way and another parable about nourishing an unfruitful fig tree in the hope of making it more fruitful (Luke 15:1–7; 13:6–9).

How far can a person drift before we consider him to be lost? One way to know is to go to him and warn him about his distance from God, lack of concern for His Word, and little or no fruit of faith. If he is humbled and admits that he needs to and wants to live a more active Christian faith, I will take that as a sign of a flickering faith. I will work with that for years if necessary. But if he tells me to leave him alone, that everything's fine, and that he doesn't need to make any changes, I'll take that as, "It's time for me to wipe the dust off my feet and stop bothering you about your relationship with Jesus." This is why constant pastoral calling and care for the delinquent Christian is so important. It does sometimes come down to this, and at the very least, we should be able to say we tried. More on this in the next segment.

In many cases, people come to us with relatives that have died and for whom we had no opportunity for pastoral care. All we can go on is the testimony of the families. Were they Christians? If the families believe they were, even though they were very inactive, I will go ahead and perform the funeral on one condition. That condition is that I have to mention something in the sermon about the importance of being an active Christian. I don't want to give the impression that continually living as a smoking flax is okay. I usually say something like this: "All of us have our times of weak faith. For some, it lasts longer than others. But God's gift of faith is not easy to get rid of. The family told me that in the end ______________ did call out to God for mercy . . . Now, I'm sure ______________ realizes how wonderful that mercy of God is and that he would definitely want us to pay a lot of attention to it in our lives today."

Burial for an Unbeliever

Many pastors would say that it is wrong to perform a Christian funeral for an unbeliever. I would agree. We cannot pronounce absolution upon the unrepentant, and we cannot give a family the hope of eternal life for someone who rejected God's grace. *But we still have to bury the dead.* If a member comes to me in her sorrow and asks if I can help bury her dead relative, even though this person showed no faith in God or may have even blasphemed God, I believe that I can help her. I wouldn't want this painful work to be done callously by a funeral director who didn't really want anything to do with it. I especially would not want this painful work to be done by an unfaithful pastor who might preach some form of universalism and that all paths lead to God, or some other falsehood, to members of my church.

Again, the conditions for such a burial would be important to explain. I could not offer the comfort of salvation for the one who was, as far as we know, lost. But in this most bitter and painful experience that anyone could go through in this life, to say goodbye forever to someone she loved—a spouse, a child, a brother or sister, or friend—there is still hope for the living and the faithful. Jesus promises that He will wipe away all tears. The best scenario for such a situation would probably be just a graveside service. I have written a committal service for those with no faith or for whom their faith was unknown (see below).

The gist of the message can go in two ways. If by their words and actions they firmly showed that they rejected God's grace, then we just have to be honest about that and say something like this: "We don't understand why some reject God's grace. It is very painful for us to consider it. But we are not the first to suffer this loss. David cried bitterly for his son Absalom. Jesus wept for Jerusalem, who stoned the prophets and rejected Him. We weep with those who weep. But we also know that God will save us and ultimately wipe away all tears. It is in His hands. He is good. He is just. We can't look back now. We will look forward. God will help us."

Another possibility is that of unknown faith. We often don't know what is going on deep inside a person's heart or especially what may have transpired in his heart as he was nearing death. I've witnessed deathbed confessions, and I'm sure there are those who confess their sins to God but may have missed the opportunity to tell anyone else about that. That is a possible comfort for those who mourn. In that situation, we might say: "_______________ never expressed his faith in Jesus to any of us. But he also did not vocally renounce the faith that he had heard about through his family and friends. The Holy Spirit may have brought him to faith in the last hour of life as He did the thief on the cross. In this case, we know that we can take comfort in the justice and mercy of God. He will save all those who trust in Him whether we know about that or not."

Committal for One Who Died without Faith or Whose Faith Is Unknown

> *Dear Father, standing beside this grave we are all reminded of the certainty and finality of death. At this time, it is good to hear the promises to those who call upon You.*
>
> *"Blessed is he whose help is the God of Jacob, whose hope is in the LORD his God . . . The LORD lifts up those who are bowed down; . . . the LORD watches over the sojourners; He upholds the widow and the fatherless" (Psalm 146:5, 8–9).*
>
> *O God, with the strength You now give us, we commit [his/her] body to the ground; earth to earth, ashes to ashes, dust to dust, and we pray that You would lift our eyes beyond this grave to*

the cross of the Lord Jesus Christ, which promises a new hope to all those who will believe in Him.

For as You promised through Isaiah the prophet, "Behold, I create new heavens and a new earth, and the former things shall not be remembered or come into mind. But be glad and rejoice forever in that which I create; . . . I will rejoice in Jerusalem and be glad in My people; no more shall be heard in it the sound of weeping and the cry of distress" (Isaiah 65:17–20).

Lord, remember us in Your kingdom and teach us to pray:

Our Father who art in heaven . . .

"Therefore, beloved, since you are waiting for these [things], be diligent to be found by Him without spot or blemish, and at peace. . . . But grow in the grace and knowledge of our Lord and Savior Jesus Christ. To Him be the glory both now and to the day of eternity. Amen" (2 Peter 3:14, 18).

(Other Helpful Passages to Comfort Those Who Mourn:)

Matthew 11:25–30; 2 Peter 5:7; Psalm 46; Romans 5:3–5; Romans 8:35–37; 1 Corinthians 10:13; 2 Corinthians 4:8; Psalm 119:28

Suicide

Suicides are usually of two kinds. The first might fall into the category above—the category of one who rejected God's Word and knowingly and without remorse or repentance took his own life. But the other kind of suicide is that which Luther spoke of in his Table Talks: sometimes Christians are driven to suicide by the devil.

One of my eighth-grade students told me that anyone who commits suicide has to go to hell because the last thing he did was a sin, and because he killed himself, he couldn't repent. That's logical; however, as he said this, he was leaning back in a folding chair on the hard, concrete basement floor of our church. I had told the students not to lean back like that because their chair could slip, and they could fall backward and hurt themselves. "Imagine," I said, "if that happened. What if you slipped, hit your head badly, had to be taken to the ER, and, tragically, you died? Would you go to heaven? I think you would!" Since we are always saints and sinners at the same time, we will all die in some kind of sin. That has to be true because no one is living a perfect life when they die. There are always "secret sins" (Psalm 19) of which we are not aware, and there are the good thoughts, words, and deeds that we should always be doing but are not—at least not 100 percent.

The real question is whether or not we die in stubborn, unrepentant sin and unbelief. Some suicides are a true spiritual battle that is lost physically but not necessarily spiritually. I believe Luther is correct on this. The devil can murder us with our own hand, depending on how hard he presses us. Mental illness can also be the cause of a suicide—and more and more so since we use so many medications that can be very difficult to control. In situations like this, we can consider the suicide to have been a Christian who did not deny his faith but struggled to live by faith, as we all do in one way or another. We can definitely commend him to the mercy of God. However, in these kinds of funerals, I am also very careful to say that this hope should not in any way be construed to mean suicide is okay. It is not, just as no murder is okay. It is something we must fight against with all our might as we hold fast to God's Word and Sacraments.

MINISTRY TO INACTIVES

When I was a young pastor, I used to get quite frustrated with Christians who only showed up for worship on Christmas and Easter. A good pastor friend of mine retired from the ministry and became a member of our church. One of the jobs he enjoyed was being an usher. He also knew the frustration we get from people who ought to have known better. I guess in his retirement, he finally decided he needed to say what he always wanted to say. Every Christmas Eve and every Easter, he used to say to the C&E Christians as they were coming into worship, "Welcome back!" On the way out, he would say, "See you again next year!" My elders were concerned, but I knew all the people he was talking about, and I seriously doubt that it did them any spiritual harm. They were hard-boiled, and they needed some prodding like that.

Delinquency is a serious matter for pastors. Again, as a young pastor, I was frustrated with my C&E Christians, but I also noticed something interesting. As frustrated as I was with them, I was always elated when visitors would walk into our church, usually people who had been estranged from the church for a long time. Now they wanted to be closer to Jesus. I was happy to see them, yet they had also been C&E Christians—for a long time in most cases. Why couldn't I take a more hopeful and positive approach to my current C&E Christians? Why couldn't I envision them with a potentially rekindled faith?

That beginning of a new attitude to delinquents was further blessed by another faithful pastor who showed me a simple way to reach them. It began by simply keeping track of who was coming to worship and who was not. We especially watched for those who had been very active in worship but who recently stopped worshiping in the last three or four weeks. In this case, something is probably wrong, and they just didn't want to tell the pastor. They might have experienced illness, unemployment, or some other setback. A quick call of encouragement from the pastor is often all that it takes to keep a bad habit from forming. These people usually welcome a pastoral call.

Many other Christians go through seasons of spiritual weakness that can last for months or years. Calling on this kind of person three or four times a year can go a long way to keep that smoldering wick burning. It's useless to make appointments with them because they will put that off just as they put off attending worship. In that case, I just show up at their door on Sunday afternoon with a bulletin and perhaps a copy of the sermon or a tract or booklet. I ask how they are doing and if there is anything we can do to help them. I tell them that we miss them at worship, and so does God. Sometimes I press a little harder, and I remind them that we all have 168 hours in a week. I truly believe that we'll get more done and be happier in the long run if we give the Lord a couple of those hours for His grace to strengthen us. As often as they don't reject this encouragement, I'm willing to keep giving it.

I also enlist my elders to help me with this so that they can share in some of this labor as well. I try a variety of approaches: personal visits, phone calls, emails, regular mail, and so forth. Now and then, a few of them (and it really is only a few) will tell me to stop visiting them, or they start rolling their eyes or tell the kids not to answer the door. In that case, I explain that I don't want to be a pest. I'll stop bothering them. But worship is not an option for a Christian. It's what Jesus wants. "Whoever is of God hears the words of God," Jesus said in John 8:47. I urge them to find a different church if that would help. But they are always welcome back.

CONCLUSION

This book covers the challenges pastors face in several different categories. My chapter was a kind of catch-all for many different problems. There are so many other topics that could have been included in this chapter: the challenges of being a young pastor or an old pastor, handling divine calls, how to be a single pastor, how to help your wife in her role as pastor's wife, and so on. But before we reach for another book to help us, there are three things that every pastor can do when challenges arise: Study God's Word and wrestle with it as you seek His will—"Make me to know Your ways, O LORD; teach me Your paths" (Psalm 25:4). "Continue steadfastly in prayer," as Paul says (Colossians 4:2). Finally, you just have to try something. In the end, pastors can't be theoretical. They have to be practical. "Be doers of the word, and not hearers only" (James 1:22). Some things will work, and some things won't.

> **God, forgive us for our sins and help us when things go wrong. Help us learn from our mistakes. And bless us to do good by Your grace. Amen.**

CHAPTER 8

THE PASTOR AND MANAGING PEOPLE

Jesse Yow

INTRODUCTION

Now that you are well into your new leadership role, you begin to realize that the work includes a wider range of tasks, needs, and demands on your time than you first imagined. Sermon preparation time runs up against the time needed to deal with an unexpected meeting to resolve a dispute between staff. Time intended for teaching or fellowship goes for unexpected hospital calls, counseling needs, or an emergency plumbing problem.

Paid staff and some of the volunteers try to help with your workload, but it takes time to let someone help you, and sometimes it seems like it would be easier to just do it all yourself. You need thirty or even thirty-six hours in a day, but God gave you only twenty-four. And since you can't clone yourself (your family probably wouldn't accept a clone anyway), you need to find a way to offload part of your work to trusted volunteers or staff. That option creates its own challenges, though, as you decide what to delegate and to whom, how to assign and coordinate their work, and how to stay on top of ownership and performance issues. You need to *manage* your situation, including the people who are there to help you!

Let's step back and take a deep breath. The most important role of a servant leader in a Christian organization is spiritual leadership, and for a pastor, this starts with the things a pastor needs to do. You need to preach and teach God's Word. You need to administer the Sacraments. You need to catechize children, and you need to catechize adults. You are leading a local manifestation of the Body of Christ, feeding and equipping the saints for now but with an eye toward eternity.

In a broader sense, a pastor's responsibilities also include discerning and explaining the vision or direction of the organization, engaging others in that vision, shepherding the people entrusted to your leadership, preparing future leaders, and serving as the visible face of the organization. Neglecting these areas is counterproductive, but you start with the fundamentals. (A baseball team may know how to dazzle the crowd with a spectacular play, but if they neglect the fundamentals, they are not going to win many games.) Personal discipleship and walking with our Lord should be a given, and Word and Sacrament are central to ministry, but other activities and roles are necessary for the ministry to be complete.

So if pastoral ministry is your top priority, then how do you find time and resources to live out that emphasis? You need to set priorities, manage your time, and manage the staff and volunteers who are there to help you. Investing time and energy in management should pay off in the form of better productivity, freedom to devote attention to what is important, and improved teamwork in the ministry and Body of Christ. This beneficial return on investment justifies the cost of your effort in setting priorities and managing people, time, and other resources.

To recap before we move on, your most important role is spiritual servant leadership, and fulfilling this role includes managing time, people, money, and property (e.g., facilities and equipment). If you ignore these stewardship aspects, your overall work will suffer. This chapter introduces how to manage time and people, and chapter 10 covers matters of money and property. Managing people almost always involves conflict sooner or later, and chapter 9 covers conflict management, so we will set aside that topic for now. We will, however, cover managing time and people in a series of interrelated practical topics: planning and priorities, time management, people management, team management, and potential problem areas that may need special attention. Some of this may already be familiar to you, some of it might be a refresher, some of it may challenge your thinking, and some of it may provide new help in the form of new ideas. Regardless, I pray that it will assist you in all your work!

PLANNING AND PRIORITIES

To manage your workload, you need to plan your activities and set priorities. First, though, you need to break down the work into its constituent parts so you can think through what tasks you need to complete, how soon, and in what order. For example, if you plan to teach a Bible class, you wouldn't just show up with your Bible and wing it for an hour. Instead, you would select the Bible passages or topic for the study, locate the reading and reference materials you need to prepare the study, do the background reading and research, prepare notes for the class, announce or publicize the class, teach the class, and then deal with any follow-up questions that might arise. This all sounds simple and obvious, but even such a simple example probably misses a thing or two. Where will you hold the class, who will set up chairs, turn on the lights, and set the thermostat? So how often do we charge ahead with our lists and calendars without fully understanding the whole of what we need to do and what it entails? Sometimes you just need to step back and ask, "What am I trying to accomplish here? What do I need to do myself (e.g., all the steps to prepare and teach the class), and what can I delegate to others (e.g., copy materials, publicize the class in a church bulletin or online, and set up the room)?" Notice, though, that you need a feel for the whole picture before you can delegate parts of it.

Stopping to take stock is particularly important to help guard against being head faked by urgent tasks clamoring for your attention at the expense of more important work that might be lost in the background. For example, someone phones an invitation to a basketball game that evening. The invitation may be urgent, but is it more important than the confirmation class you plan to teach? Maybe that choice is too easy, so let's up the ante. Someone phones to ask you to attend a city council meeting that will decide about zoning laws that affect your church. It conflicts with the confirmation class, so do you ignore the meeting, send the president of the congregation in your place, cancel the class, or ask one of the elders to teach the class for you?

Tyranny of the urgent must be kept at bay, or urgent demands will frequently crowd out work that is more important. Competing priorities come up all the time, so you will often need to sort them out, or do triage, on short notice. Often, it may help to take time for the decision process. Stepping away from that urgent email, text message, or phone call gives you a moment to put things into context and into perspective. Matthew 14:23, Mark 1:35, and Luke 5:16 and 6:12 give us examples of Jesus stepping away from His very busy schedule to spend quality time in prayer. What do you suppose He prayed about? Perhaps His prayer time included praying about His plans and priorities. A few minutes spent in prayerful reflection will help you sort out the important from the urgent as you plan your work and judge between competing priorities.

As you set priorities you need to know which tasks are in progress and which still need to start. You need to visualize which options might be available for performing the work. For example, let's say you have a retired shut-in whom you visit twice a month. You might be able to hand off every other one of those visits to an elder, Stephen minister, or other mature layperson with the appropriate skills and personality. For a more utilitarian example, you might be used to producing a monthly newsletter for the congregation, but you might be able to let someone with administrative skills format and assemble the newsletter if you provide the lead articles. In a larger sense, then, you need to understand your personal role and responsibilities; just because you are the pastor does not mean taking responsibility for every detail of ministry or its support and operational activities. Some responsibilities are uniquely yours, while you can and should delegate other work to staff and volunteers. However, that may mean letting go of something you enjoy doing so that you can save time for the things only you can do.

Once you analyze your workload and set priorities, you can get to work and never look back, right? Well, no. Now you need to communicate priorities to your staff and volunteer help, which we will discuss below, and you need to record the priorities in the form of action items or a task list to be able to track their progress and due dates. You can record and update tasks and priorities with any of several apps available for smartphones, with management tools for your desktop or laptop computer, or with notes written into a desktop or pocket planner. Electronic formats make it easier to share with a secretary, administrative assistant, or business manager. Tracking the workflow over time also helps refine your judgment in defining the work, estimating how long it will take, and identifying resources it will need.

Setting priorities is a dynamic process because priorities can and will change, depending on circumstances. Some tasks will need to move up or down in priority. For example, you plan your routine work for the month, but an unexpected death in the congregation forces you to rearrange priorities. Scheduling issues aside, some tasks might need to be subdivided or combined, and some tasks may need to be reassigned. For example, you are preparing a statistical report for your district, but you discover that someone needs to assemble some data that you had not realized was missing. So now the report task spawned some subtasks, and you involve your treasurer or financial manager to do something you thought your secretary already had in hand. But who gets to decide what is important, and who gets to set the priorities and then assign and reset them as needed? That would be you. Even if you happen to lead an organization large enough to employ a professional planner, and even if your organization uses elaborate calendar and planning software tools, you still need to be able to plan your own work and related activities to be able to lead your team. You will find that setting and managing priorities for your staff and volunteers and for your own work will be time well invested. Of course, defining priorities will itself take time, which leads to our next topic.

STEWARDSHIP OF TIME

Time is the one resource you cannot expand, duplicate, or replace. You can buy back time by having someone else work for you (e.g., manage the budget, draw an illustration, or research a question for you), but even buying back time takes some effort just to arrange the transaction and receive the results. Regardless of how much work you hand off to others, effective time management pays off by making your own work more productive.

Your first step in time management is to understand the demands on your time, your priorities, and how you already spend your time. You should have some grasp of time demands on a daily, weekly, and longer basis from your planning and priority setting discussed above, and you probably have some idea of where your time goes. We need to be aware of two types of potential self-deception, though. First, our energy level, stress level, and personality (are you a Tigger, an Eeyore, or something between those two extremes?) will affect how you estimate the time and possibly other resources needed to complete a task. Second, despite all your best intentions (and your resolve to stay off Facebook and to avoid letting every incoming email interrupt your work), you may not really know where your time goes.

Some years ago, I spent a full week carefully planning and monitoring my time because I wanted to understand where my time went, and I wanted to improve my planning. In the process, I discovered that any given task would take much longer to complete late in the day when I was tired than it did early in the day when I was fresh. No surprise. However, I also found that my time estimates could be off by as much as a factor of two, depending on when I did the planning. Early in the day, I would estimate an hour to draft a letter the next morning, for example, but if I planned my work late in the day, my estimate would be two hours for that same letter. I did not realize this variability came into play until I went back over my time and task records to examine my planning. Here is the point: you need to be brutally honest with yourself in work planning and time management, and the only way to assure honesty is to track enough of your tasks and time usage to be sure that you plan and spend time where you intend.

After you understand your time demands, priorities, and how you spend your time, you are ready to sketch out a daily, weekly, or even monthly budget for your time. You can use a private or shared calendar app, office planner, or paper calendar, but you need to be able to schedule meetings and standing commitments and then block out the rest of your work around those events. If you have a staff person or volunteer helping you with phone calls, scheduling, and the like, this is where you really need them in the loop.

Managing time like we are discussing does not usually require extreme precision; it is not like scheduling trains to avoid collisions (unless you really don't mind double-booked meetings). Management does not mean filling each day and each week with as many activities and tasks as possible; it must allow for unexpected opportunities and unexpected problems. Life does not always go as we plan, and we need to allow the latitude to adapt to new situations and needs. Of course, this may require declining or deferring some work or task commitments, but that is where your priorities come into play.

As you allocate time, you should also be intentional about setting aside time for personal spiritual disciplines, including reading, study, and professional development; for family time, including chores, recreation, and eating meals together; and for protecting your health. I once worked in an engineering office in a for-profit organization, where we worked against project deadlines and rigid design decisions. Nevertheless, our management expected us to set aside no less than 20 percent of our time for reading and professional development to stay abreast of developments, issues, and trends in our field. Your work is demanding, but you still need to set aside time for similar investments in your vocation. More broadly, you are a professional and probably working well over forty hours per week, but you need to protect time for your family.

Once your plans and calendar are in place, it is time to follow through and get your work done. In our earlier discussion of setting priorities, we listed four passages from Matthew, Mark, and Luke showing Jesus taking time to be alone in prayer. Perhaps most striking is the example recorded in Luke 6:12–13, in which Jesus spent the night in prayer before selecting His twelve apostles. Following His lead, a few minutes spent one-on-one with our Lord in prayer asking His blessing and guidance at the start of each day and at the start of each major meeting adds value to our efforts. Sometimes it adds midcourse corrections too. As you move through the day and the week, try to balance patience and tenacity against the sense of urgency that will intrude from time to time. You will need to protect against unnecessary interruptions to be able to stay the course, and at times, this may require stepping back from text messages, email, and phone calls. Time management, like life, is a contact sport, and as things come up, you will need to be ready to do triage on the fly, deciding when to say no, when to say yes, when to defer or ask for more time, and when to hand something off to someone else.

As time passes and you manage and complete your workflow, you should periodically take a pause to evaluate your use of time, the success of your planning, and your fidelity to priorities. You don't need to overthink it, but consider taking a few minutes to prayerfully reflect at the end of each day and a few minutes more at the end of each week. Monthly, quarterly, or annual reviews each deserve more time, and it is up to you to decide the right frequency for these evaluations.

Let me step back and share one more thought about how we use our time. Over the past year or so, many of us have made more use of teleconferencing and videoconferencing technologies to reduce the time and cost of travel and to pack more work into each day. This trend can improve our efficiency, but sometimes the nature of your work will make it more important to do things in person. Do not hesitate to invest personal time to build new relationships, strengthen trust in old relationships, or deal with high-value situations that need your personal touch if that is what the situation requires. You may need to rework your calendar, but that's why time management must be dynamic and flexible.

PEOPLE MANAGEMENT: GENERAL

Among the different kinds of resources at your disposal, people are your most interesting, challenging, and valuable resources. With your priorities and time management in hand, now you need to find people to whom you can delegate administrative work and other responsibilities. These human resources might include professional associates; staff (rostered and laity) who can serve below you in the organization[2]; and trusted volunteers who have the time, ability, and interest to serve in appropriate, specific roles. These people may already be serving, each in their own slot, in your existing organization; they may be new people you need to recruit and bring onboard to fill vacancies; or they may be staff or volunteers that you recruit and train to fill new positions.

As you consider the people already working in your team[3] and the ones you might be able to bring into your team, remember that most people can learn new skills, so motivation, talent, and commitment are more valuable than training or experience alone. Further, you should think outside the box and try to identify more potential current and future human resources than you think you may need just now. Additional human resources can fill gaps as they arise, and they can help you develop new opportunities if you are willing to dream about what might be.

Matching skills with needs is a continuous process, and you need to keep it in mind on two levels. On a task-specific level, you need to match task assignments to the skills, knowledge, and abilities (SKAs) of the people available to perform the task for you, regardless of whether these are staff or volunteers. If they don't have the right skill set, give the task

---

2 *Organization* refers to the group of paid and unpaid people who help in ministry and its support operations. It could be as minimal as a church secretary and treasurer, or at the other extreme, it could include an office staff; associate pastor; director of Christian education; board of elders; board of directors or a church council; principal, teachers, and school staff; Sunday school teachers; nursery or daycare staff; property maintenance staff; and more. Regardless, the common thread is people who help in ministry and support operations in the broad sense.

3 We will often use *team* interchangeably with *organization* in this discussion. *Organization* implies a definite structure of distributed responsibilities and lines of accountably. Many churches do not have a useful organization chart, but still have commonly understood responsibilities and accountabilities. *Team* implies mutually beneficial working relationships in which the team can do more working together than the individuals are able to do working on their own (i.e., the whole is greater than the sum of its parts).

to someone else. On a higher, broader level, you need to fill positions with the right people to do the job over the long term. Be ruthless but kind and discreet in assessing and matching people's skills, knowledge, and abilities with the needs of a position or task, and keep an eye on how people are likely to fit in with the rest of your team.

When you do have the opportunity to recruit someone for your team (e.g., to hire an administrative assistant or secretary), a question may arise about whether you should tap a member of the congregation or someone from outside. The answer will be somewhat situation-dependent, but let me offer a few observations. A member of the congregation will already know people, the culture and history of the congregation, and possibly something about current needs and workload. However, he may come with baggage and preconceived notions. A person from outside the congregation will come with a fresh perspective and may have a better set of SKAs but will not know the people or the context of the position. The advantages of tapping a member may outweigh the value of bringing someone in from outside, but sometimes you may have to bring in an outsider because the SKAs are simply not available from within the congregation (e.g., you need an information technology specialist).

Turning our attention back to the ministry aspect of your work, time will be your biggest constraint, so it may not be possible to personally mentor all future staff or volunteers. Therefore, leverage your time by focusing on those who are already in place and willing to take their servant or servant leader roles seriously, along with focusing on a few other hand-picked individuals that you can influence. Groom these people for growth in spiritual service, and then equip and challenge them to groom others as a force multiplier. Your immediate circle of support staff and volunteers will change as people move in or out of the loop or as their interests and availability change, which is why it is important to have some idea of whom else you could tap for help.

PEOPLE MANAGEMENT: JOB DESCRIPTIONS

Your basic starting point for managing your human resources is a job description for each paid or volunteer position in your team. This is important, even if your ministry does not have a good organization chart; you or your administrative support can draft a chart later to show how different parts of the ministry fit together. Meanwhile, a good job description will outline the SKAs needed for each job, and it will sketch out the roles, responsibilities, kinds of authority, and accountability (e.g., who does this position report to?). These are all important for finding the right people for each job, and they provide a basis for evaluating each person's workload and performance[4]. The roles and responsibilities also provide a general descriptive framework within which you can spell out and assign specific tasks and types of work.

You need a written position description for each member of your team, but it makes no sense to start developing a job description from scratch if someone has already written something that you can adapt to your needs. Your organization may already have some job descriptions on file, in which case you can dust them off and update them as needed. If you don't already have viable job descriptions in place, The Lutheran Church—Missouri Synod web pages offer draft job description resources (or templates) for several categories of ministry work at lcms.org/resources/church-and-school-administration (or try searching lcms.org for the terms "ministry staff positions," "congregational officers," "administrative staff positions," or the like to find descriptions for compensated staff). They include descriptions for compensated staff, and some of the templates would work for volunteers too. The web page provides a surprisingly wide range of templates, includes job descriptions for eighteen types of ministry staff, ten different lay leader functions, sixteen kinds of administrative helpers, and thirteen different facilities and program support positions. The web page provides these materials as pdf files for download, and it is easy to copy and paste the verbiage into a different file format for editing. The LCMS web page also provides a draft human resources manual for HR policy needs and worksheets for performance appraisals. Whether your staff is only a half-time secretary or includes an organization of dozens, think of the draft job descriptions,

4 Suggest this to your nominating committee if they are not already using this approach.

policy manual, and performance appraisal templates as work-saving starting points to edit and adapt to the needs of your ministry team.

With the job descriptions and, more importantly, the SKAs of your team members in mind, you are prepared to delegate work to free your time for the work that only you should do. For example, you should prepare your class and let someone else set up the room, and you should provide material for the bulletin but let someone else format, print, and make copies. As we noted in the introduction, your most important role as a servant leader in a Christian organization is spiritual leadership. This is a complex role, to be sure, but you need to take a clear-eyed look at what you can delegate to others and then cheerfully hand it off so that you can focus on the work that is uniquely yours. Lutheran polity places every aspect of the ministry under the leadership of the pastor, but that does not mean the pastor needs to personally perform every aspect of the ministry. Therefore, you should continually delegate administrative tasks to others. Some tasks can be handed off completely; others will need your imprimatur or signature. In the latter case, delegate the assignment and then put the finishing touches on it when it is ready for you. Regardless of the kind of task, have your administrative staff track assignments, action items, and deadlines in a written work log to help avoid things being lost and forgotten.

PEOPLE MANAGEMENT: MOTIVATION

As spiritual leader, you are responsible for the care and feeding (think shepherding) of the ministry, the congregation, and the shared vision or mission[5] of the ministry. Keeping the vision means nurture and protection, but it also requires sharing that vision with the whole congregation and

5 *Vision* and *mission* are organizational terms that are often confused. For our purposes, we define *vision* as "a concise statement of an organization's purpose." Think of it as "why we are here, what we do, and what we are about." In the 1960s, the NASA vision was simply, "Put a man on the moon." A vision for a congregation might be the Great Commission (although that is a lot of words for a concise statement), or it might be shortened to something like, "Make disciples in Christ." A mission statement, then, would expand on the vision to provide more details or context. For example, the mission statement might include details that reflect ministry in and to the community around the church, or it might mention a school if education is a special emphasis. Vision and mission statements are not easy to write, and they will be somewhat unique to each congregation. And yet a congregation should be able to recognize themselves and their best aspirations in their vision and mission statements, and they should see Jesus, the Lord of the Church, at the center of those statements.

particularly with your staff and volunteers. That shared vision is key to motivating your team. Churches (and most other organizations) rarely pay enough for compensation to be much of a motivator; few, if any, people in ministry are there to get rich. Rather, they are there because the Holy Spirit draws them into the vision, opportunities to serve, and the chance to make a meaningful difference.

If you are pastor of a Lutheran church, the vision you keep probably has its roots in the Great Commission and the Office of the Keys. Most church vision statements seem to be either a paraphrase, an expanded restatement, or a direct quote of the Great Commission. I would be surprised to see anything much different. However, as you teach, share, and apply the Great Commission, you usually need to work with people to help them understand how Jesus speaks to them through those words. They need to understand how, as children of God and as His ambassadors, they fit into God's plans and directions as expressed in the Great Commission.[6] This is also important for your team members: they are not working to fill out a timecard or to earn a living; they are working as members of a multipart team intent on fulfilling God's ministry in that place. Just as if they were members of a baseball team or football team, they each have different roles to play. If they play the wrong position or sit out the game, the whole team and ministry suffer. Sincere positive reinforcement as you unpack and explain their roles will help with the motivation.

PEOPLE MANAGEMENT: COMMUNICATIONS

Communications are important in every part of the work, and this involves more than just information flow. All team members supporting the ministry (and supporting you) need to understand their roles, responsibilities, accountabilities, and assignments. They need to engage the larger mission of the ministry, and we will discuss this later in the

---

6 To unpack this a bit, understanding how we (the congregation) fit into God's plans and directions starts with understanding who we are as redeemed sinners, as children of God, and includes understanding how God nurtures us by Word and Sacrament. Then it includes looking at the community around us, including its strengths, interests, needs (and especially spiritual needs), demographic makeup, and dynamics and then exploring why God placed us here as His ambassadors. God desires all to be saved (John 3:16 and 1 Timothy 2:3–5).

context of motivation. They need to be able to come to you for help if they hit a snag or for redirection if needed, and they need to have feedback and encouragement about their performance. And you would like your communications to be two-way and perhaps to generate new ideas, new collaborations, and new opportunities. All of this takes time, but remember that time invested in helping your team succeed will pay back manyfold in freeing the rest of your time for your own work. And, in fact, leading your team is part of your work.

You have a few, or perhaps several, tools at your disposal for communicating with your staff members. You can choose from face-to-face (either one-on-one or in groups), telephone calls, email, text messages, handwritten notes,[7] teleconferencing, or other communication tools, but you should choose carefully based not just on convenience and personal style but also based on the level of trust, level of understanding, timeliness, and strength of the working relationship.

Communicating involves more than words; the richest communications include body language, facial expressions, tone of voice, and variations between loud and quiet speaking. You can use ALL CAPS to shout at someone in an email, but it is not the same as a phone call, and a phone call is not as good as face-to-face conversation. Sensitive topics, such as performance feedback, should be in private and preferably face-to-face, or you risk damage to the working relationship. Initial assignments and problem-solving after project start-up may require personal time for more in-depth discussion. Other kinds of communications—for example, to hand off information or to answer a question—are more amenable for less personal tools like email. Frequent communications will help avoid problems and, as a fallback approach, help identify issues soon enough to resolve problems. If communications are not working as well as you would like, you can switch to a different tool or try multiple approaches.

Communicating also goes both ways. Asking people for their views is important and empowering, but you should try not to leave a false expectation that anything they suggest will be done or that they will

7 Handwritten thank-you notes or notes of encouragement can carry a lot of weight. Few people write notes by hand or send hand-written letters, so a personal note can be very special.

always have their way. You can ask for their advice, but you may decide not to take it. Also, while you can ask people what kind of supervision and communications would benefit them in their work, they might not be able to tell you. They might not have ever thought of such a question, so you may need to draw ideas out of them with further questions or some suggestions of your own.

PEOPLE MANAGEMENT: DELEGATION AND SUPERVISION

Managing people requires supervising people rather than just dropping work onto their desks and turning away to something else. Supervision involves giving people work to do, arranging for them to have the resources they need to do the work, monitoring their progress, receiving the results, and giving them feedback. It may also include integrating the results of their work with results from other people's work to create a final product, but in many cases, the integrating will be your job rather than theirs. Let us consider a simple example, such as preparing for a voters meeting to review and approve the annual budget, to look at the steps of the workflow process.

First, as you give people work, you need to be clear about the assignment, its timing and due date, and the expected results. They need to understand how it fits in with their other work, particularly if it is different in content or disruptive because of schedule. You may need to answer questions or do some brainstorming with them to achieve the necessary mutual understanding.

In our example, you work backward from the approximate date of the voters meeting to lay out the work schedule to prepare for the meeting, and you decide what the meeting will include. Perhaps you want to review membership changes and discuss a possible new ministry opportunity in addition to presenting the budget for discussion and voter approval. The budget discussion will need to review current income, expenses, and types of costs and then rack up projections for next year. If you have a business manager or treasurer with the right SKAs, you can ask her to draft the budget under your supervision, or you can do it yourself.

Regardless, you need the treasurer to assemble data for income and expenses, and you need input from leaders in each area of work (e.g., music director for choir and music expenses, altar guild for worship supplies, DCE or Sunday School superintendent for class materials, treasurer or church leadership for salaries, and so on). The more you can delegate this work to others, the more you have time to thoughtfully consider how their work comes together, and the more you can shape it for understandable presentation to the voters. You would ask your administrator to pull together information about membership changes, and perhaps you would ask the chairman of the board of elders or the president of the congregation, or both, to work with you and your key professional ministry staff to put together the discussion of the new ministry opportunity (depending on what it is). You set deadlines for all these parts of the work, and you ask your administrator to collect them as input for your review, understanding that the administrator will then prepare the briefing materials for the meeting.

Second, as you assign the work, you may also need to arrange for, or at least authorize, them to have the resources they need to do the work. These resources could include special information, access to data, authority to disrupt other activities, spending authority, or support from other members of the team. This may be part of the discussion where you kick off the project, or it may be a follow-up discussion after they have had a chance to review and start thinking through the assignment.

By now, your team realizes that this simple example is not simple. People assigned to work on the budget are a little squeamish about reporting salaries, and to ease their fears about privacy, you give them permission to show salary costs by lumped category rather than by individual. Maybe the treasurer hesitates to give the numbers to someone else on staff until you make it clear that he has permission to see the data. Someone is reluctant to take time away from important other work to meet your deadline to prepare for the meeting, so you help her sort out her priorities. This is all par for the course, though.

Third, once the work is underway, you will need to monitor their progress. Some leaders are very hands-off (this extreme can let problems fester) while others tend to micromanage (this extreme can impede work and may drive people away). Some workers need a lot of attention, while others may need much less or sometimes even resent it. Your management approach needs to reach a happy medium to balance these preferences, and it will likely be a little different for each person in your team. You need to get along, but they need to give you feedback for you to be able to help if problems arise, and you need to know how the work is coming along. You can afford a certain amount of trial and error in your approach, but you still need to assess what kind of supervision (and how much) each person needs and adjust on the fly if it is not working well. In our example, you might be able to track progress through your regular staff meeting, but some of the lay leaders are not likely to be in your staff meeting, so you will need to check with them separately. If everyone knows that you asked your administrator to check on the progress on a weekly basis, that will make your life easier.

Fourth, when they finish the task, you need to receive the results in a form that you can use. For our voters meeting example, the results might take the form of draft tables and pie charts along with verbiage to explain what they show. You need to be able to present and discuss the information in your own words, so you may have questions or may need to ask for revisions. There may be follow-up tasks to discuss and assign, such as preparing a final version of charts or handouts for the meeting. Discussions along the way should set the stage for successfully bringing all of these activities to closure.

Lastly, you should give your team members constructive feedback. It may be a mix of negative and positive, but you should try to provide enough positive to be encouraging, to build up rather than tear down. And it should include enough specifics to be unambiguous and actionable (i.e., the person understands what to feel good about and knows how he needs to improve). Public recognition may be appropriate when an accomplishment truly merits it, but some people are genuinely afraid of public recognition, so be discreet.

TEAM MANAGEMENT

Leading a team of multiple people requires all the skills and concepts we discussed in the previous sections, plus attention to a few additional things. Several situations may require you to manage a team. Sometimes you simply need more manpower for the work on hand because it is too much for one or two people. Sometimes the work needs a broader range of SKAs than you can find in one person. More often, you need a team for both reasons. A classic example might be a building committee when it is time for a new sanctuary, school building, or ministry center. Launching a building project is too much work for one person, and you need a team that can work on the finance, design, contracting, permitting, and other aspects of the project in an integrated approach.

Updating the congregation at an annual voters meeting would be a smaller example; in addition to discussing various parts of the ministry, you also need to include data about contributions, expenses, and the budget, a recap of changes to the congregational membership, and perhaps information about relevant changes in the surrounding community. Rather than pulling all of this together on your own, it makes sense to have your team (perhaps this includes your administrator, treasurer, head elder, and president of the congregation) help assemble the material you need.

If you are in a ministry that is quickly outgrowing its staff, such that your team of staff and volunteers is forced to grow, then you may have the opportunity to expand by recruiting and bringing several new people into the team at once. On the other hand, your ministry may not be growing or shrinking, but you need to add people to the team from time to time as people retire, move on to other interests, or leave for other positions. In either case, your team is the people God has given you. While you rarely have the chance to select your dream team all at one time, you do have the opportunity to work with the people God raises up or calls to your attention.

In a similar vein, unless your organization is new, allowing you to build from the ground up, you will need to work within the existing organizational structure. The situation may call for a different framework of positions and lines of accountability, but organizational change takes time and energy, and it disrupts productive work, so you need to count the cost before driving forward. On the other hand, if you are patient and watch for chances to move the organization in an incremental fashion, it should be doable to reshape things over time and as needs and opportunities arise. An artist's lump of modeling clay provides an illustration: if you set a hammer on top of a lump of stiff modeling clay, the steady pressure will gradually reshape the lump. If you swing the hammer as hard as you can and hit the lump of clay, the lump will shatter. Slow, steady, incremental change will usually be more productive than sudden forced change.

Sometimes you need to delegate work (e.g., a complex project like starting a preschool, renovating the sanctuary, or creating a new outreach to your community) to a team rather than to one individual. The basic principles are still the same, though: understand the work, know to whom you are delegating, and do not neglect any of the steps of assigning and supervising the work. You will need to identify a lead person among the individuals forming the team. A leaderless team is like a committee without a chairman: it will either thrash along with low productivity, or it will eventually identify its own leader after some amount of lost time. If you are blessed with strong enough people (in terms of SKAs), you can find and designate someone who can lead the team. That individual will still need supervision, though.

If your organization is large enough for multiple staff and many volunteers, you should consider cross-training, or rotating people through different roles, so they can pick up multiple skills and experiences. Cross-training can be as elaborate as formally moving people from one position to another for a set length of time,[8] or it can be as simple (if less beneficial) as having a person shadow another team member to get a sense of their work functions and responsibilities. This will give you depth of bench so that if someone retires or moves to another position, you

8 Work tends to self-organize around periods on the calendar, such as a monthly payroll or expense cycle, a school year or a quarter within the school year, or even an entire Church Year. Cross-training may be more productive if planned around one of these cycles, as appropriate to the position.

have people available with a SKA match that is close enough for them to be able to fill the gap.

When working with a team, you still need to know when to help and when to stand back as you supervise the individuals, the team lead, and the whole team. This requires judgment and some understanding of individual and group personalities. Candor and humor will give you some latitude to adjust as you go along. However, regardless of whether you are managing individuals or a team, staff or volunteers, you should be ready for some potential problem areas. This is our next topic.

POTENTIAL PROBLEM AREAS

The concepts covered above have broad applicability to managing people and time, but some situations deserve special attention. You should back up your special attention with special prayer. Pray that you may properly discern the situation, pray that you may hear and understand the people and their thinking, and pray for God's help in working out a peaceful, constructive, unifying solution to the situation. With our prayerful approach in mind, here are some special, but not all that unusual, challenges you will likely encounter sooner or later:

But we've always done it that way!

Ministries and people tend to develop their own inertia over time. This helps explain the proverbial "but we've always done it this way" attitude we have all seen. Sometimes this arises as an objection to a new idea for ministry, with a claim that we cannot or should not try the idea, although the specific reason why not remains murky. For example, you would like to replace the old worn-out hymnals with the new *Lutheran Service Book*, but a vocal minority drags their feet, insisting that the old hymnals are good for another year or two. Sometimes this comes up as an appeal to return to the way some good thing used to be, even if a return is impossible. For example, someone wants to return to the NIV translation rather than continuing with the ESV but does not understand that the 1984 NIV translation is no longer available for general use and that the new NIV translations have serious flaws. Both kinds of objection tend to be oblivious to the damage done by not moving forward and to the potential loss of keeping things static.

Examples abound where a new pastor takes a call and arrives at a congregation that has been vacant for an extended period of time (habits form in a leadership vacuum), a congregation where a well-loved pastor recently left (habits also form around the previous pastor's leadership style), or a congregation where a few lay leaders or staff resist the new pastor's efforts to step into his leadership role (people resist changes in general). The common threads in this include a fear of loss, such as a loss of the familiar, the comfortable, or the known past as compared to the unknown future. Often these objections involve putting self-interest ahead of the Lord's work. Sometimes they reflect a lack of trust, and often they reflect a lack of understanding the new idea or the proposed change.

Transparent communications are often the best remedy for problems of inertia. Whether done one-on-one or in a group setting, you need to identify and address the issues behind objections. Most people don't like confrontation. They also want to be part of the ministry community and not left behind. You can use these perspectives to insist on a calm discussion to clarify the issues and decide on a path forward to facilitate, rather than impede, the ministry. Start by assuming that everyone involved has the best interests of the ministry at heart. After all, God's work (God's ministry) is more important than individual preferences. Then explain clearly and lovingly where and how the inertia affects ministry. This approach really needs a face-to-face conversation with the people concerned. Make frequent reference to your mutual interest in the success of the ministry as you explain what success means for the church. Identify specifically what needs to change to relieve the inertia but without promising to completely avoid discomfort. Nobody ever said the church was meant to be a comfortable place!

While most people dislike confrontation, a few people enjoy it, either overtly or covertly. Confrontation gives them the chance to feel that they are in the right while others are sadly misinformed, misguided, or simply wrong. Perhaps they need to hear from God's Law to remind them that contentious behavior, arguing, gossip, pride, and wrath are all symptoms of our lost, sinful nature. They may need time to understand this, but behavior is really a spiritual issue rather than anything to do with ministry, and they need to seek repentance and absolution. As we discussed before, a steady effort toward moving forward is often more productive than a sudden, forced fix.

Occasionally, someone will become so worked up that he threatens to leave. If someone threatens to quit his work in ministry or leave the congregation, keep your cool and try to depressurize the situation. Immediate pushback may put him on the defensive, leading to rash decisions that he may regret later. You can ask him to prayerfully reconsider the whole situation. If, after a cooling-off period, he chooses to step away from his job, you can express sincere regret about his choices, but you cannot afford to be held hostage by a selfish threat. Whether his position was staff or volunteer, work with the rest of your church leadership to move ahead and backfill behind them.

Silos, stovepipes, and ministry monopolies

Ministries often tend to develop internal degrees of separation over time. We call these separations silos or stovepipes, as the figurative walls keep different parts of ministry from cooperating or communicating with each other. This helps explain "we versus they" or "us versus them" attitudes we sometimes find in voters meetings or other discussions of plans and priorities. In other cases, we may not run into a sense of competition between parts of the ministry as much as we find a sense of apathy, where one part of ministry appears indifferent to another part.

Examples might include Sunday School teachers who do not coordinate with those working in youth ministry or a lack of integration between a day school and its parent congregation. This is not necessarily any one person's fault, and we do not mean to point fingers, but silos by their nature each tend to have a constituency of supporters and participants. Inertia and pride can come into play, as people in different parts of ministry may resist integration or may find excuses (e.g., why should the church support the school, or why should the school support the church?).

It is important to recognize silos (or stovepipes, if you prefer that metaphor) where they exist and then take steps to break them down. Breaking down silos can help the team (and the congregation at large) realize and follow up on missed opportunities that come with better cooperation and integration. Breaking down silos can lead to better use of resources, and this itself may reduce a potential source of competition and division among staff and in the congregation.

Many of the communications and management approaches that apply to the inertia problem discussed above also apply to the silo problem. These would include candor and transparency in communications, honest examination of goals and motives, and a call to repentance as appropriate. Each silo may have somewhat different goals, so it would help to review the overall vision for ministry and then take time to review how each silo reflects and accomplishes part of that larger vision. Follow this up by discussing the value to be gained with a more integrated, cross-cutting approach to ministry.

As mentioned above, silos can tend to have a constituency of supporters and participants. In some cases, these constituencies have developed their own private communications networks and have developed habits of gossip and mistrust about the other silos. This ungodly behavior must stop. As mentioned above, use God's Law to call out this sin and to call for repentance and a fresh start. If some attempt to sabotage the work, this calls for candid discussion of their values and behavior, in hopes of helping them understand how they should behave and function as part of the Body of Christ.

Personal investment: who owns the scope of work?

Sometimes you find people who think of their job as their own, who believe that they own some given task or function. Nobody could ever do it better than or even as well as they do, and they will kindly urge you to take your time, energy, and interest elsewhere if you attempt to change anything. After all, they are just trying to protect you from wasting your limited time by looking into something that they already have well in hand. Or they feel a calling to this special job and don't see why they would ever do anything different.

Examples might include the lady who has run the Sunday School nursery for many years and will not let anyone else help, the secretary who knows all about her business and uses information for power, or the treasurer who does not want to bother or distract you with those boring numbers. They may each be very good at what they do, but they think of it as their private ministry rather than seeing it as part of God's work, which is much larger and Christ-focused rather than self-focused.

Your best strategy here involves reminding your team about who owns their work as well as the entire ministry. It is God's ministry, after all, and we are only stewards. God's work in and through our congregation goes on for years and, hopefully, for multiple generations. We carry the baton until we hand it off to someone else, so our job is to carry it faithfully, avoid stumbling in pride, and then take care to not fumble the handoff. Further, in the spirit of each of us being a valuable part of the Body of Christ, we must each work as part of an integrated whole, meaning that there is no place for something to be done as a private hobbyhorse.

Again, it will help to have a clear discussion of how individual roles fit into the larger integrated whole of the ministry. This may be an opportunity for cross-training, such as we discussed earlier. These conversations need to include members of the lay leadership, such as two or three of the elders. Their explanation of integrated ministry will have a broader base of support, and it leaves you in a better position to provide pastoral support and offer God's grace if people feel hurt after giving up their hobbyhorse. In that vein, some congregations are blessed to include members with professional experience in personnel management or human resource policies. If you have a mature, trustworthy member with that expertise, do not hesitate to tap him or her for help with personnel matters.

The non-ordained ghost pastor

Although perhaps not as common as the problem areas described above, sometimes an individual or a couple essentially rules a congregation by their strength of personality, dominant financial contributions, or a deep-rooted history of personal involvement. These people might serve as elders or as officers of the congregation, or they might wield their power behind the scenes. They can block your leadership of the ministry, whether through passive-aggressive behavior or by challenging your decisions and leadership. This is not a tenable situation.

Once again, candid communications and clear expectations must be part of your approach to deal with the non-ordained ghost pastors. They probably believe sincerely that love of the ministry drives their behavior, and they hold only the best of intentions for you and for the congregation. The challenge, then, is to help them understand how their constructive activities need to be part of a larger whole, one that you lead as pastor, and to understand how their destructive behavior works at cross purposes to the ministry. Even if they think they already know these things, explain to them the Lutheran understanding of the role of a pastor and the value of an integrated ministry led by the pastor. Remind them of the role of the Good Shepherd who lays down His life for the sheep, and that they are sheep and not the shepherd. Point out their role in the Body of Christ and examine how a healthy body is not dominated by one of its many parts.

You do not need to cover every one of these topics, but they need to see that dominating the congregation is not healthy for them or for the congregation and that stepping back into being one among a congregation of diverse peers is healthier for all concerned. If they are not willing to consider and accept such a different view, then a more direct call to repent may be in order. Again, it may help to include one or two strong lay leaders in this conversation if any such leaders are available. If the lay leadership is intimidated by the ghost pastor, then perhaps you could ask your circuit visitor or another pastor from your circuit to join you in the meeting.

If they decide to take offense and leave, you will need to work to maintain the unity of the rest of the congregation. This will include teaching them about the importance of unity among believers, drawing from Jesus' discourse in the Upper Room and perhaps from Paul's teaching in 1 Corinthians regarding playing favorites and separating into sects. And it may require extended peacemaking as the congregation navigates the loss of what it thought to be its most important member.

NOTE IN CLOSING

After considering such very difficult situations, it is always helpful to recall that this is God's church, not ours. These are God's people, and Jesus died to save each of them. The gates of hell will not prevail against the Church, and neither will any inertia, silos, ownership issues, or grievous departures. Our unity and perseverance are in Christ, and it is beneficial to teach these things.

The advice outlined above should fit well with the work of a pastor serving as the functional spiritual leader of a congregation or, in a more general sense, a Christian ministry. If we think of the purpose of the organization and its leader as being the work of the right-hand kingdom, then left-hand kingdom work needs to facilitate the right-hand functions and is not an end in itself. Managing people, such as staff and volunteers, and managing time are important tools to help facilitate both areas of work.

ADDITIONAL READING FROM CPH

The Calling: Living a Life of Significance, Kurt Senske, 2010

Godly Man: Men at Work, John H. Auble, 1996

Mentoring, Henry Simon, 2000

Overcoming Pastoral Pitfalls, Kurt Brink, 1997

Servant Leadership: Setting Leaders Free, Jane Fryar, 2001

Strengthening Integrity and Accountability in Church Leadership, Christian Okon Ekong, 2019

CHAPTER 9

THE PASTOR AND MANAGING CONFLICT

Rev. Ray Hartwig

I remember reading of a play years ago that pictured hell as a place so crowded that its inhabitants could not help but constantly rub against one another, producing continual conflict and a miserable, eternal existence. The play contained at least one element of truth: regular contact with other human beings can rub the wrong way—true in this life, true even in Christian congregations.

This certainly was the case for the congregation at Corinth in early New Testament times. Founded by the apostle Paul (Acts 18:1–22), it nevertheless fell prey to the "spirit of the world" (1 Corinthians 2:12), fertile ground for the rubbing and chafing that leads to "jealousy and strife" (3:3). To make matters worse, the members of the congregation stopped talking to one another and working things out, instead, regularly looking beyond their congregation for resolution:

> When one of you has a grievance against another, does he dare go to law before the unrighteous instead of the saints? . . . So if you have such cases, why do you lay them before those who have no standing in the church? I say this to your shame. Can it

> **be that there is no one among you wise enough to settle a dispute between the brothers, but brother goes to law against brother, and that before unbelievers?** (1 Corinthians 6:1, 4–6)

Today's congregations exist in similarly secular times, a spirit of the world not only engendering disputes but tempting members to look for solutions outside the church, often ending up with lawyers in courtrooms. Thirty years ago, when secular lawsuits were an extensive and expensive practice within The Lutheran Church—Missouri Synod, the Synod took upon itself the development and application of a Christian conflict resolution process that was and still is today scriptural and effective, an "exclusive and final remedy for those who are in dispute" (LCMS Bylaw 1.10.1.1, 2019 *Handbook*, p. 38). Since its adoption, this process (Bylaw Section 1.10, pp. 38–53) has been used successfully with very few exceptions to address disputes in the Synod, restoring harmony, while at the same time saving huge amounts of money and the shame mentioned by the apostle.

However, most of the disputes that take place within Christian congregations cannot ordinarily be addressed by using the Synod's *Handbook* process, per se. That process, with relatively few exceptions (Bylaw 1.10.2, 2019 *Handbook* p. 39), provides help for resolving theological, doctrinal, or ecclesiastical issues involving rostered church workers and rostered congregations as a whole. This leaves the resolution of the more common kind of disputes that erupt within congregations, most often involving individuals or groups of members and their pastors and other church workers, to be addressed locally following Jesus' instructions in Matthew 18:15–20. It is this use of the Matthew 18 process that is addressed by this chapter.

Dispute resolution is a very important part of a pastor's care of the congregation(s) he has been called to serve. This chapter will address the four rules of thumb listed below that I have found important and helpful when providing assistance to disputing parties in a congregation, both as a pastor and as a district president. Perhaps they will also be helpful for you to bear in mind when you are faced with a dispute in, or perhaps even with members of, a congregation you are serving, when you find yourself contemplating, "What do I do now?" It may help you to remember—

1. The Instigator Is Not an Alligator—It's the Lion
2. What the Church Needs Now Is Love, Sweet Love
3. One Should Not Swat at Every Fly
4. The Congregation Is Queen

1. THE INSTIGATOR IS NOT AN ALLIGATOR—IT'S THE LION

I remember listening years ago to a group of pastors discussing what at the time was a popular topic, said to be the key to peaceful ministries and prosperous congregations. That key was to identify the "alligators" in a congregation, namely those stubborn-minded members found in every congregation, often the so-called "pillars of the congregation" (who hold everything up). These members are those who always think they know best, resist reason, hold court in voters meetings and coffee shops, are intent upon having their way or no way, and are therefore the common source of most of the trouble in a congregation, especially for the pastor who wishes to move his congregation forward.

The discussion by the group of pastors concluded with what seemed to be general agreement that such members had to be dealt with sooner rather than later, even if it meant isolating them or even facilitating their departure from the congregation. Doing so was said to be the key for peaceful ministries and prosperous congregations. After listening for a long while, I remember finally speaking up, admitting that I cringed at the thought of calling any of the baptized children of God placed into my pastoral care "alligators." I also remember while driving home from the meeting looking back on my years of pastoral ministry and trying to identify any members who might have been alligators in the congregations I had served. Although I did my best, the following list was about all I could come up with, even these hardly meriting being compared to an ugly reptile.

I supposed one might have been the elderly retired farmer who lived across the street from the parsonage, one whose self-assumed role in the congregation was to keep an eye on the pastor on behalf of the large German-Russian contingent of the congregation, whose last three pastors' average stays had been twenty months. On the Sunday afternoon after conducting my first worship services, I had changed out of my dress suit and clergy shirt and was walking across the parsonage lawn to inspect our newly tilled garden area when my neighbor came storming out of his house, calling out to me across the street, "Oh, Reverend, Reverend! Around here, we wear our church clothes all day Sunday!" before abruptly returning into his house. I remember finding myself thinking, "What do I do now?"

Perhaps another alligator might have been the wife of the perpetual chairman of a congregation I served (she was very active in the life of the congregation, and her husband was the president of the local small-town bank), who, without her usual smile, on her way out of church one Sunday morning, called attention to the facial stubble I was beginning to grow and show in preparation for our community's 1976 bicentennial patriotic beard-growing contest. The next morning, I received a succinct letter from the chairman of the congregation, its message very clear: "Reverend, our pastors don't grow beards!" I remember asking my wife, "What do I do now?"

Probably my best candidate for an alligator list was the assistant pastor with whom I served for three years. He was fresh out of the seminary with somewhat different ideas and talents for pastoral ministry, who, behind a veil of peaceful coexistence and cooperation, had made himself available to a group of younger members advocating significant changes for the century-old congregation. His response when I expressed concern, if not in so many words, was that he also was pastor of the congregation, with rights and responsibilities of his own. I remember asking myself more than once, "What do I do now?"

These candidates for "alligator" that came to my mind were not, as I knew in my heart, alligators—they were two sheep and an assistant shepherd of flocks that our Lord had called me to serve. I also knew that they were, if anything, instruments of discord being used by the real gator, the "instigator," the lion of whom the apostle Peter warned in his first epistle:

> **Be sober-minded; be watchful. Your adversary the devil prowls around like a roaring lion, seeking someone to devour. Resist him, firm in your faith, knowing that the same kinds of suffering are being experienced by your brotherhood throughout the world.** (1 Peter 5:8–9)

In the case of those early New Testament Christians to whom the apostle addressed these words, the lion was indeed roaring. Peter was making reference to the suffering of early Christian martyrs, who all too often faced death in the jaws of real lions in Roman arenas. Perhaps more often, however, this lion doesn't roar. Martin Luther spoke of a stealthy evil foe who "tries every trick and does not stop until he finally wears us out, so that we either renounce our faith or throw up our hands and put up our feet, becoming indifferent or impatient" (LC V 26). One of this lion's stealthiest tricks is to lure God's children into disputes that do harm to faith and loving concern for one another, thereby often also doing grievous harm to their congregations and to Christ's Church on earth.

C. F. W. Walther calls attention to the same lion at work on a broader scale and in a different manner, with a purring that leads to devouring:

> **My dear brothers, let us be on our guard! Satan is sly. Right now we are brothers, living together in peace and love. But Satan will most certainly lay for us snares by which he hopes to destroy the sweet, brotherly love we now have in our hearts.** (*Essays for the Church*, Vol. 2, p. 56)

Suffice to say and important to recognize, it is the old evil foe who means deadly woe and is seriously busy among us, tempting pastors to look the other way or fail to look deeper or merely to lay blame upon the usual troublesome people. And although invisible, the lion is readily seen in the great harm that he has already caused in many a congregation's history, especially when disputes instigated by him were left unresolved and smoldering for years or were allowed to increase in intensity and participation until the entire congregation had become involved and its ministry to its community seriously injured, hopelessly divided, and sometimes even destroyed.

So "What do I do now?" when faced with a dispute? We do well, first of all, to bear in mind that this is not about alligators but about the lion and that his is not some kind of devil's play, as though the old evil foe is merely fooling around and harmlessly having his way with unreasonable and undesirable members. Better, we do well to be ready for spiritual warfare, bearing in mind St. Paul's reminder regarding who the enemy really is and how best to meet him on the field of battle:

> For we do not wrestle against flesh and blood, but against the rulers, against the authorities, against the cosmic powers over this present darkness, against the spiritual forces of evil in the heavenly places. Therefore take up the whole armor of God, that you may be able to withstand in the evil day, and having done all, to stand firm. Stand therefore, having fastened on the belt of truth, and having put on the breastplate of righteousness, and, as for shoes for your feet, having put on the readiness given by the gospel of peace. In all circumstances take up the shield of faith, with which you can extinguish all the flaming darts of the evil one; and take the helmet of salvation, and the sword of the Spirit, which is the word of God, praying at all times in the Spirit, with all prayer and supplication. (Ephesians 6:12–18)

Included in that armor is everything we will need to take on the lion and "be able to withstand in the evil day," but it also requires our stepping forward to address the conflicts that threaten the congregations we serve, motivated by the love of which the apostle John speaks in his first epistle. This will be the subject of the second section of this chapter.

It should also be borne in mind when faced with a dispute in a congregation we serve and we find ourselves asking, "What do I do now?"

2. WHAT THE CHURCH NEEDS NOW IS LOVE, SWEET LOVE

Jackie DeShannon's 1965 single, "What the World Needs Now," was perfectly timed to be a hit, given the racial unrest and violence that had begun to trouble American cities at the time. Its words by songwriters Burt Bacharach and Hal Davis offered the solution:

> **What the world needs now is love, sweet love**
> **It's the only thing that there's just too little of**
> **What the world needs now is love, sweet love,**
> **No not just for some but for everyone.**[9]

The pop hit went even one better, identifying the source of such love:

> **Lord, we don't need another mountain . . .**
> **Lord, we don't need another meadow . . .**
> **Oh listen, Lord, if you want to know.**

As we Christians know, the Lord listened to the plight of His creation and its human beings long before Jackie DeShannon won her Grammy, immediately assuring humankind of His love when shame, guilt, strife, envy, and blame replaced "love, sweet love" as the norm of life on earth. His deliverance required extreme measures, far from sweet, provided by His offering of His own Son to be the only sacrifice that could suffice "not just for some but for everyone."

But even for those who are moved by the Spirit to receive the benefits of God's great act of love, such faith does not rid them of the constant pursuit and temptations of the lion during their lives on earth, the evil foe particularly rearing his ugly head in what should be the most unlikely of places, the Church on earth where the Holy Spirit-laden Word and

---

9 Text of *What the World Needs Now is Love* is used under license with Hal Leonard LLC.

Sacraments are regularly preached and administered. What's more, the most serious and devastating strife occurs in what should be the most unlikely of places: in relationships between pastors, other church workers, and the congregations they serve.

Numerous books have been written, offering help to resolve strife and restore peace and goodwill, good-hearted attempts to flesh out the instructions provided by Jesus Himself for handling disputes in His churches:

> **If your brother sins against you, go and tell him his fault, between you and him alone. If he listens to you, you have gained your brother. But if he does not listen, take one or two others along with you, that every charge may be established by the evidence of two or three witnesses. If he refuses to listen to them, tell it to the church. And if he refuses to listen even to the church, let him be to you as a Gentile and a tax collector.** (Matthew 18:15–17)

During the years that I served as secretary of our Synod and administered its dispute-resolution process, I became familiar with many of those numerous books on the subject, calling on what I considered to be the best of them to help prepare our Synod's 140 official reconcilers for their tasks. But as a parish pastor, circuit counselor, district president, and Synod secretary faced with the "What do *I* do now?" question, my resource of choice for fleshing out Jesus' Matthew 18 instructions came to be the instruction and encouragement provided by the apostle John in his first epistle, specifically chapter 4, verses 7 and 8.

John's words became my go-to passage after I heard them sung, not by Jackie DeShannon, but by a group of young people at a youth outing at Outlaw Ranch in South Dakota, the words not by the likes of Bert Bacharach and Hal Davis—but straight from I John 4:7–8 in the King James Version of the Bible:

> Beloved, let us love one another:
> For love is of God; and every one that loveth is born of God, and knoweth God.
> He that loveth not knoweth not God; for God is love.
> Beloved, let us love one another.

This is the love-sweet-love song that I personally have found to be most effective when disputes erupt, its words already known and probably even memorized in confirmation class. But do we *know* them, really? Not really, or else the prowling lion could not have his way with us so often and do such damage in the Church as he too often does. We may be tempted by the purring lion to think, as I was first inclined, that the song was just a contemporary music rendition of a nice biblical thought, one that young people fifty years ago liked to sing around campfires. Over the years, however, after further education in the proverbial school of hard knocks, I learned that the song is much more. It is heavy-duty Word of God with the right balance of Law and Gospel to engender thoughtful consideration, followed by careful attention, followed by personal application when relationships become strained or even broken.

This really registered for me as a district president at a time when a division was clearly developing among the pastors of our district. One group was essentially saying, "We have to stick together and do something about the problems we are seeing in our Synod and our district!" Other pastors found themselves essentially saying, "We have to close ranks and muster our collective strength to counter what we see this new group of pastors doing!" Faced with "What do I do now?", I was pleased when the officers of the district pastors conference that year asked if I would provide the Bible study for the conference. I chose 1 John 4:7–8 for us to consider together, that study summarized as follows:

> In the first three chapters of his letter, John already made the point several times that fellowship with God and with His Son includes fellowship with one another. We belong together in love (1 John 3:10, 11, 23). We do not belong together with those who have a spirit of deceit (1 John 4:1–6).

Αγαπητοι, "Beloved," is a term of endearment John uses six times in this letter (1 John 2:7; 3:2, 21; 4:1, 7, 11). A very loving man, John looks upon his readers as his "little children" (1 John 2:1) out of pastoral love and concern. Although he is addressing heavy matters, including exposing false teachers (1 John 2:26) and calling out their lack of morality (1 John 3:8–10), he is tender and encouraging in his manner, quick to give "dear friends" assurance of salvation even when they are less than perfect (1 John 2:1). When we are faced with "What do I do now?", we do well to note that before John looks for love from his readers, he first shows himself to be loving and caring.

With the words Αγαπωμεν αλληλουσ, "let us love one another," John demonstrates that same kind and encouraging manner with his choice of verb tense, literally "let us go on loving one another." Here John puts the best construction on his readers' behavior as if assuming that they have been doing this all along, even though they, as is true in our case, had surely failed time and time again. The present subjunctive verb tense indicates that this expectation is continuous, stemming from the similar directive of Jesus (John 13:14–17, 35). The first person plural "us" is inclusive, John asking no more than he himself is ready and willing to give. In dispute resolution, much depends upon our manner in approaching brothers (and sisters) who are misbehaving.

Οτι η αγαπη, "for love," repeats what John has already written in 1 John 3:11 and 3:23, lending full support to his exhortation to love one another. If there is any concept that clergy in particular and all Christians in general understand, it is this agape love that is able to love even the less than lovable, so necessary in dispute resolution. But this verse is more than mere repetition of what had already been said before. Here there is progression of thought. Here and twice more in this chapter (vv. 11–12), John introduces a fresh idea, in other words, the fundamental basis for the command to love. It is far more than even a command of Jesus, although it is that (1 John 3:23). Nor is it merely to be evidence of living in the light of life (1 John 2:10; 3:11–18). It is grounded in the nature and being of God Himself.

Εκ του θεου εστιν, "is of God," makes clear that all love originates in God, that it belongs to the divine dimension, and, when found in a human being, is a reflection of divine nature abiding in that human being. This is the predominant implication in John's discussion of the source and revelation of love for the case he is making.

Και πασ ο αγαπων, "and everyone that loveth," or better, "everyone who is loving," begins a new sentence in which John makes clear the spiritual source for anyone capable of truly loving, the use of "everyone" characteristic of God's style (1 John 3:4; 5:1), emphasizing the need for such love to be evident in every individual believer. This is to be love in absolute terms and in all forms, love not only in attitude but in practice, not only in intention but in action. Claims to love God that are accompanied by hating one's brother are in every case a lie (1 John 2:9–11).

Εκ του θεου γεγεννηται και γινωσκαι τον θεον, John had earlier made reference to the believer as one who is "born of God" (1 John 2:29; 3:9) and who "knows God" (1 John 2:3–4, 13–14; 3:1; 4:6). John here speaks of a relationship that is not only intimate but also continuing. Being loving of itself is not a mark of being a child of God, contrary to much current popular thinking. After all, there are loving people to be found outside the Christian Church. As in 1 John 3:23, the command to be loving is directly linked to the necessity of faith, of knowing God.

Ο μη αγαπων ουκ εγνω τον θεον οτι ο θεοσ αγαπη εστιν, While love by itself is not the criterion for knowing God, and

> lack of love does not in itself prove that no relationship with God exists, yet because God's nature is love, knowledge of God should lead to love of others. Stated in positive terms, anyone who enters into a true relationship with our loving God can and is likely to be transformed into a loving person. The obverse is also true. One who claims a true relationship with God should reflect this relationship in loving others, or else the relationship is suspect. The present active participle speaks of one who "keeps on not loving," allowing that Christians will sometimes slip into loveless moments and deeds but will not continue in such behavior. It is the Christian who keeps on doing otherwise who "knoweth not God" (aorist active indicative), who has no real acquaintance with God and never has really gotten acquainted with Him, "for God is love," not merely the source of love but love itself. It therefore stands to reason that anyone who is "in Him" will also have and demonstrate this love.

I have used the 1 John 4 text often when involved in one way or another in dispute resolution, not always entirely successfully but always for the better. On one occasion when I was a circuit counselor/visitor, I was called upon to referee a dispute between two pastors called to serve in a team ministry. The question never gets old: "What do I do now?" What I did was to open our meeting with prayer, after which I actually sang to them the words of 1 John 4:7–8, which certainly got their attention. They were too young in the ministry to be familiar with the campfire song, but we discussed the words together. As a result, I witnessed their confessions of faults that each had contributed to the dispute between them, as well as their requests for and acceptances of forgiveness from each other.

Such moments are quite wonderful. They undoubtedly also cause great disappointment to the prowling lion, now scooting out the door with tail between legs. But in this case, it was also a sad moment, their strife having become public and their congregation having become increasingly involved, making it prudent for the pastor who had only recently arrived to resign and leave the congregation and community while awaiting another call. It was not an ideal ending, but very importantly, it ended with each pastor having gained the brother.

In my own personal disputes with brothers in the ministry, and there have been too many, the 1 John 4 passage has helped me to take steps in the right direction, that is, in the brothers' direction. One dispute involved two fellow clergymen, one living in my city and the other two thousand miles away. We had already been going back and forth via emails and getting nowhere. When, however, I learned that the more distant brother was about to attend a meeting in my city, I recognized this as the time to take the first step. I asked that we meet, he and I alone, when he was in town, to which he agreed. All I can say is that Jesus knew what He was talking about when He prescribed face-to-face meetings. After meeting with the one brother at the hotel where he was staying and resolving our differences, I stopped at the church where the other brother was serving, with the same result. In both cases, the combination of Matthew 18 and 1 John 4 caused the prowling lion to vacate the premises—no one left to devour there.

It behooves especially us who are pastors (or other church workers) to strive to preserve the true fellowship of the faith, nothing doing greater harm than loss of unity of faith and practice in full view of the church public. When we see a fellow Christian, especially a fellow pastor, fall into serious error, we must deal with that error as soon as possible and in a brotherly, kindly manner, speaking the truth in love, each helping the other remain in the true faith. And it must be done in love, always ready to allow for harmless differences among us, as Martin Luther encourages in his response to a pastor's complaint regarding the insubordination of an assistant pastor:

> Oh, my dear God, how the devil hates us! He even creates disunity among the servants of the Word, so that one hates another; he is constantly starting new fires of dissension. Oh, let us put those fires out with prayer, reconciliation, and by overlooking minor faults, so that both parties put the best

> **construction on things and get along with one another! Let us recognize that we are not the same in our life and conduct; each of us has his [or her] own peculiarities and way of doing things; we simply have to overlook that. You cannot turn everyone into the same kind of peg and make them exactly alike, as far as customs and habits are concerned. It's enough if we are united in pure doctrine.** (*Essays for the Church*, Vol. 2, p. 58)

Actually, it was those words, "It's enough if we are united in pure doctrine," that also enabled me and my assistant pastor to endure our mutual irritations and even cooperate during the three years that we worked together. Some people just rub the wrong way, and we may never be able to wholeheartedly like them and regard them as close friends. But part of being united in pure doctrine is to love them nonetheless as friends in Christ, with the love that John implored when he wrote, "Beloved, let us love one another."

But those words of Luther bring to mind two other rules of thumb that can also make a difference when it comes to dispute resolution, warranting their being kept in the forepart of our minds as the devil prowls about, seeking whom he may devour. These are the subjects of the remaining two sections of this chapter. A German proverb has helped me always to remember the first: *Mann muss nicht nach jeder Fliege schlagen.*

3. ONE SHOULD NOT SWAT AT EVERY FLY

At least in my experience, most damaging disputes in congregations involve the pastor in one way or another, as when a member of the congregation continually rubs him the wrong way; when a group in the congregation opposes something he really wants to do; when the congregation is accustomed to doing something that he really doesn't want to do; when he publicly takes a side in a growing disagreement between members; or when, all too common, he does rub elbows every day with another not entirely likable church worker.

Take, for example, the three scenarios offered earlier in this chapter. Damage to my ministry or even to the congregation could easily have resulted when Mr. Retired Farmer living across the street from the parsonage in my first parish expected that I would honor his congregation's and the local community's Sunday dress code. I had already been warned about this community by a gas station attendant eighty miles away while my family and I were on our way with our U-Haul trailer to that very place that our Synod's first president described as "the dearest, most beautiful, and most pleasant spot on earth" (*The Proper Distinction Between Law and Gospel*, p. 207). When the attendant heard where our family was headed, he mumbled something about a "stubborn bunch of people."

I wasn't prepared, however, for the Sunday afternoon dress code. When faced with having to decide on the spur of the moment how I would dress Sunday afternoons, I might just have ignored the old man, or I might have made up my mind to make it clear from day one that there was a new pastor in town, or I might have decided that this was a good time for a teaching moment and followed him into his house for a lecture regarding the dangers of Pietism. What I did do, however, was an about-face, returning to the parsonage and re-donning my black shirt and collar before continuing on to check out the garden area.

Likewise, disagreement could easily have led to damage to the congregation when Mrs. Bank President persuaded her husband to write his Monday morning note asserting that pastors of their congregation don't grow beards. I might have written a note back asserting that I was growing a beard for a good reason (our community's bicentennial celebration of our country), that I had been asked to serve on the community's Bicentennial Park Development Committee, that I had also been asked to be the speaker for the community's bicentennial banquet, and that such wholehearted participation in the community on my part would be a credit to the congregation. Or I might have sought support from other members of the congregation who also were growing beards for the contest. Or I might have requested a meeting with the elders or even a special voters meeting to ask the congregation to decide. What I did do, however, was to get out my razor.

Or again, a damaging dispute could easily have developed when I was serving with the young assistant pastor, who, early on in our team ministry, had made it clear in actions that spoke louder than words that he, too, was a pastor of the congregation with a following of his own. Chafing almost daily because of that attitude, I was tempted to treat him unkindly, or amass my own support group, or direct public attention to his shortcomings, or inform the congregation that things were not working out and suggest requesting his resignation, or accept the call that I had received from another congregation that had much to say in favor of its acceptance, including the opportunity to leave the strife behind.

But what I did do was to make the best of the situation for three years, taking care not to involve the congregation, prayerfully awaiting divine intervention and resolution, which did happen when the assistant pastor accepted a call to serve as sole pastor of a congregation located closer to family and in a warmer climate. I will admit, however, that upon his departure, I did follow the example of a well-respected elderly pastor, who had shared with me how he had endured a similar situation in his own ministry and how, when appropriate goodbyes had been exchanged, he drove around the block three times that day singing the Common Doxology to his heart's delight.

In each of the above situations, of course, I merely followed the apostle Peter's words: "Above all, keep loving one another earnestly, since love covers a multitude of sins" (1 Peter 4:8). I probably shouldn't say "merely" since human nature and the prowling lion's temptations could easily have led me to do otherwise, the old evil foe always lurking not far away, already salivating at the prospect of dissension in the Body of Christ, eager to roar with delight at the serious harm soon to be suffered in the Body of Christ.

But how does one respond properly and necessarily quickly when faced with such situations? And what if the pastor or congregation doesn't always handle every little thing well? C. F. W. Walther, in his "Duties of an Evangelical Lutheran Synod," including a quote from the Apology to the Augsburg Confession, speaks to congregations and pastors alike:

> See to it that you don't expect too much from your people. . . . You can't turn every [piece of wood] into a dowel. It simply can't be done; not all wood is suitable for dowels. . . . "Divisions also will easily develop if the people immediately want to master and nitpick everything in the life and conduct of the bishops or pastors," says the Apology [Ap IV]. Also our dear congregations should note this carefully. When a pastor makes an occasional mistake, they should not be too harsh in their judgment but should consider, "Did he do that out of weakness? Is it really serious enough to sound the alarm or not?" And if you determine that it was done in weakness and is [a matter] of little importance, then you should either ignore it or tell him in a friendly way, "You did not handle that correctly." Otherwise, if the congregation insists on nitpicking (*ausecken*) about every little thing, then the beautiful relationship . . . will come to an end. Then the devil laughs up his sleeve, when the people no longer heed the pastor's word; then he has torn the members from their orthodox pastor. *We must support one another!* The pastor should not expect the members of his congregation to be nothing but angels, and the members should not demand that their pastor be an angel either, for that he cannot be. (*Essays for the Church*, Vol. 2, p. 56)

When the lion tempts and we have very little time to respond, it has been helpful for me to recall the rule of thumb that I came upon during my vicarage year. It had been printed in a church bulletin of a neighboring congregation just weeks before the pastor suffered a serious heart attack that left him debilitated. In the absence of any other workable arrangement and authorized by my vicarage supervisor pastor, I filled in for the pastor for the remaining six months of my vicarage. Early on, as I was looking through a stack of recent church bulletins left on the pastor's desk in his office, I came upon the nugget of wisdom that easily became the most memorable and important lesson of my vicarage year, a German proverb that the pastor had included in the bulletin to augment his sermon one Sunday: *Mann muss nicht nach jeder Fliege schlagen.* It struck home as being really important: "One should not swat at every fly."

That proverb became a go-to in my life. At the time, it addressed my smoldering dissatisfaction with the first six months of my vicarage experience, now resolved by my change of duties but now also recognized to be a mere fly on the picnic table of life. It became the default response to many of the "What do I do now?" situations I faced in my years of ministry, times when I may otherwise have been tempted to wear out my little swatter, to the jubilant roar of the lion.

When, therefore, Mr. Retired Farmer shouted from across the street that I shouldn't have changed out of my Sunday clothes, and when Mrs. Bank President prompted the note I received from her husband that instructed me to get rid of the facial hair, and when I was quite regularly tempted to take a swat at my co-worker pastor for what, after all, were flies of little consequence, "*Mann muss nicht nach yeder Fliege schlagen*" prompted my response.

When this becomes a pastor's first response when tempted to grab the swatter and also becomes his way of life and ministry, he also gains necessary time to be able to distinguish between pesky little flies and that one fly about to land on the potato salad. More often than not, situations will be less than crucial, probably someone stepping a little out of line, begging a soft response to "What do I do now?" The pastor will also have greatly improved his prospects for a ministry in "the dearest, most beautiful, and most pleasant spot on earth." Most importantly, he will have averted real potential for more serious consequences, which Walther had in mind with the already above-quoted words from his essay to the 1879 Western District Convention, where he then continues:

> My dear brothers, let us be on our guard! Satan is sly. Right now we are brothers, living together in peace and love. But Satan will most certainly lay for us snares by which he hopes to destroy the sweet, brotherly love we now have in our hearts. We dare never think that it is enough if we just remain united in our faith and doctrine. No, once love has been destroyed,

> it won't be long before one person believes what the other person rejects, and the other teaches what the first considers an error.... For example, one person takes a stand [on a given issue], and another person takes the opposite stand. Perhaps the one person dislikes the other; he simply can't stand him, and for that reason he inflexibly maintains his position. It is frightening (*schrecklich*) what harm can result when members of a church organization do not vigilantly guard their fraternal love. (*Essays for the Church*, Vol. 2, p. 56)

Further, having been taught by their pastor, possibly by sermon but hopefully by example in not so many words, *Mann muss nicht nach jeder Fliege schlagen* is an important response also for the members of a congregation to learn to practice in congregational life, where elbows rub frequently. The Apology to the Augsburg Confession warns against the kinds of conditions that threaten to prevail in the church of our day, for the same kinds of reasons:

> In all families and in all states unity should be nourished by mutual offices, and peace cannot be maintained unless people overlook and forgive certain mistakes among themselves. In a similar way, Paul commands that there should be love in the Church in order that it may preserve unity, bear with the harsher manners of brethren as there is need, and overlook certain less serious mistakes. This must happen or else the Church will fly apart into various schisms, and hostilities and factions and heresies will arise from the schisms. (Ap V 111)

I have had, in my various pastoral roles in the Synod, the opportunity to observe firsthand this lesson modeled by pastors toward their congregations and by congregations toward their pastors, due in large part to their high regard and respect for the pastoral office but also because of their Christian love and its resulting disinclination to swat at every fly.

A case in point was one of the rural congregations I was privileged to serve, where my predecessor had been the pastor for twenty-eight years, who then retired as pastor but remained in the parish to serve as master of the beautiful pipe organ that adorned the congregation's worship. He was not very personable, nor was he a very good preacher or teacher by most standards. He used no liturgies in worship (preferring to provide his own simple orders of worship), conducted no Sunday Bible studies ("because people can't digest two big meals in one day"), and administered Holy Communion four times a year ("lest it become common and cheap"). He did present topics at Ladies Aid meetings but then exited to a separate room to eat his lunch alone (plated for him by his wife and eaten with his own utensils, which he kept in his suitcoat pocket). His sermons were usually prompted by articles in *Time* magazine, he crossed the street rather than greet people on the sidewalk, and he was a master of outrageous comments in public ("With the price of sugar, who can believe in God?"). In short, his ministry today would prompt a call to his district president within two weeks of arrival in the new parish.

But the pastor preached and taught God's Word as best he could and was loved by his congregation and respected in the community. He was loved and respected because of the office he held among them and the Word of God that he preached and taught among them, without a single swat at the swarm of potential flies that accompanied his ministry. The congregation demonstrated its love and respect by taking good care of one another and their church building, maintaining a 90 percent Sunday morning church attendance, and contributing the district's second-highest total offerings to district and Synod missions each year. They loved and respected him for twenty-eight years and then gave him and his wife the parsonage to live in upon his retirement, prior to my arrival as their next pastor.

Equally impressive was a situation I came upon as district president when, as I was gathering names for a vacant congregation's call list, I missed a caution signal from another district president regarding one of the pastors whose name I had included on the list, who had suffered an injury that called into question his ability to remain in the pastoral ministry. Before I could change the information that I had provided to the congregation, this was the pastor who received and had already accepted their call.

Already when the pastor and his family arrived, I recognized some concerns and expected sooner rather than later to receive the inevitable telephone call from the congregation asking that something be done. It took eight months for that phone call to arrive from the president of the congregation, and when it did, I was surprised to hear not criticism but a question: "A number of us were talking after the service last Sunday, and could it be that there has been a serious physical injury in our pastor's past?" They had noticed that sometimes his thinking seemed to skip a beat, a difficulty much like that of two other persons in their community who had suffered serious head injuries. They didn't want to speak to the pastor himself because they didn't want to hurt his feelings. They just wanted to know so that they could be helpful.

I asked how the pastor was doing otherwise. The response was that he was doing just fine. He preached good sermons, well thought out and prepared. He faithfully visited the sick and, although he was not as good at working with their young people as their previous pastor had been, gave them his attention and support, helped them plan their activities, and really did okay. For the first time ever, the youth of their congregation even had a float in the town's Fourth of July parade. And then the royal priest spoke frankly about the pastor: "Oh, we know that he is not the perfect pastor, but his heart is in his ministry and we are just a small parish. We know he serves us as best he can, and we want to help him as much as we can."

I know that the above are amazing stories, illustrations to the extreme of what it means for a congregation not to swat at every fly. And the histories of both congregations give testimony that the prowling lion had over the years enjoyed little success with either of them, pretty much going hungry, certainly not enjoying the feasts that he must have anticipated.

On the other hand, I have also seen pastors and congregations who were very quick on the draw with the flyswatter, things turning ugly very quickly. And all the while, there is the roaring lion having a veritable banquet at the expense of the congregations—the expense that brings me to the fourth and final section of this chapter.

4. THE CONGREGATION IS QUEEN[10]

While this final subject pertains primarily to pastors, it can also apply to other church workers and individual members of congregations. I became most aware of it during another experience in team ministry, when the assistant pastor with whom I was serving was a former district president. We rarely had a conversation about goings-on in the congregation without his reminding me that "the congregation is queen." I must admit that although I heard those words countless times, I didn't fully recognize their significance during the seven years that we enjoyed working together.

I became more aware that "the congregation is queen" during my district president days when the district agreed to give me a sabbatical to allow me to teach at the fledgling seminary of the then-emerging Evangelical Lutheran Church of Ingria in Russia. This was shortly after the demise of the Soviet Union, when Lutheran congregations were emerging from the rubble of seventy years of Soviet persecution. Undoubtedly to the devil's great dismay, while nearly all of these congregations no longer had ordained pastors, they (and their church schools) were being served by promising young men (and women) "evangelists," all of whom were being sent by their congregations to the new seminary.

Our four-hour classes (two a day) met in the basement of a newly constructed church outside of St. Petersburg in the village of Koltyshe. My assignment was to provide a review of Christian doctrine to determine the extent of the students' biblical knowledge and doctrinal comprehension. With the aid of an interpreter, I walked the class of young pastor and teacher candidates through *A Summary of Christian Doctrine* by Edward W. A. Koehler. I was humbled to learn that the Ingrian students'

10 As used in conversations with my co-worker, use of the word ***queen*** in reference to the congregation served the sole purpose of reminding each other to put the best interests and well-being of the congregation above other considerations.

knowledge of Christian doctrine and the Lutheran Confessions sometimes more than equaled my own.

It was during one of our discussions that the students asked about our Synod's practice of calling church workers, having already heard that it differed from what they had anticipated. They were quite amazed to learn not only of the efforts that were made to assign candidates who would "fit" calling congregations but also to learn that the average stay of a pastor at his first call was three to five years and that pastors and other called church workers usually received and accepted multiple calls during their years of service. By way of contrast, these young Russian Ingrian candidates expected to serve the same congregations they were already serving until parted by death, without interest in mobility or advancement. In their minds, the congregation each was already serving was "queen," and they were privileged to serve.

During those four months with those eager young men and women, I received more than I gave. Not only did I receive a fresh and stimulating review of Christian doctrine, but I also received the important reminder that the congregation is indeed queen, with Christ as the King, that is, that when you are a pastor, it is not all about you, especially in your own mind—a real temptation in the pastoral ministry. Nor is it only about the individual members of a congregation and the doctrine and practice that they may prefer. It is all about the congregation, the Body of Christ, the queen.

I offer a painful case in point. As district president, one of my privileges was to participate in the Call Day services at our Synod's seminaries. These were grand occasions, the graduates receiving their assigned first calls ceremoniously embedded in splendid worship services. The excitement of all present was always at a high pitch, rivaling the first tenors of the seminary choir in the balcony.

But for me, while these services never lost their importance and significance, they began to lose some of their luster. I began already then to get a whiff of brimstone—the lurking presence of "the old evil foe" now meaning "deadly woe," ready with his "deep guile and great might" (*LSB* 656:1) to spoil the early ministries of the inexperienced young pastors and the ministries of the time-tested congregations they were being called to serve. To be sure, the candidates had received the best pastoral formation, education, and training that seminaries had to offer, but the lion was already planning how he might use even their seminary formation, education, and training to trouble, if not even destroy, not only their ministries but those of the congregations they would be serving.

I of course paid closest attention to the graduates who were being assigned calls to congregations in my district. Each congregation had its own history, some including conflict with prior pastors. Each had its own way of doing things, a sum total of earlier pastors' practices, not all of which lined up nicely with what had been taught at the seminary or experienced on vicarage. Most would have within their memberships groups of people already short on patience and determined in their ways, usually a product of frequent pastoral changes and often corresponding changes in pastoral practice. Often these congregations did not realize that by issuing a call for a candidate, they were continuing their new pastor's training and that mistakes would likely be made. Because they did not realize this, each was a promising hunting ground for the lion already prowling about the seminary chapel, seeking opportunities to cause trouble early and often.

I remember thinking that one candidate assigned to a rural parish in my district was likely to be safe. He was a second-career seminary graduate, a former dairy farmer who was eager to put his first-class seminary education into practice. The congregation to which he was assigned was suitably rural, and although wounded by recent pastoral experiences, eager to start anew with a new pastor straight from the seminary.

The first reports that I heard from the congregation after the new pastor was installed were favorable. Pastor and congregation did indeed seem to be an ideal fit, the pastor feeling right at home in rural South Dakota and the people thankful that they didn't have to explain what a combine was to their new pastor. As a matter of fact, the pastor's fame quickly spread as one who actually knew how to tear down and repair a combine and to help with the harvest. The proverbial honeymoon was on.

It was also brief. Both parties soon were unable either to discuss or overlook even the smallest of issues between them, unable to put into practice Solomon's proverb: "A soft answer turns away wrath, but a harsh word stirs up anger" (Proverbs 15:1). By all reports, the pastor had been an excellent and eager seminary student, and he brought his considerable knowledge of the Holy Scriptures and Lutheran Confessions with him to the parish, ready to be put into practice. He may have, however, missed the seminary class where the importance of listening and learning and becoming familiar with his pastoral setting and its people before advocating changes was emphasized. Believing in doing things the proper, and even ideal, way learned at the seminary, he found it difficult, even impossible, to settle for less, beginning already on day one.

For starters, for the first Sunday's worship service, he insisted on chanting the liturgies he had learned to love from seminary chapel services, a practice foreign to the congregation already astir after finding the baptismal font moved when they had entered the church. For their part, the members of the congregation had not been good students of the Scriptures and Confessions, Sunday morning worship being more of a family event than one of confessional commitment. Accordingly, its Communion and worship practice had varied of late, the congregation recently having been served for short periods of time by a variety of pastors, including a pastor of another Lutheran denomination. Two pastors ago, the congregation had practiced open Communion and participated in joint holiday worship services with other churches in town. One pastor ago, it had experienced serious tumult when the new pastor made an abrupt attempt to return the congregation to proper fellowship practice—at the price of his early departure.

All of which quickly led to serious strife. Encouragement to study together the issues that were dividing the congregation and pastor—and to talk together to work things out—fell on deaf ears. As divisions developed and disgruntled members began to absent themselves, a number of members had already left the small and struggling congregation, noisily and permanently.

Involving myself as district president, I arranged for opportunities for the members individually to discuss with me the issues that were causing the strife, which they were quite willing to do. A small number supported the pastor, believing he was doing his best, admitting he might have done some things differently, for the most part blaming other members. Other visits produced a list of issues to be addressed, including the pastor's chanting, his moving the baptismal font, his declaration that the Christmas tree lights not be turned on until Christmas Eve, his too-lengthy Bible studies, his declaration that confirmands leave the worship service prior to the celebration of the Sacrament, his decision not to allow parents of confirmands to commune with their children at the time of their first Communion, his unwillingness to commune visiting relatives and family members now belonging to other denominations, and more.

For his part, the pastor insisted that the changes were in keeping with his seminary education. He also had issues of his own with the leadership of the congregation, especially their interest in relaxed worship and fellowship practices, influenced by practices members were experiencing when attending other Missouri Synod congregations.

Faced with the question that is also quite common among district presidents, "What do I do now?", I asked for a weekday morning meeting to bring the two factions together to begin to discuss these issues. Suffice to say, the looks and words that were exchanged by pastor and people—beginning even before I had opportunity to remind them that the old evil foe was present and winning, or remind them of the apostle's words in 1 John 4:7–8, or encourage them not to swat at every fly but instead consider the well-being of their beloved congregation—are best left in that meeting, except to say that pastor and church leaders had come with their swatters, soon wearing them out, along with what little remained of their fellowship in Christ. There were no alligators in the room, of course, but the lion was very present, the same evil foe that C. F. W. Walther regularly warned about in his writings, as in his essay, "Duties of an Evangelical Lutheran Synod":

> You see, the devil's great craftiness is that if he cannot plunge a church group into false doctrine, nor destroy their unity in confession, he then tries [to destroy it] through their lives. He creates divisions among the members. One person offends another, perhaps without wishing to do so. The second person then becomes angry and imputes malice to him. And if the offense was great enough, perhaps even intentional, then true brotherly fellowship has been destroyed, and the result is that there is no longer any real joy of standing in confessional fellowship with the offender. And that is precisely what the devil wants! (*Essays for the Church*, Vol. 2, p. 55)

What *does* one do in such a situation? For one thing, we should do our best never to allow disputes to get that far along. For another, we should help everyone involved remember that the congregation is queen and that her welfare is of primary importance. This is important, first of all, for the members of a congregation to remember, especially those in positions of leadership. When there are issues and its members must be saved from the serious consequences of bad behavior, it is the queen's best interests, that is, the best interests of the congregation and its proclamation of the Gospel, that must also be kept in mind. When a member of the congregation or its pastor is confronted with an issue that could well end up serving as the devil's weapon to tarnish its past, destroy true brotherly fellowship in the present, and seriously harm the congregation's welfare well into the future, it is the welfare of the queen and her kingdom that must be of first importance, for which Jesus provided the instructions recorded in Matthew 18.

Such is the primary responsibility of clergy, to look after the best interests of the queen—past, present, and future. "What do I do *now*?" should be an ever-present question for those who serve the queen, even, and perhaps especially, when everything seems to be peaceful and going well. This is a subject that warrants a book of its own: "Is the service I am providing to the queen the best that I can provide?" In short, am I really using the gifts that God has given me in the best way possible to serve the good of this congregation? Or am I using this congregation, even its Communion practice and worship life, to suit my own talents, interests, and druthers? Am I tailoring the practice of my ministry to be and remain popular so that I will be more likely to receive calls from other congregations with greater prospects and benefits? Am I considering accepting a call I received from another congregation primarily because of family or salary considerations? Am I overlooking hard issues in the congregation at the expense of confessional theology, matters certain to cause issues and perhaps even harmful difficulties for the queen and her subsequent pastors?

In short, does my ministry to my queen, the congregation, look out for her bests interests or for mine? Do the pastoral decisions I am making now serve the future best interests of the queen's future pastors or those of the lion? We have all been faced with this particular "What do I do now?" many times. It does us well to ponder again and often who we are and who this congregation that I am privileged to serve is. She is queen.

IN CONCLUSION

There is another German proverb that pretty much says everything said in this chapter, one that I first learned as a child from a plaque on my grandparents' living room wall. Its message is proverbially simple:

Wo glaube, da Liebe
Wo Liebe, da Friede
Wo Friede, da Segen
Wo Segen, da Gott
Wo Gott, keine Not.

Which is to say, "Where there is faith, there is love." 1 John 4 reminds us that faith in God comes from knowing God and that knowing and loving God is to be born of God, who is love.

"Where there is love, there is peace." Knowing God and His love is where true peace is found, which in turn motivates us to live in peace with one another.

"Where there is peace, there are blessings," which brings us around full circle: "Where there are blessings, there is God." Among those blessings is the full armor of God, enabling us to defeat the prowling lion walking about, and Christian love to enable us not to swat at every fly but to truly care for one another as we walk together.

And "Where there is God, there is no need"—true also even when faced with the question, "What do I do now?"

CHAPTER 10

THE PASTOR AND FINANCIAL CHALLENGES

Rev. Billy Brath

INTRODUCTION

MONEY IS NEVER THE PROBLEM.

> "If resources were not an issue, what should your congregation do in the next year?"

I have asked this question to dozens of congregations across the country. I serve as the vice-president of ministry support for the Lutheran Church Extension Fund (LCEF), an organization with The Lutheran Church—Missouri Synod (LCMS). I will dive into what LCEF is later in the chapter; for now, know that I am one of the called pastors who helps congregations and ministries around the country understand who God has called them to be, discover what He is calling them to do, and build and execute plans to do the work. This includes engaging and raising up congregation members to respond as faithful stewards, another concept I will explore later in the chapter. Back to the question.

> **"If resources were not an issue, what should your congregation do in the next year?"**

It is posed during an early event of the ministry clarity process I facilitate in congregations. This process guides the discovery and planning mentioned above.

This is a trick question.

It is designed to hear what people think their congregation should be up to, sure, but it also reveals what barriers to ministry exist in the mind of the congregation. Answers emerge:

> **"Fix the building."**
>
> **"Add another worship service."**
>
> **"Expand the school."**
>
> **"Get more members."**
>
> **"Do more fundraising."**

Yes, these are real answers from actual congregations. All of them tell a story, especially when taken in context. The last one was my favorite.

This congregation was so deep in perceived financial ruin that when asked a ministry future question with all resource barriers removed, the person could still only think about raising funds. This answer stuck out, but it is the same for all the others.

See, when we work with congregations, even if the healthiest one is flush with cash, we need to see if money is on the mind. Why fix the building? So we can stop spending money on maintenance. Why add another worship service? So we will get more members and have more offering revenue. Why expand the school? Well, you get the idea.

Do church folk want their ministries to expand and people to come to know Christ? Absolutely. In fact, this is true for all the examples above. Yet no matter what, behind every answer looms at the very least a glimmer of financial worry.

"Are resources ever an issue?" I will ask the crowd during the event. Most immediately reply, "Yes!" The elephant in the room is revealed. I pause just long enough for everyone in the room to remember that a pastor has just asked them the question, and inevitably, a few folks soon blurt out, "No!" Oh yeah, they remember, if Jesus is in control of His Church like our pastor has been telling us for years, then resources should never be an issue.

Let us lay some groundwork.

First, Jesus is in control. Period. Whatever He wants done will happen. Whatever resources are required to make it happen will be provided.

Second, He has chosen to do His work in the world through us, the Church on earth.

Third, the Church is people actively living as His hands and feet—proclaiming, serving, loving, bearing fruit, you get the idea. It is not the institution.

Fourth, the institution, congregations, agencies, and denominations are clumps of His chosen people brought together to do His work together. They do not exist apart from this.

Fifth, every individual congregation that existed in the first thousand years of Christendom exists no longer as it was constituted in those first thousand years. Keep your perspective—everything in its own season.

About that last point: it is not comforting, but it should be. It is one of the many proofs that God's work in the world continues.[11] The pressure is not on us to preserve our current iteration of the Church. Instead, we are free to continually pursue Him, to follow Him, and collectively do the work He has called us to. If that means continuing that work through your individual parish, agency, or denomination, great! If not, then do not despair; the Lord is in control, and His work in the world continues.

11 Ref: Colossians 1:15–18. A reminder to the Lord's church in a letter to a parish that no longer exists.

I do not often bring that final point up with congregations I am working with; it sends the wrong message during most of the events and meetings I facilitate. But it does bring me comfort. Our role as church leaders is not to figure out finances so that our institutions continue. Our role as church leaders is to remain faithful to the work the Lord calls us to by living as His faithful stewards in the world.

In this chapter, I will first get ahead of problems by laying out a financial framework that all our congregations should implement and then look directly at problems that often arise. To begin, we need to get back to the basics and set a firm foundation.

THE BASICS

What Is Money?

My seminary classmate had a part-time job with an engineering firm. Part of his job was to collect data on what we would call paper money so that vending machines could recognize money when inserted into the machine. This meant he was paid to insert and re-insert money into a data-collecting machine over and over again like a kid trying to get a soda ("pop" for you Midwestern folks) with a crumpled-up bill. He would handle large amounts of money from all over the world, sometimes tens of thousands of dollars worth of cash from countries oceans away.

The money was worthless, though.

Yes, if I were not in school, had the ability and means to travel around the world, and ignored the Seventh Commandment, the money would be worth something. However, in a St. Louis dorm room, thousands of yen and three dollars would buy a cup of coffee at Kaldi's Coffee Shop.

Money is a storage device. It stores goods and services. I give you some of the grain I've grown, and you give me some of your wood you've grown to build my home. I give you a chicken I have raised; you help me seal my walls in preparation for winter. In a modern economy, this exchange system becomes much too complicated, so we created money to help these exchanges.

Put another way, money represents work and time. I work, and that work is stored in money. Instead of me doing direct work for someone else, I give them a marker of my stored work.

Modern economies are more complicated and include more devices than what we call money, but for our purposes, money is a simple thing that really is not anything at all.

It is important to remind ourselves and our congregations that money represents a portion of what the Lord has given to us, a portion of our time and work. Before we can talk about money, our offering, or the tithe, we first have to be reminded who we are actually called to be: faithful stewards.

Faithful Stewards

A steward manages what someone else owns. A faithful steward manages what someone else owns according to the instructions of the owner.

We are always stewards of the gifts God has given us. We are not always faithful stewards.

Being a faithful steward begins with the answers to the following:

- → **What have you been given to steward?**
- → **What are you asked to do with what you have been given?**

Traditionally, we immediately answer the question:

- → What have you been given to steward? **Time, talent, treasure.**
- → What are you asked to do with what you have been given? **Tithe.**

Note: we are sure to place treasure third in the list, so people do not assume we are only after their money.

These answers are not only oversimplified; they are wrong. The first question is better answered:

- → What have you been given to steward? **My life, my relationships, my passions, my skills, my experiences, my stuff, my salvation, Jesus!**

Everything—*everything*—is given to us to steward, to use, for His purposes. You and your people are more than simply time managers, talent managers, and treasure managers.

→ What are you asked to do with what you have been given? **Bring glory to the Lord! Make disciples! Bear fruit! Proclaim the Gospel! Care for the sick, the hurting, the orphaned, the poor, the widowed, and so forth.**

I will point you to the Bible for an expanded answer set.

Here is the big connection: everything you have been given is for Kingdom use. Not 10 percent, not some talents, not a portion of time—everything. To be a faithful steward is to actively use everything and every moment for God's work in the world.

You are a faithful steward when you decide to spend an extra twenty minutes talking to a co-worker in need, even though you know it will cause you to stay twenty minutes later at work to finish your tasks. You are a faithful steward when you take a different route home so you can stop by the ASPCA and walk dogs to give relief to the day volunteers. You are a faithful steward when you choose to remain in your current job instead of taking the better paying one on the other side of the country because you recognize the Lord has placed you within your current group of friends as the light of Christ. You are a faithful steward when you plan and execute a neighborhood block party, at your own expense, so your neighbors can meet your new pastor. You are a faithful steward when you take a vacation to recharge yourself so that you can serve in your vocations more effectively. And while you are on that vacation, you intentionally interact with people so the joy of Christ can be shared and the Holy Spirit can guide conversations for His Gospel purpose.

All these examples involve faithful decisions and actions that use all that the Lord has given you for His purposes. Faithful stewards are active Kingdom workers, from Baptism until death retires them into the arms of Jesus.

YOUR MISSION AND MINISTRIES

Scripture has many "really?" moments: Abraham, Moses, Jonah, Isaiah, asking God in their own way, "Really? Really? This is how You want this to happen?"

The Book of Acts leads the way in laying out the Church on earth. Surround this book with the canon of Scripture, and we see that Jesus prescribed this system, clumping Christians into groups around His Word and Sacrament, to be the way He comes into the world. His kingdom coming, here and now.

This means your congregation is an intentional group, a clump of Christians curated by God. He curated your parish, bringing together all the passions, experiences, relationships, stuff, jobs, handbell acumen, and so on.

What is He asking you all to do with everything He has gathered through your people? The answer is your mission.[12]

How do you execute that mission collectively? Through your ministries.

Note that I am defining these terms for our conversation here. I understand there are many nuanced ways to define mission/vision/purpose/values.

The intentionality of it all is important. God intentionally gathers people, gives them their mission, and provides all they need to accomplish that mission, and we create ministries to assist us in living it all out.

Facilities

Facilities facilitate.

Facilities facilitate ministries.

Facilities often distract us from our mission by not facilitating our ministries effectively.

Facilities are most often the top issue I work through when working with congregations.

Facilities are not holy in and of themselves.

12 Ref: John 3:17, 1 Corinthians 12:27. Jesus saves and has chosen to work through His Church.

Facilities are made holy when they facilitate ministries that execute mission.

Facilities should not distract from the mission.

Facilities must facilitate ministries.

Facilities facilitate.[13]

People

People facilitate.

The congregation is not the customer. The congregation members are employees.[14]

Your people execute the ministries. Participating in worship is executing a ministry, not receiving a service. In this, I am not referring to the divine implications of the worship service held for Sabbath. The worshipers absolutely receive from the Lord and are blessed. However, worshipers are not the customers of a church, receiving a service from the church like a person attending a concert or dining at a restaurant. For our purposes in this chapter, those leading the service and attending are in it together, people executing the ministry. Similarly, participating in a Bible study is executing a ministry as much as leading the study.

Your congregation is a clump of people who live out the mission through your ministries. Sometimes those ministries equip the people to live out the mission; sometimes they facilitate those people living out the mission. Either way, the programmatic institution of the church, the ministries, only exists to aid people in living the life to which God calls them.

Finances

Finances facilitate.

We understand this in every other part of life, but many struggle with the concept in the church. I understand that my finances support my life

---

13 Ref: John 2:13–22. Among other teachings, facilities are not the focus, Jesus is.

14 Ref: Matthew 20:1–16. Jesus spoke of laborers in the vineyard. The same principle is involved here. I used ***employee*** here as a reminder that our members aren't consumers of church, they are the laborers, workers, or employees serving Christ.

now and in the future. They have no other use. Sure, I can store money up in banks, but unless I use the cash to facilitate my life, then it is worthless.

In the church, because we talk about the offering as a sacrifice, we confuse what finances are. I am not suggesting that bringing a sacrifice to the Lord is not good, right, and salutary. Instead, I want your people to see that everything they have been given to steward, finances included, is for the Lord to use.[15] Everything is a sacrifice, not just the money you place in the plate. Within that life of sacrifice is the slice of one's finances that gets pooled together with fellow Christians within a congregation to execute that congregation's God-given ministries.

A clear connection between one's offerings and the ministries they support is critical. It is also critical to have a clear and constant teaching that to live as a faithful steward is to live a life sacrificed to the Lord.

For example, I have three thousand dollars to use this month. I use two thousand of that for life operations—housing, insurance, utilities, and so forth, everything that facilitates my life of service in this world. I use five hundred of that to interact with others—evenings out, recreation, and so on. I use another five hundred of that, along with fellow members of my parish, to support my pastor, run ministries, keep my church campus running, and support other sister ministries in town. Every dollar is consciously used for Kingdom purposes: some to support my daily service; some to support my interaction with family, friends, and community; some used in conjunction with other members of my church.

The Offering

> **I appeal to you therefore, brothers, by the mercies of God, to present your bodies as a living sacrifice, holy and acceptable to God, which is your spiritual worship.** (Romans 12:1)

Your entire life is an offering to the Lord. You belong to Him, and He has placed you in the world for His purposes. Everything you have and everything you are has been handed to you to steward, to use.

---

15 Ref: Acts 17:25. Jesus does not need our money yet invites us into this generous relationship or worship and service.

This includes every dollar.

The offering has two parts. First, in the vertical, it is one form of worship, an important and special interaction between steward and owner, beloved and the Lord.

Throughout Scripture, we learn about this important action. However, in the Old Testament, when we were under the burden of the Law, the tithe was built in, a law-based act of worship. This compulsory act, well the deviation from it, led to the first murder. This law was at the center of many a controversy Jesus stepped into. Yet He became the ultimate tithe for us, a full and complete offering that paid all the tithes for all of humanity for all of eternity.

Now, free from the tithe law, the offering in this first sense remains an act of worship, a free response propelled by the Gospel. It is a confession of our relationship with our Lord and Master, a perfect and pure relationship. This offering includes everything, as I have mentioned before, but we are zooming into the offering as it relates to the life of a congregation. When you place your offering in the plate, you are continuing your lifelong practice of worshiping the Lord with all you are and all you have.

The offering in the second part, the horizontal, is a confession that God has intentionally brought you together with other Christians. He has chosen you to pool yourselves for His purposes. These include internal pooled work—the worship service, Bible studies, fellowship, and the like. These also include external pooled work—social ministries, outreach, human care, and so forth.

The monetary offering is one slice of a person's life of offering. How much should someone contribute to the congregational pot? Three ways to inform the answer:

1. **Deuteronomy 16:17—Give according to what you have been given.**
2. **What does the congregation need financially to accomplish the work the Lord is calling it to?**
3. **The tithe, while not a law, is a good tradition to start the contemplation.**

Pointing to Jesus

A portion of my work this month is stored up in dollars. Those dollars will be placed in my congregation's offering plate. That offering will be pooled with others' offerings to support my congregation's ministries by paying salaries, maintaining the building, and funding programs. Those ministries will assist my congregation in living out the mission Jesus has given us. All of this because Jesus said so.

An extra portion of my work this month will be stored up in dollars. Those dollars will be contributed to my congregation's capital campaign. The capital from the campaign will pay builders to expand our preschool facilities. The expanded preschool facilities will allow our preschool ministry to double in size. More kids will hear about Jesus. Our mission, in part, is to teach kids about Jesus. All of this because Jesus said so.

Everything must point to Jesus.

The test is simplified by the question, "Why?" Why does your congregation do anything? The answer must always ultimately end with "because Jesus said so."

Funding

With all the previous points established and operating in this faithful steward framework, let's dive into the practical. The remainder of this chapter will lay out financial guidance in the context presented beforehand.

THE OFFERING

The offering supports your operations, your regular expenditures to make your congregation's ministries function. This includes workers, facilities, ministry operations, benevolences.

With some exceptions I will mention in a moment, the offering should cover regular operational costs that sustain your ministries year after year. This includes maintenance and capital improvement. Let me say that again for Bible-style repetitive emphasis; this includes maintenance and capital improvement.

I grew up in South Florida in an active church family. Growing up in Florida means understanding how air conditioners work. To oversimplify it, for most homes and buildings, central air conditioners have two main parts, an outside unit and an inside one. The system relies on both units working together to cool a home. The outdoor unit, exposed to the elements and working hard in the Florida heat, has a predictable working life of about ten years. It's just how it is. Everyone in Florida must replace their outdoor units every ten years. This includes churches.

You can see where this is going. Every ten years, when church air conditioners break, the congregation's leaders stand in front of the congregation, tell them what happened, and ask for an extra contribution to the fix-the-air-conditioner fund. It's Florida, it's hot, the money shows up, people are frustrated.

Instances like this, predictable operational expenses, aggravate congregations and erode institutional trust. People think, "If this organization cannot properly manage its facilities and build in real operational costs like air conditioning repair, then what else are they missing?"

Build your capital improvement plan into your budget. Do the work to predict regular operating expenses even if they only pop up once every ten years.

One last point in relation to funding regular operations through the offering: there are some ministries of your congregation whose operations require extra funding outside the regular offering. A youth group is an example. The congregation is not expected to pay the tens of thousands of dollars it costs to send the youth group to the National Youth Gathering. Your preschool is another. The congregation is not expected to pay all the operation costs of the school. In both instances, most often, congregations subsidize those ministries, and the ministry makes up the difference. The congregation may budget ten thousand dollars a year to the National Youth Gathering fund and pay all the utilities and maintenance of the campus in support of the preschool.

Let me challenge this.

Your offering supports your regular operations. That is, the congregation pools its resources to support the ministries God has placed in your midst. Your youth group's trip to the National Youth Gathering is part of your congregation's ministry to your young people. The trip should be included in regular operations and funded by the offering. Your preschool is a primary outreach and Christian training center. Its entire operation should be included in the regular operation and funded by the offering.

I know, you just read that paragraph and think I am living in la-la land. Maybe, but you know I am right. If the goal is to pool resources to fund ministries, then do it! Yes, we want the youth to have buy-in, to understand the financial reality of their slice of the ministry, but have them participate in the ministry work of the congregation, not do random fundraising events to fund a ministry of the church just because it's expensive. If parents have the means to support the trip their kids are going on, great! They can contribute through the offering like the rest of the congregation.

Yes, it is great if preschool parents can contribute to their children's education and preschool care. In that case, you will have more funding to bless other missions or ministries with.

I am writing this in my own thought bubble; I understand that. Yet do not skip this section because it sounds too difficult, expensive, or far-fetched. Challenge your congregation to think about their ministries and offering in this way.

One final point about the offering. Online giving is a great tool to teach your people about the offering. It shows that pooling financial resources is not tied to worship attendance. Yes, it removes the physical action of placing the sacrifice in the plate, but let us not forget, the passing of the plate is adiaphora. Teaching people to live as faithful stewards, to sacrifice their entire lives in service to the Lord, and to pool a portion in response to the Lord's calling on one's congregation is required. I recommend using the offering time in your service to continually do this.

FUNDRAISERS

Fundraisers in this chapter are defined as individual ministry groups asking for funds for a specific purpose. The youth car wash to support a school in Kenya, the baby bottles passed out to collect change in March to support the crisis pregnancy center in town, and the LWML mite boxes are all examples of fundraisers. Fundraisers are not ministry groups of a congregation asking for money to operate their ministry; the offering does that.

Fundraisers by their nature highlight the ministry they are connected to. The youth car wash reminds the congregation of the importance of the youth group and the work of the church in Kenya. The baby bottles remind the congregation of the importance of caring for moms and babies and the work of the pregnancy center. The mite boxes remind the congregation of the great work of the LWML and the missions around the globe they make happen.

Fundraisers also often educate and engage the fundraiser. The youth washing the car is taking responsibility and learning about the church's financial and ministry situation in Kenya. The young adult group distributing, collecting, and delivering the baby bottles is learning how to serve as part of a congregation. The LWML, well, all those ladies are fully educated and fully engaged, so no need to discuss further. (Support the LWML. They are one of the greatest blessings to Christendom we will see.)

Fundraisers should be planned and scheduled appropriately. Do not have multiple fundraisers going at once. This diminishes the funding opportunity and clouds the messaging of the ministry. Try to only highlight one at a time and master plan a rotation each year.

Finally, fundraisers must be clearly communicated. Provide clear and simple information that includes what the money is for, how the money will be managed, and how to learn more or connect with the ministry effort being funded. In effect, the donors simply need to see their dollars make a direct impact.

The ASPCA is famous in the advertising world for its Sarah McLachlan-sung commercials. You know them—the distressed animals, emotion-evoking music, narrator pulling at your heartstrings. For just a few dollars, you can save these distressed animals you are seeing on the screen. The direct connection is the key: your dollar, given to us, saves this dog staring at you. Manipulation removed, the connection of dollar to tangible result remains.

Fundraisers can happen in various ways, and it is helpful to explore them.

Fundraisers: Galas

Celebrations, in the budget, and direct funding to mission

Primarily, galas and events like them are celebrations of the ministries the Lord gives to us. Examples include school auctions, ministry celebration dinners, and golf tournaments. Secondarily, they provide a robust platform to inform and engage people in ministries. Third, they give ministry leaders the chance to publicly thank supporters, staff, and volunteers. Finally, and only after the first three have been realized fully, can galas and events like them have fundraisers within them. The fundraising portion of these events follows the guidelines of the section above. The funding message must be clear, concise, and point people to a specific ministry fund or project that is outside of operations.

The school auction is a celebration event with a fundraiser; it just happens that the fundraising mechanism is an auction. The ministry celebration dinner celebrates the workers of a specific ministry; it just happens that the funding mechanism is acquiring new regular donors. The golf tournament promotes a specific ministry and uses various means to raise funds: entry fees, course challenges, mulligans, and so on. Some end with an actual gala and auction.

Galas can be effective fundraising events because they can connect with a diverse group of people. Most often, the event will include nonmembers or people who are not directly connected to the ministry. This presents challenges and opportunities. The challenge is effectively communicating during the event in language that embraces the ministry-connected folks while still fully informing the new people. The opportunity arises from an engaged group of people who are prepared to hear about the ministry by their attendance.

To effectively connect with attendees, a full ministry picture must be painted at the event. Also, while not the central message, financials should be presented or made available. Showing how the ministry's operations are funded and how the fundraising goal that evening is unrelated to operational costs is part of that reporting. This builds trust that will lead a donor to give to the fundraising initiative that evening.

Finally, effective galas will have a fundraiser that is focused on one tangible item or project. Show the new modern playground, story-tell the food bank's direct impact, have a model version of the church van being purchased. The guests of the event need to see how, by the end of the event, something will happen.

Fundraisers: Annual Appeals and Annual Funds

Specific, targeted, for a purpose

Annual appeals are part of a larger communication and funding strategy for a ministry. If unfamiliar, annual appeals are just as they sound: appeals for donations toward a specific fund, typically toward the end of the calendar year. The timing is a function of the tax cycle, assuming people are more likely to contribute over and above regular giving for personal tax reasons.

As you can expect, within a congregational context, annual appeals should follow the fundraising guidelines presented above. The appeal is toward a specific item or project, not for general operations.

Although it sounds like annual appeals occur once throughout the year, they should be a yearlong strategy that culminates with the direct appeal. For instance, an annual appeal goes out in early December to raise funds for the community organization that provides Christmas gifts for families. Around Christmas, a final total communication is sent out to all who received the original appeal. A few months later, another message is sent out storytelling a family that received assistance. In early fall, a communication reminds people of the ministry's general needs, volunteer opportunities, and how to connect needy families. All communications thank donors. The cycle then repeats. The first and last message of an annual appeal cannot be the appeal itself.

Fundraisers: Scholarships

An exception to the rule, maybe

Scholarships, specifically Lutheran school-related scholarships, can be an exception to some of what I have said above. Let me explain.

Lutheran schools are more than private schools; they are important ministries that equip young people to live faithful lives for Christ. From infant education through post-doctoral work at a Concordia, the Lutheran system has sent out missionaries in various vocations for generations. Our schools should be full.

Therefore, scholarship funds are connected to the student, not the congregation. This makes scholarship funding abide by a slightly different set of rules. Let us explore the various ways this plays out.

First, all congregations, with or without a school, should create a fund within the budget, a benevolence, that provides scholarship dollars for students to attend local Lutheran schools, Concordia Universities, or an LCMS seminary. Promote the fund and connect your young people appropriately.

Second, congregations in associations for Lutheran schools or with their own school may have a separate fund, with specific fundraisers, for scholarships. This is an exception only as these congregations work to fully fund their school out of the general budget.

In a perfect world, all congregations would fund schools across the church 100 percent out of budget and benevolences. Until then, scholarship funds fill the gap. They are tangible; this amount of money will send this student to this school so that he or she learns about Jesus. School ministry in the church is a powerful ministry, and no seat should go unfilled.

CAPITAL CAMPAIGNS

Ministry future—capital step required

It is 1890 in central Kansas. You are a faithful farmer and member of Zion Lutheran Church. The parish was formed by you and all the families who farm the land around you, miles outside the train stop town where your grain meets the railcars. Your pastor, newly married, and his wife, now pregnant, can no longer live in the room built off the back of the church building. After the worship service this Sunday, you, along with all the members of the congregation, begin building a parsonage next to the sanctuary. Over the next few weeks, you all take extra time throughout the week, all day Saturday, and Sunday afternoons to complete the new structure. You just participated in a precursor to a capital campaign.

Capital campaigns are not fundraisers. Fundraisers can masquerade as capital campaigns, though. Spend a couple of months pitching a big funding need, have people commit to giving to that need, and allow them to fulfill that financial obligation over a few years. That is a fundraiser. The focus is funding the need.

Capital campaigns are movements. They *increase collective stewardship to take capital steps forward for future benefit.* I will break that statement down in reverse order.

"Future benefit" reminds us that campaigns look forward. The project within them may be immediate, like fixing a broken boiler or reducing debt, but for the process to be a capital campaign, the connection of the current project to the future is imperative. For instance:

We must replace the boiler so that our facilities can be efficiently heated throughout the week. This allows us to expand our midweek ministries and invite the community to use our space throughout the week.

We must reduce our debt so that we have freed up cash to hire a DCE. This allows us to expand our family education and service ministries.

To round out the examples, what is the future benefit of building a new sanctuary?

We must build a new sanctuary to give us dedicated worship and gathering space while freeing up what will become the fellowship hall. This allows us to expand our worship offerings, wedding ministry, fellowship events, and community events.

Any of those projects could simply be fundraisers if they are not connected to the future.

We need to fix the boiler; it's cold.

We need to reduce our debt because it would give our budget some margin.

We need to build a sanctuary because we want a dedicated place to worship.

That reasoning is not bad, they are funding arguments that keep things relatively the same. When it is time to enter into a capital campaign, connecting to the future and pulling your people into that future is critical.

"Capital steps forward" refers to the project portion of the campaign. There must be a tangible capital change the campaign is promoting. Fundraisers can collect cash for general ministries or ideas; campaigns point at something tangible. For reference, "capital" refers to wealth, a congregation's assets in buildings or funds. Therefore, the term in question links the capital change to the previous clause; campaigns make a change to the capital of a congregation to step forward into the future. In the three examples, the term "capital" has a double meaning. Note the examples:

We are taking in extra capital (money) to make a capital (excellent) change (boiler, loan reduction, sanctuary).

"Increase collective stewardship" is where capital campaigns fully diverge from fundraisers. As noted above, fundraisers are great tools that connect donors to ministries. Campaigns do the same and then engage the donor in the ministry future.

Faithful stewards give all that they have in service to the Lord, a portion of which is pooled together with others to support collective ministries. Campaigns make the argument that a select group of faithful stewards, members of a congregation, or supporters of a specific ministry, reassess their stewardship and allocate more of what they have to the congregation or ministry. Note I have not used the term *money*. Yes, campaigns have a financial component, but the larger argument is for increased stewardship across the board. Our examples again:

We must increase our stewardship to expand our midweek and community ministries. This includes extra dollars to accomplish the project, extra volunteering to manage the ministries, extra leadership to guide new ministries, extra prayer to bless campus visitors, and so forth.

We must increase our stewardship to expand our family ministries and service opportunities. This includes extra dollars to reduce debt, personal support for the DCE, leadership and volunteering, and so on.

We must increase our stewardship to expand our ministries across the board. This includes extra dollars to build the sanctuary, extra volunteering to service the expanding ministries, extra time spent participating, and so forth.

Campaigns are powerful tools that raise up stewardship among a group of faithful stewards toward a common future goal. They are not fundraisers; they are movements. Use campaigns often, continually connect your people to the future the Lord is calling you to, and never make it about just raising cash.

Finally, never run campaigns alone. Bring in professionals to guide the process. You and your congregation's leaders need to continue to lead your ministries and make the case for the future. You should not be focused on process and campaign guidance. Allow professionals to do that alongside you. If you are part of the LCMS, connect with LCEF; we will guide you.

FUNDING—LOANS

Is it the church helping the church?

In the classic movie, *It's a Wonderful Life*, during the run on the savings and loan, George Baily, the main character, explains the general concept of banking. As people attempt to pull their savings out, he reminds them that their cash is not sitting in the safe waiting for them. Instead, their money has been given out as loans so that fellow community members were able to buy homes. You pool your dollars with others so that someone can use that money for their own purpose. The interest on your savings is the borrower saying, "Thank you for letting me use your money."

Church extension funds, CEFs in general, LCEF specific to the LCMS, are organizations that help churches, members, and the organizations themselves pool their dollars so that other churches or church workers can use the money for their own ministry purposes. The modern concept began in 1902 when LCMS congregations pooled four hundred dollars to help Zion Lutheran Church in Bridgeport, Connecticut, build a school. That money was returned over time and, as the pool was increased, was loaned out to build and expand churches around the country.

Today, CEFs exist in many denominations, with LCEF growing from the original to be the largest in the nation. While they operate with the most basic banking concept, they are not banks. They transparently show how invested dollars are pooled and used to benefit the church directly. Moreover, LCEF specifically offers adjacent services to congregations that banks simply cannot provide. These include everything from strategic ministry planning to campus planning, stewardship training to real estate management. They guide congregations through capital campaigns, decreasing loan demand, and even assisting congregations in paying loans back faster. Can you imagine a bank having a department that assists borrowers in a way that reduces their interest income?

All this talk of LCEF and CEFs is to bring us to this point: loans are not intrinsically bad. Loans, in their pure form, are people helping people. Loans through LCEF is the Church helping itself do the work the Lord is calling it to. In other words, debt is a tool that can be used for the good of the Kingdom. Like any tool, though, it can be used improperly and lead to issues. How can this be avoided?

First, congregations should only borrow through LCEF or their specific CEF. This is the only way to hold to the church-helping-itself concept. Moreover, LCEF exists in service to the church; they are for the Kingdom. Banks are not.

Second, loans should be acquired as part of a larger financial plan in response to ministry plans. A clear repayment strategy must be created, vetted, and approved by leadership. The loan, as a tool, should be part of a larger ministry argument made to the congregation. For example:

> We need to expand our school building to accommodate more families so that more young people can learn about Jesus and bring the Gospel into the world. This is the core of our capital campaign, which will generate a million dollars. The project

> is two million. We will borrow one million from LCEF. Monthly payments fit into our current budget, and we will engage in a second capital campaign in a few years to pay the entire loan back and bring the congregation fully into the future the Lord has prepared.

Third, loans are tools to avert disasters. We explore these scenarios later in the chapter but have in mind this basic concept: people help one another in times of crisis. Taking out an emergency loan, without the ability to fully plan, is just like a brother loaning a sister money to get her through a trying time. Use your extended church family.

Finally, let the professionals guide you. Loans, the planning, the paperwork, the financials, are quickly overwhelming. People like me are called in service to the church to help you. Connect with your local LCEF or church extension fund representative.

WHAT IF?

All the planning in the world does not change the fact that you are in the world. Things break before they are supposed to, natural and manmade disasters roll through, people go through chaotic periods, and finances get messy. With honesty and transparency, built from the systems I have laid out so far, your ministries will get through the craziest of times.

MINISTRY EMERGENCIES

Honesty amid the best planning possible

For our purposes here, ministries are organized congregational events that equip people to serve and facilitate their service. A Bible study, for instance, is teaching people Scripture so that they can live as Christ directs, the Bible study leader serving. A fall festival event facilitates outreach and personal evangelism, assuming people invite and interact with the community.

Ministry emergencies arise from the people who run the ministries. Moral failures, personal chaos, and leadership mistakes all lead to ministry emergencies. They will happen; do not be surprised. Respond pastorally, inform your denomination's leadership when appropriate, and follow the laws of the land. I want to address the financial fallout that can occur as a result.

Financial troubles will arise because of broken trust. The emergency may have no financial impropriety at all, but financial crisis follows scandals because trust is broken. Your people, pooling their resources to support the ministries of the church, will pull back because they do not want to support ministries that are not effective, which is the immediate perception in the midst of a ministry emergency. What to do?

Be as transparent as possible. Understanding that the situation may not allow you to divulge all the information, be as open as possible and even honest about what you cannot share and why.

Keep the ministry's narrative alive. What did the ministry do? Is it still able to do what is intended? Who is the leader? What changes have been made in reaction to the emergency? Are people still being blessed despite the mess?

As financial issues arise, communicate them in parallel to the previous two. This will fight the financial regression and give others the chance to step up and fill the void.

An example:

> A youth group and confirmation leader is indicted for illegal drug use and sent to prison. The man has faithfully served for years, and no direct issues were observed. The pastor calls all the parents, informs them of the situation, explains the public legal record, and shares his observations as appropriate. He allows the parents to vent and process. Other youth and confirmation leaders come together to connect with the parents to assure them that their young people have been cared for and blessed, regardless of the personal failures of the one leader. They promise to continue their service to the

> kids and work with the parents to explain the situation to the youth. The congregation is informed of the entire situation, moral failure, pastor-to-parent connection, leaders-to-parent connection, the plan forward, and the impact of youth and confirmation work in the congregation. Finally, anyone is invited to meet with the pastor to talk through the situation. A few families leave the congregation over the incident, including the now-jailed leader. While dealing with that pastorally, the new financial reality is shared with leadership. This changes the offering-giving pyramid. A few leaders step up to fill the gap. The next budget year, a revised pyramid is presented, and people respond accordingly.

Crisis is not averted; you do the best you can to faithfully lead your people forward.

MINISTRY OPPORTUNITIES

Be nimble and prepare your people

Financial crisis in a congregation can arise from ministry opportunities.

A congregation in Texas finds themselves at the center of flood relief.

A congregation in Pennsylvania has a grief share ministry expand exponentially.

A congregation in New York is given a closed church property for replanting.

Without proper planning and execution, these stories could continue:

A congregation in Texas closes its doors to flood victims because the members were afraid of the liability and expenses.

A grief share ministry in Pennsylvania moved from a Lutheran to a Unitarian Church to accommodate its size.

A congregation in New York sold a neighboring church property to cushion their budget. That property is now a gas station.

Alternatively:

A congregation in Texas, in response to the flood, has built a community resource center and distributes food and social care to hundreds of families a week in partnership with the county. These families are loved, prayed for, and connected to Jesus through the work of the congregation.

A congregation in Pennsylvania ran a successful capital campaign to build a community hall and adjacent classrooms which now house multiple ministries, including the largest grief share in the area. People are loved, prayed for, and connected to Jesus through the work of the congregation.

A congregation in New York, in partnership with synodical partners, replanted a successful congregation in a neighboring town. They did the hard work so that local people are loved, prayed for, and connected to Jesus through the work of the congregation.

Ministry opportunities are passed over by congregations because they are not prepared. Be prepared.

First, you and your leaders must keep your eyes open. Opportunities arise all the time, but if you and your leaders are only focused on keeping your operations going, they will pass you by.

Second, know who you are and what God is asking you to do. No, you cannot do everything, and having a solid framework will help you understand what God has uniquely curated your congregation to do.

Third, be flexible. Yes, you do need to know what God is asking you to do, but do not let that be your out to responding to opportunities. There is a tension, as with all good church teachings. On one side, stay in the lanes the Lord has set you in. On the other, understand He is free to make you change lanes.

Fourth, equip your congregation to respond. You do this by consistently reminding them of who they are as faithful stewards and neighbors. From proclamation to testimonials, keep your people mindful of the opportunities God has laid before them with the expectation of opportunities to come.

Fifth, have a cash reserve. Well, you expected this from me by now, but it's not what you assume. I do not want you to have a few hundred thousand sitting in a ministry opportunity fund. Instead, have a cash reserve that sits above your operating budget, like a personal checking account that has enough liquid in it to float for two months to buffer against any financial hiccups. This takes the immediate worry out of the conversation when big ideas need to be pursued.

Sixth, communicate. Since you already have solid communication channels set with your congregation, a congregation that trusts your financial reporting, and a congregation that knows its calling as faithful stewards, you can communicate the ministry opportunity immediately and empower your people to rise up and respond.

Finally, the money will show up. Not magically, rather it will come with your people as they respond. You do not need the ministry opportunity fund because that fund is your congregation, both in person and in wallet. Do the work of sorting the costs and communicating the needs, but know that when God's people respond to ministry opportunities, money comes with.

FACILITY EMERGENCIES

Fix and honesty

All the planning in the world will not prevent facility emergencies. The most robust and exhaustive capital improvement plan cannot account for the randomness of this world. Through transparency and built trust, you can weather the worst of emergencies.

It all begins with the capital improvement plan being communicated to the congregation. Folks need to know that leadership has done the work to predict facility needs as best as they can. Having the capital improvement plan in the budget and making mention of it as regular repairs occur is sufficient.

Know your insurance company. Know your agent. Know your coverage. During the emergency, you do not want to be sorting out who to call and what your coverage is.

Have connections to plumbers, electricians, HVAC companies, fix-it people, and so on. Mine the connections through your congregation: Who do they trust? Who do they use? Most importantly, have these connections in a conspicuous location in the office or wherever people know to access the info.

Think like a stoplight. Here is what I mean:

Red: It must be fixed immediately. The facilities are not safe, are out of code, or are not usable.

Yellow: It should be fixed within a year but allows for some fiscal planning.

Green: It can be wrapped into the capital improvement plan.

We will review in reverse order. The green items may present themselves as emergencies but can realistically find their way into the cash flow of the capital improvement plan. These are typically items that can be fixed temporarily, like patching a roof or repairing an old boiler. They will need to be dealt with soon but do not affect the budget dramatically. The expenses incurred by green items being dealt with can be factored into the cash flow of a capital improvement plan.

Yellow items provide some time to plan for the emergency expense. With small items, adjustments to the budget may accommodate. For larger items, private asks to understanding congregation members may suffice. For the biggest issues, a capital campaign or loan may be used. Intrinsic to biggest issues is clear, open, and honest communication to the congregation.

Red items are why organizations like the Lutheran Church Extension Fund exist. Do the work, make things right, use your line of credit, or get an emergency loan. Again, communication with the congregation is key. After the crisis, to deal with the debt, you can treat the project like a yellow, dealing with it via the budget, private ask, or campaign.

I cannot state this enough: be clear, open, and honest with the congregation. Here is the situation, here is why we were not prepared, and here is the solution. Yes, some members will be angry or put off, but with due diligence, a culture built on transparency, and a forward-looking mission, your people will accommodate the emergency and move on.

One final note: do not let reds slide into yellows or greens. If it is a red, deal with it. If you are reading this and are part of the LCMS, call LCEF or your district CEF immediately. They are here for you.

PERSONAL FINANCIAL CRISIS

Stop being an individual—get help, be honest

You are not alone. Yes, other people have personal financial issues, but that is not what I mean. God did not put you in this world, redeem you through your Baptism, and send you off alone to navigate the world. You know this. Most parts of our lives are shared with our families, friends, and community. We do this face-to-face and through social media. We talk about our health, our home drama, our passions, even our personal emotional struggles long before we will talk about finances with someone, including our spouses.

First, stop that. Money is not a real thing—we discussed that already—so do not give it power that it does not have.

Second, we all have struggles in life. Everyone knows this. Whether directly caused by your own actions or the regular chaos of life, all our struggles stem from the fall.

Third, there are people who are called by God into the vocation of helping people financially. Use them. You are not expected to be a financial professional, just like you are not expected to know how to fix an air conditioning unit or remove your own appendix.

Fourth, if and when you find yourself in a personal financial mess, do not be embarrassed; get help and follow their guidance. Financial worry will eat at you and overcome your ability to lead.

Finally, if appropriate, bring this to your leadership team or elders. Discuss the situation and ask them to support you with prayer and guidance where applicable. If you serve as the pastor and are underpaid, which has led to the situation, bring it up your denomination's leadership chain and follow their guidance. Congregations will support you; they often are unaware of underpayment.

FINANCIAL MISTAKES

Honesty, transparency, get help

There are too many examples of financial mistakes in congregations to discuss here, so I will summarize in three areas: intentional, accidental, and systemic mistakes.

Intentional mistakes are bound up in the Seventh Commandment. People sin, people steal, and congregations often discover long after. I will lay out your organizational response in a moment, but here let me remind you that at all times you are the Church. Sin is real, and forgiveness is greater. While the assailants will face legal repercussions, they should not be pushed out of Christendom. If they have stolen, there is likely a major issue that led to their action. Whether requiring a diagnosis of kleptomania or discovery of a life crisis, pastoral care is required.

Accidental mistakes occur because we are human. I took Calculus 3 in eleventh grade (yes, I was good at math). One day, late in the school year, my class of fifteen was given a ridiculously complicated problem that we worked on collectively for a solid hour of class time. We filled up a wall of whiteboards and came to our answer. Our teacher, Mrs. Woerner, a faithful Christian genius who devoted her life to us kids, said simply, "Wrong." We were aghast. She rose, walked to the far end of the whiteboard, toward the beginning of our work, and circled a few numbers with a little giggle. We were in shock. This class of fifteen high-level math students had forgotten that 6 - 4 = 2. Yeah, we made a simple error in kindergarten arithmetic. Mistakes happen. Everyone knows this; grace may abound.

Systemic mistakes are the result of antiquated processes or programs. Even the smallest congregation should have their finances tracked and managed by professional software, not the treasurer's checkbook (yes, I still see this around the country). Counters should double-check each other's work, receipts documented, expenses tracked, reporting made regular. Even with a seemingly perfect system, though, things can get messed up. So how do we respond?

I will deal with prevention in the last section of this chapter; here I want to lay out a simple response list:

1. Involve the authorities immediately when appropriate, absolutely in the intentional case. Not only is this proper in the kingdom of the left, but it also shows your congregation that you recognize how serious this action was.
2. Involve your denominational leadership. There is legal and pastoral help available, and you are not alone.
3. Involve your LCEF, CEF, or other church financial organization to assist with immediate needs. Do not let this sin impede the work of your congregation. There are financial products to give you the buffer to sort out the situation.
4. Be transparent. Your congregation's financial trust is critical to the life of a parish. The only way to rebuild that trust is to show the effort being made to discover the issue, remedy the failure, and execute the plan for recovery.

Mistakes happen. They can be overcome.

FINANCIAL LEADERSHIP

Be involved

I end this chapter with the hardest section. If you are reading this book, you are likely a pastor or church leader. If you are reading this chapter, you recognize the complexity of church finances. If you have made it this far, you may be wondering how to implement all that I have laid out. Be a financial leader.

Financial leadership is part of being a leader in any organization. In the church, it is often downplayed, ignored, or discouraged. Someone somewhere made up the idea that church leaders should stay away from financials. They cite anecdotes of impropriety or inability or declare that they would not have the time. Regardless, leaders of organizations are financial leaders.

Let us begin with debunking the lies.

"I shouldn't know what people give because I don't want to treat people differently."

This is by far the most repeated phrase to me around the country. I hear it from seminary students, pastors of all ages and experience, and from congregational leaders referencing why they do not want their pastor looking at church finances. It makes sense: if I know that the Johnson family gives a lot of money, and they ask me to do something, I will be more inclined to do it.

Note the subject of that last sentence. The issue here is not with the leader knowing financials; it is what they do with that knowledge. The response to the person saying this lie: that is your problem. Yes, knowing what people give should make you treat people differently but not how you are thinking.

Let us say the Johnson family faithfully gives one thousand dollars a month for years. Then one month, out of the blue, they start giving one hundred dollars. What happened? Remember all we have already talked about regarding money and faithful stewardship. This giving shift reflects a change in their life or their devotion to the congregation to which God has called them. In both instances, the Johnsons require pastoral care.

Conversely, the Johnson family begins giving ten thousand dollars a month. They are faithful Lutherans and absolutely do not want recognition for what they are giving, but they are also humans and do need that recognition. This is not to spike their pride or shame others; rather, privately, they may want and need to share why they have increased their giving. It may simply be a celebration of a new financial reality or a devotion to the congregation; either way, a pastoral conversation is warranted.

Another example, one often overlooked, is the lack of giving by seemingly devoted members. If a member of your council is not living as a faithful steward, giving part of what they have been given toward the congregational financial pool, are they fit for congregational leadership? Do not read this wrong, they are not paying for a seat at the leadership table. Rather, the leadership table of a congregation should be filled by people devoted to the congregation. As we have mentioned before, devotion to a congregation has the offering as a marker.

Yes, there are extenuating circumstances when people seemingly cannot give. Some will say they are on a fixed income. All of us are on fixed incomes. We all receive a finite amount each month, whether on welfare, social security, salary, or stock dividends. We are still called to pool a portion of our resources to support the collective work. Some will say they simply do not have a margin to give from. While you can throw the widow's mite story at them from the Gospels of Mark and Luke, chapters 12 and 21 respectively, a better approach may be pastoral and financial care. How can this person be assisted so they are not so worried about money that they cannot part with even a mite? What financial education needs to be shared so the person can reassess and reprioritize their expenditures?

Bottom line, pastors, spend time in prayer and ask the Lord to guide you to use financial information for the benefit of His people and His church. Release the worry that has been cast on you regarding treatment of your people. Love all of them and give attention to families according to spiritual situations. May their offering be one window into their lives.

"I'm afraid I will mess things up and get caught up in a scandal."

The argument of incompetence aside for now, this lie emanates from fear of the anecdote. Yes, congregations have scandals. There is the chance you will be wrapped up in them. However, you will be wrapped up in the scandal whether you are involved in the finances or not; you are the leader!

Instead of hiding behind this lie as an excuse, use it to motivate you to dive in. Since you will be implicated in any scandal, at least via proximity, it is in your personal interest to be engaged so you can stop issues before they arise. Moreover, to weather scandal, you will need to be transparent with your congregation, as I mentioned earlier. If you are not engaged at all, your attempt at transparency will fail, and people will wonder why you let the mess happen. If you can show you were involved, were diligent, and the scandal still arose for whatever reason, people will be more willing to forgive and move on.

It is advisable, right, and good for the pastor to never be involved in counting the offering. Two reasons: First, there are other people fully capable and willing to do this important work. It does not require pastoral attention. Second, the view of passing the plate, bringing that plate to the pastor, and him counting it confuses what the offering is, even if the pastor counts privately after worship. The offering is collected and handed to the pastor during the worship service in the stead of Christ. In other words, the offering is laid before the Lord, not the man in the role of pastor. Allow no doubt to leak into the minds of the congregation; the pastor is not collecting and counting the offering handed to him.

Note, I did not make the argument that the pastor should not count so that he is not tempted to steal from the plate. Need I expand on why?

"I'm uncomfortable talking about money. People don't want to hear about money from their pastor."

First, this lie is like the first, an issue you must deal with personally. This is like a pastor saying he does not do funerals because he is uncomfortable with death. Funerals are part of the job, as is financial leadership.

Yes, your people do want to hear about money from you; you are the leader. No, you do not have to lay out all the details of the budget during the voters meetings, but you do need to show that you understand the budget and how it supports the ministries of the congregation. No, you do not have to do annual stewardship drives to guilt people into tithing. As you can assume from the rest of this chapter, I am not a fan of the annual Sunday before Thanksgiving "tithe or die" sermon. Financial stewardship is one thing a faithful steward does. Every sermon should have a faithful steward thread running through it, and sometimes the financial action should arise when appropriate and helpful.

Your people want to know their offering is facilitating the work to which God is calling you all. This reporting must start from the top. It should show up in anecdotes in your sermons, inside comments around announcements, in newsletter articles, in board reports. The pastor must continually connect the financials of the church to the work of the church, lest we forget what the Lord is up to.

"I don't have time to deal with finances."

If this statement really is true, then you are not doing your job fully and something has to change. Either your workload needs to be decreased to allow you the time to be in financial meetings and to analyze finances, or your leadership needs to rearrange the way your congregation operates so the pastor can be involved in the financials.

Just to be clear, this line is usually a lie, a cop-out. Being engaged in finances does not require a full day of accounting. You should have volunteers and professionals who are managing the day-to-day. However, weekly check-ins, monthly analysis, and annual deep dives are part of the job as church leader. Period.

"I don't understand financial stuff or budgets, so I'm going to leave it to my members."

I did not understand how to preach a sermon, but I learned so I could serve as pastor. I did not know how to lead a premarital counseling session, but I learned so I could serve as pastor. I did not know how to do budgets or analyze financials, but I learned so I could serve as pastor.

I admit that last line was true for my second parish, a church I planted. I happily lived this lie in my first parish. They did not need me; we had a multibillion-dollar corporation executive accountant as our treasurer.

Yes, they did. No, they did not need me for the day-to-day, but the congregation would have benefited from my devotion, ministry leadership, and pastoral responses.

Learn how budgets work. Learn how church finances work. Spend the time with your treasurer and interview your counters. Take a course online. Read your denomination's treasurer's handbook. Yes, they exist. Call your LCEF, CEF, or other church financial company rep and ask him or her for a crash course. Take it from me, I was my LCEF district vice president's pastor. He tried to teach me many times. Oh, if I had listened! (I would have written this chapter a decade ago!)

Now, with lies aside, let us build an image of financial leadership with some simple statements.

Financial leaders lead with a team.

Never do this alone. As crazy as it sounds, I have had congregations where the pastor is the only one who manages the finances, from counting through spending, budgeting through accounting. I cannot imagine many reading this think it is a good idea! This is far from the vocation of pastor and introduces too many opportunities for error. Not because pastors cannot learn how to do it all, but because humans make errors.

The team approach requires multiple people working together to review and double-check one another. Build a team of counters who proof one another. Turn the counter group into a small group that prays together; this is a blessing to many a congregation I have worked with. Have a treasurer and an apprentice or two. Train up the next generation of leaders, and have the team double-check the work. Build a team to work and review the budget. Do it right, and it will not take a lot of time throughout the course of the year.

Commission and celebrate these people publicly. Let your congregation know who faithfully and properly manages the finances; seeing them maintains trust. Thank them often. They need to know from their leader that they are part of a critical team in the congregation.

Financial leaders know the whole picture.

You must have access to everything and understand how the whole process works. Understand how dollars go from plate or online giving site to bank account, how checks are cut, and bills are paid. Know where your savings, dedicated accounts, and endowments are housed, how much is in them, and for what they are intended. Have full access to whatever accounting software your congregation uses—giving, recording, and accounting sides. Understand what each of your people oversees and how their roles intersect.

Here is the test. If a member walks up to you and asks where his or her offering goes, can you answer without just saying, "It goes to church operations"? Track a dollar's path through your congregation's financial pipelines with reporting and exchanges.

Financial leaders can do all financial operations, kind of.

There is a practical reason for this—people cannot always do their jobs. Sickness, life crisis, death, and so on can all leave your congregation void of the worker required. Without the time for transition, your financial management could suffer and important details and nuances could be missed. You, as the leader, must be the institutional bridge.

Leaders are better leaders when they model competence to their team. It shows them you understand and appreciate the work they are doing. It enables you to converse with them at the level of the work and problem solve in the weeds when required.

No, you do not have to be certified in accounting principles or get an MBA. Yet you must have a working understanding of every part of the financial process, even if you must google a term here and there.

Financial leaders check in at all levels regularly.

To thank your team, check in with them as they serve in their roles. Show the effort to greet your counters—just do not do it while they are counting! Show up to your treasurer's house in the days before the budget is due to praise and pray for him or her. Go to your bank and meet everyone and thank them for their service. Meet with your LCEF, CEF, or other church financial organization and show you appreciate their service to the Kingdom. Financial leadership happens in those special moments.

It must also be said that when you are regularly checking in, you are also looking over shoulders for quality control purposes. Yes, you may catch impropriety, but you also may catch innocent mistakes and process errors. Check in, thank people, and keep your eyes open. You can do all three without one being in service to the other.

Financial leaders understand the big picture.

Remember, all this financial consideration is in service to the Kingdom. You must be the person who brings that big picture into every financial meeting, conversation, or budget voters assembly. The role of financial leader in the church connects the finances to the ministry and mission of the church as we have discussed. The only way to do this: know His "big picture" and connect your congregation's work to it. Finances are part of that story.

CHAPTER 11

THE PASTOR AND DIGITAL AND FUTURE CHALLENGES

Rev. Joshua Duffy

WESTCLIFFE, COLORADO

In October of 2019, I sat in Dr. Paul Looney's office in The Woodlands, Texas. Dr. Looney is highly respected not only for his overall counseling practice but also for his work with ministry leaders. I was closing in on the five-year mark in ministry (July 2020) and nearly broken. I had undergone two EKGs and one stress test. Maybe it had something to do with enduring forty-nine deaths in my church and forty-two funerals (forty-one from my church, one personal) in forty-eight months. And if that wasn't enough, both our campus and our home flooded during Hurricane Harvey, and we had to evacuate.

So there I was in a counselor's office, trying to figure out what to do next with my life. At the tail end of our session, Dr. Looney asked me this question: "When is the last time you got away by yourself, prayed, sat in His presence, and listened for Him?" My answer: "You mean alone?"

He already looked dumbfounded and shocked at the trajectory of my response. "Yes," he said. "Alone." I simply said, "Never."

It was in this moment he made an offer to me that had a profound impact on my life. Dr. Looney offered me his home in Westcliffe, Colorado, to get away and figure out what God had for me next in ministry and in my life. My wife, Mallory, could not have been more supportive, so I went.

In Westcliffe, Colorado, I fasted, read, sat silently, and prayed for God to guide me through His external Word to His will concerning my marriage, my family, my life, and my ministry. I can honestly say I was truly open to going wherever God wanted me to go and doing whatever God wanted me to do.

I have to say, it was one of the most powerful experiences I've ever had with our great God. And it was from that experience that I would come back and lead our church in an additional forty days of prayer. And from that entire experience came a direction for our church that connects beautifully to this chapter, the challenges and opportunities of digital technology for ministry and future challenges.

In light of COVID-19, I now know that God was pointing us in a direction in which we could minister to our most vulnerable, our elderly, and our church family, and still maintain a sense of family in the middle of a global pandemic. He was equipping us to make Him known literally to the ends of the earth, and He was empowering us to reach the lost in a completely new way. Some of what you will read was planned and strategized. And much of it was reacting to the constantly changing landscape the external circumstances were imposing upon us, in which we had no control. In short, we were along for the ride, and God was in the driver's seat! We took on the mindset that this isn't just about doors closing or being limited in some way. In fact, this is God wanting to do a new thing. There is a path for innovation, a blessed path and an ordained, God-honoring path. We just had to trust, pray, and move in faith, and that is what we did.

CULTURAL CHALLENGES

But to set the stage, let's talk roads. I'm from the polar opposite of Westcliffe, Colorado. I'm from Houston, Texas, and that is also where I have the great honor of being the senior pastor of Pilgrim Lutheran Church. In my entire life, I cannot think of one four-week period in which there was not some highway or road on my commute that was not under construction.

I remember when toll roads were first introduced to my city. The selling point was that by charging a toll, the construction of these roadways would be funded and paid for only by the people that used them. And for special measure, we would call them "tollways." And so what was meant to be a method of paying for a new freeway became a method of collecting revenue long after the freeway was completed.

So you think, "I'm not gonna pay these tolls. I'm gonna just use the FREEway." But the freeway isn't free. Why? Because they keep the freeways just barely broken enough so that every couple of weeks, somewhere on Houston's freeways, one guy in a reflective orange vest and hard hat can move three pounds of rocks with a shovel from one side of the road to the other while three other guys dressed the same watch him intently. And who pays to fix the free? We do! The same people who pay at the tollways!

What's strange is that ancient Rome managed to build roads and bridges that are still in operation to this day! In fact, Roman roads and bridges played a pivotal role in many aspects of their infrastructure, growth, efficiency, expansion, and power. But one additional key purpose of Rome's roads was that of communication. It was via their roads and bridges that news and urgent messages would be carried.

The internet, social media, and the greater online world, in one sense, are the equivalent of Rome's roads for communication. Two thousand years ago, information traveled at 1G speed (as in one guy on a horse), and today it's 4G or even 5G. However, in another sense, I'm afraid the digital world is more like our tollways and freeways! I wish I could say that communicating via the digital road in our world and landscape is flawless and efficient. I also wish I could tell you that engaging our culture through this medium comes with fewer issues than pre-social-media eras. The methods and strategies, in their own right, require constant maintenance and upkeep and are laid upon the backdrop of technology that is constantly changing. Oh, to go back to 1G when people sat in a room and listened to one person read one letter!

While information travels much quicker than it did back then, there are still principles and values that we will discuss in this chapter that stay the same no matter the era, time, or context. In order to best dissect the challenges and opportunities of digital technology for ministry and future challenges, it's important to get an idea of the value system you are now encountering, the shifts in how people are communicating, and, quite possibly, why they are communicating the way that they do.

Let me hit you with a few things staring at you every day but that you may not have stopped to consider before.

Number one is how we communicate now. The two-faced nature of people online (I almost put "younger people" solely under this category until I remembered that I know older people that are just as bad as younger generations). Have you ever noticed people sitting next to one another at a restaurant while all looking down at their phones on social media? They are sitting next to their real friends, preoccupied with telling their emoji friends (maybe that's too harsh; how about "digital disconnected"?) that they are out with their real friends. But that's the problem—they are not really with their friends; they are lost in cyberspace somewhere. In fact, it's worse than two-faced. At least with two-faced people, they pretend to be one way when in fact they are something else entirely different. In this case, there is an odd intimacy issue that seems to be lurking.

Or how about the mild and timid male or female that you speak to in person who can hardly muster the courage to string three sentences together, but online he or she has a radically different persona than what you would meet in person!

Or the family that posts never-ending digital documentation of their personal highlight reel of happiness and success when actually their lives are falling apart.

Or the people who reveal nothing about themselves over coffee but online will divulge their most personal experiences, just hoping for the true depth of human empathy in the form of a tear-faced emoji or a red-faced emoji. Nothing says how much care and thought I put into your tragedy like spending a second and a half choosing which emoji best encapsulates my solidarity with you and your pain.

Here's one of my favorite posts, and it starts like this: "I don't normally do this" (wait for it, wait for it, wait for it . . . *now*!) "buuuuut" (ah, the classic "but"! There are a lot of big "buts" online these days). And sure enough, after the "but" disclaimer comes eighteen paragraphs of thought, the equivalent of standing on a folding chair in the middle of a Houston tollway or a supposed "free"way, yelling your guts out as traffic passes you by. The only thing that actually draws interest is not the message, just the fact that you decided to stand on the folding chair called your profile, in the middle of the freeway called social media. And it's on this platform that we villainize, demean, and reduce one another.

The next factor is time and how we spend it. When I started in youth ministry in 2006, Sunday nights were solid, and Wednesday nights were golden as well. Within two years of ministry, Wednesdays were almost a no-go. By the end of my five years in student ministry, Wednesdays were a no-go, and so were Sunday nights. Soon the only option left was Sunday mornings. So what did that create? It now created the possibility for the family unit to be split up during church. I'm not here to criticize if that is your church. I'm simply pointing out a progression that has taken place. And why? Why did we find all of these slots of time were slowly swallowed up? They gave up Wednesdays and Sunday nights—and now, even Sunday mornings because their kids must be in club baseball, or club volleyball, or club basketball. No, wait. It's dance or cheer; maybe it's actually band, piano, gymnastics, or chess or badminton (nothing would surprise me).

Think about heart and brain surgeons. You know that kid, little Johnny; he can't throw, catch, shoot, whistle, or chew bubble gum and walk at the same time. And no one wants little Johnny on the team anyway. Little Johnny is thirteen, and he is free most evenings and Sunday morning to worship the Creator of all things because when Little Johnny is thirteen, he doesn't have heart or brain surgeon practice, recitals, games, or competitions. Nope, one day Little Johnny becomes Doctor Johnny, and when I'm lying flat on the operating table, I won't care that he can't throw a curveball or play the piano. But that's our world, a world of time commitments and priorities that are absolutely upside down.

Our culture and our people are terrified of their kids being left behind or left out. I honestly believe this issue is directly tied to the first issue. It's all connected, and it's a spiritual issue. There's nothing wrong with leagues, extra coaching, and putting extra time into our passions. But with what's happening in our culture, the message to our youth is not "the goal is to maximize what God gave you, to be good stewards of however much or little talent He gave you." Instead, what kids and parents are being promised is this: "Your kid is one more practice, one more league, one more recital from a new identity, a higher plane, the next level." And it's simply not true.

Fathers who may have known very little about a certain sport used to go outside and dribble, shoot, throw, catch, and hit with their sons and daughters. Again, nothing wrong with specialized and extra training, if it's in addition to that time with mom and dad together. But too often it is usurping what used to be quality time between a father and a son or a mother and a daughter, or father to daughter or mother to son. Now what you have is a parent sitting at a distance, arms folded, watching intently. He has become one more critic, one more judge, and the games and the recitals and competitions each day become a little less of what they were meant to be—fun.

And are you ready for this as pastors? We, in a way, directly or indirectly, have contributed to this movement in culture. Now I'm not saying it was or is malicious. I'm just saying we have a part to play, and in fact, we have played a part in what's happening culturally.

You want to know what I mean? Well, I have a theory that most—not all, but most—pastors fall into one of two categories: 1) pastors who will say hard things, who are honest, true, and infused with the Gospel or 2) pastors who skirt tough issues that challenge cultural norms, live to please culture, and are infused with the Law. Now your role in this is to honestly analyze and self-diagnose. And if you aren't sure, trust me, your staff already knows which one you may or may not be!

We are called to set a culture—a *cultus Dei*, or culture of God— like it or not. And that culture will be tied to our proclamation of the Gospel message. We have to be bold, and we have to speak in opposition to culture, while also speaking life into culture. We are called to highlight what is broken, wrong, miserable, and sinful in our world and in ourselves and why Jesus alone could take those same things and redeem them. If I could put plainly what I'm trying to say, then it's this—are you saying "hard" things in church?

For example, have you ever told your congregation that they love their church more than they love Jesus? Have you ever told people to stop talking about our church because our church isn't interesting—Jesus is interesting and compelling? Have you ever told your church that the cross in the front is not a glorified hood ornament for this building, but rather, it is proof that you have been outed by God that you are messed up and need what He freely gave and gives in this moment? Or maybe tell them to stop comparing themselves to their neighbors? Or my favorite, have you ever asked your church why is it they can sit in Bible class for forty straight years without missing a Sunday, but they still can't tell their neighbor about the groom named Jesus because they believe they don't know enough about Him still? And yet, if they hear two minutes of hearsay from someone completely removed from the situation, person, and event, and in fact know less than even 10 percent of the actual story, they have no problem gossiping about the Bride of Christ (His Church members) to that same neighbor. You know what you call that—little old lady gossip. I call it murdering the Bride of Christ. That one goes over great every time. Try telling people during the next election that they worship a King and not a president.

My question to you is simply this: are you preaching a message centered on Jesus and therefore infused with grace and truth to our culture? Are you avoiding the hard topics, the topics and values that are shaping our culture? I'm not advocating being a jerk and throwing verbal haymakers and pile drivers at your congregation to be a spiritual, mental, and emotional bully. Do you have angst in your soul when you get up and preach? Do you ever feel led by your convictions to say hard and honest things to the people that God has entrusted to you, even if culture no longer values your perspective, and maybe even if people would leave your church?

To this day, I toss and turn the night before a sermon that I know I must give to my people by the conviction of the Holy Spirit that is not a "preaching to the choir" type message. I am a people-pleaser by nature, and that alone creates an interesting collision inside of me. My desire to be liked sometimes slams into my conviction and the truth that must be shared may mean that the people-pleaser in me will have to look at disappointed faces, folded arms, and stiff upper lips. Maybe you are like me. And if you are, please be encouraged. It may sound cliché, but when you have messages like that, and the conflict is happening inside, you have an audience of One, and He is pleased. Sometimes that's the only consolation I have and should be the only consolation I would ever need.

There are some Sundays when I preach the Gospel and grace with even more passionate, reckless abandon because the person I'm really preaching to is myself. I know I have no right, if not for the grace of God, to stand before this group of people called Pilgrim Lutheran Church. I'll never forget the Sunday when I got home and Mallory told me, "That sermon was awesome." She then paused, composed herself, looked at me, and said, "And you didn't do a word of it yesterday."

Just a quick pause. My wife is my best friend, unbelievably wise, and the love of my life. To be married to a godly woman is a gift! I only wish I would have listened to her earlier in my ministry!

Saying hard things isn't just about an intellectual transfer of information from your brain to the listener. Saying hard things has to start in your soul, your gut, and your own desperate need for Jesus.

Gay marriage, sex, money, divorce, hell, gender identity, and politics, just to name a few, are the very topics that pastors must speak about in a godly, Christ-centered, compassionate, bold, and clarifying, Gospel-driven way. These are the very topics that are now more and more infused into our public-school curriculum, already being introduced in some cases at the elementary school level and younger.

The public square is now dominated by pop culture icons and politicians. Still don't believe me? Take abortion. What do you think it does to followers of Jesus when a politician says, "I am personally against abortion" (that just got your vote, but wait for it, there's more to the statement) . . . "*buuuuut*, I don't believe in imposing my view on someone else." What does that do for the conscience of followers of Jesus, to feel like you have to defend those kinds of lukewarm convictions? But in a way, at least that politician is honest. Weak, but honest. How about the ones on the same exact issue that tell you they are against it, say they will do something about it, but never seem to be able to quite get there to get it done, and if you'd just vote for them one more time, they think it's possible to get it done next time. Make no mistake, the state, our government, our school systems, and our leaders are discipling the Church, and for good measure, so is pop culture.

It is not that we don't still have something relevant to say; it's that the culture has shifted the public square to a different platform, a different plane, a different medium. It's that our people are taking in information differently and in different ways than ever before. And in some cases, we simply are not as bold about our convictions as the culture. I know this may be somewhat disturbing to consider, but what if our model of church has gotten out of control and possibly is not even biblical anymore? And I don't mean megachurches, even small churches. Think about it—does Jesus honestly care or really want you to have a three-million-dollar worship center? Or do you think He is really passionate that your organ is from Germany and installed and tuned by real Germans from Germany?

I live near Galveston. The last time there was a vessel with Germans in it off the coast of the United States, it was full of sailors in U-boats during WWII. At the same time, the only other strategy we've implemented, which is not the one we used to reach immigrant Germans, was what evangelicals did to reach Baby Boomers. Both of these strategies were wildly successful for their time and in their context, but now what? What if God is watching the collapse of congregations around the country and is fully supportive and pleased? What if God actually is closing doors—maybe even our church's doors—to open to us the path He wants for us to take to reach our people in this era and in this context?

Please know, I am proud of my own Lutheran heritage. So please don't misunderstand what I'm trying to say. Different eras, at different times, needed a different kind of approach. The only constant is Word and Sacrament ministry. How it looks, how it manifests itself, cannot drive what we do, how we do it, and most importantly, why we do what we do.

I once asked my congregation the following question: "If leaving this campus, selling this church, and moving meant that God would bless us beyond our wildest imaginations and reach more people through this ministry and baptize more people than ever before, would you do it?"

To some, that may seem like an extreme question to ask your congregation. But really stop and consider the biblical legacy we are all a part of: loving the lost, loving your people, loving your community, and doing whatever is necessary for all three to receive the grace of Jesus and have a saving faith in Him.

Consider St. Paul's love for his own Jewish people in Romans 9:2–3, expressed in his willingness to be cursed for them if at all possible. Or Moses' passion for his people, expressing to God his willingness to be cursed to hell forever while the Israelites were carrying on in blatant, shameful, and egregious sin as they worshiped the golden calf in Exodus 32:32. Or what of our Savior's self-sacrifice? Romans 5:8 says, "While we were still sinners, Christ died for us."

Isn't that Jesus, though? So powerful that His love is different than ours and brings dead things back to life. His love is different. How great is His love that its depth is yet to be discovered, hidden below even the depths of the deepest sea; so high its summit yet to be conquered or realized; and so wide that all of humanity and time is swallowed up by it. And yet so powerful is He that His one death and resurrection can save billions of souls. And yet so great is His love that He'd die that wretched, miserable death to save the soul of one.

There's the disconnect. And we aren't being honest about it. We do love what we've created, and it's almost indistinguishable from the

Creator. And He knows. He knows the difference. Think just for a moment about how you even spend your time. I don't know about you, but I feel like many weeks I might use my degree maybe thirty minutes a week. Just saying. If your head is spinning, welcome to the party.

Bottom line, the message of Jesus was a message of grace, but it was not a message of compromise. Look at the ministry of Jesus. By the time He entered the scene, there were so many rules and regulations in place, implemented, at one point I am sure, with the best of intentions, that the people couldn't and wouldn't recognize the Messiah if He was standing in front of them—and He was! Jesus, at multiple times, exposed people the disciples respected and people that the disciples thought would make great candidates to join the team.

Here's the reality—your church wouldn't hire Jesus! It's true, and it's okay because if I were honest, which I'm trying to be, I wouldn't hire Jesus either. Why? He is a human relations nightmare. Heck, not only would your church not hire Jesus, it wouldn't issue Him a call. He wouldn't even graduate! Jesus gathered massive crowds and seemingly ran them off; He healed people and then told them not to talk about it. Can you imagine that conversation between Jesus and His supervisor?

> **"Jesus, I really love your preaching. Would you mind, though, actually preaching in our brand new sanctuary? It has intelligent lighting, 4K cameras, a line array system, and we are livestreaming! We just notice that You spend a lot of time at the synagogue down the street or the Jewish community center, or the parts of our city where organized crime, prostitution, and general corruption are prevalent. You don't seem to be promoting our brand."**

And talk about leadership? After three years, He had only twelve guys and dissension in the ranks; one doubted, one pretended to not know Him, and another with the moneybag seemed to be spending a lot of time with the Pharisees. I don't know if Jesus' actual ministry would meet any of our modern-day metrics! But maybe that's the problem. My goal isn't to tell you what to do in this chapter but rather to ask the questions that drive you to prayer and to seek the leading and prompting of the Holy Spirit in your context.

The truth is, Jesus is an HR problem and will always be a PR problem that will persist until He comes back. And if you walk too closely to Him in this life, you will become an HR and a PR problem yourself. And that idea should be distinguished from being relevant and pop culture-ish as a pastor or a church. Because you see, only the church has a problem being relevant. Jesus has no problem being relevant. He has never had a problem being relevant. While Jesus may be an HR nightmare and problematic in the realm of PR, He is always relevant. He is always in the conversation.

So let's talk "prescription" and "description." When we look at our practices in worship, our models of what it means to be a church, outreach, connection, and community, we all on some level tend to view Scripture and even the life and ministry of Luther through one of these lenses or even a mixture of the two.

Prescription is when we look at something and say, "This is literally how it is to be done or what it literally means." Therefore, the practice, experience, definition, method, or context is to be followed to a T. Conversely, we also have that of description. Scripture, or even our Confessions, is not prescribing what to literally do line by line but rather is offering a description of what can be applied to a larger context or altered depending on the context.

So when we look at the challenges before the Church in 2020, I believe those challenges exist because it may have unintentionally gotten off track. For example, the Early Church had many of the following attributes that you may find in your current context are lacking or wanting, to say the least.

As an example, you see in the Book of Acts a description of worship but not a prescription of worship; in other words, we see described to us that the people worshiped and a high-level view of how they worshiped. However, we do not get from Scripture in the New Testament a book of liturgical rubrics—in other words, a how-to manual for Christian worship.

Here were the circumstances to consider as well: the Early Church was first built on the foundation of the prophets and apostles, with Christ as the cornerstone, but it also had a sense of mutual and shared alienation from places of trading, selling, buying, and participation in every social, civil, and religious element of life. In other words, the Early Church was a community that needed one another's mutual support, encouragement, and the meeting of their day-to-day needs. As a result, and central to the mutual and shared exile, their faith in Jesus was the reason for being pushed to the outskirts of society.

Now compare that to today. We have community groups, life groups, or small groups. There is nothing wrong with these groups if you have this ministry in your church. In fact, they can be, and usually are, incredibly beneficial and necessary to the lifeblood and health of your congregation. But in many cases, this has become an addition to the calendar for our people. One more time commitment and one more program. Two thousand years ago, it wasn't a program; it was survival with Jesus in the very center of it all.

Think about houses of worship. They were literally houses where people worshiped! Only synagogues and state-sanctioned temples were what would foreshadow what we think of as sanctuaries and churches today. I wonder if the Early Church ever foresaw the need for building a separate house with a parking lot, playground, gymnasium, family life center, and a full industrial kitchen. Again, none of this is bad or against Scripture, but the question is, are these things enhancing, attributing to, or supporting the mission of God, or are they becoming what takes our focus off of the mission of God? Here's another question: is the model of your church enhancing or contributing to fulfilling the mission of God (not your mission statement)?

DIGITAL CHALLENGES

Remember that time that everyone became an online church? Lent 2020 will go down for many of us as one of the strangest seasons in any of our ministries. Every church became an online church (well, almost); every school became an online hybrid homeschool. Parents, by and large, became work-from-home or stay-at-home parents. And if that wasn't enough, we struggled with how to navigate this new world that seemed to evolve every four to seven days. If that was enough for your chaos quota, in some states the president didn't agree with the governor, the governor didn't agree with the mayor, the mayor didn't agree with the county judge, the judge wasn't in agreement with the local sheriff, and maybe the officer on the ground was on a different page from everyone else! Wow, how exhausting! And in the midst of all of that, the Church had to figure out in short order how to cut through all of the noise and chaos and get to the heart, soul, and minds of our people who were often gripped with fear, worry, uncertainty, and skepticism about it all.

Now what I am going to share is by no means prescriptive but merely descriptive. Our course of action was based on what we prayerfully believed would best meet the needs of our congregation. Sometimes I think we get tripped up as Lutherans trying to make things that are merely meant to be descriptive into mandates that become prescriptive. I think we have a word for this kind of freedom: adiaphora!

So here is what we did: we utilized freeconferencecall.com for all of our people who had no computer and no internet. We found that we could set up our personal cell phones through this service and set them on our podium for the service. Our members were able to call in and listen to the service over the phone. For the period of time in which we had no live services at all, we put the prerecorded services on the computer, then held the phone to the computer speakers as we played the services on the computer. This did an adequate job of putting our prerecorded services online.

This brings me to our next course of action—we prerecorded worship services by Thursday of each week at the latest. Through Amazon, we ordered ring lights that allowed us to record liturgy and sermons online. To be fair, there are pros and cons with the course of action that we chose. One con was that this method was less efficient than simply filming the whole service either live or once through with one camera. Our choice of action also required a person to be very proficient in film editing (we used Final Cut Pro). This also meant that we needed to have our sermons pretty well worked out each week before Thursday to record as well.

So you may be wondering, why on earth did you do things the way you did?! Well, the pros of our course of action included the fact that we did not have the budget or the means to have separate dedicated cameras for filming and placing our services online. As a result, we used our personal cell phones, as the camera quality was excellent (1080p). Our method also allowed us to give the feeling that we had more cameras than we actually had at the time. One pastor filmed his message on his phone; the other pastor filmed each part of the liturgy on his phone. We got efficient at setting up each shot so that the frames were lighted pretty well and the images were close-ups of us as pastors looking directly to our online congregation and viewers. We felt that this method allowed for the best possible quality and allowed for the best connection and intimacy for the congregation/viewer for an almost nonexistent budget.

We offered two different worship services each Sunday that kept the exact same liturgy with either contemporary or traditional music. This way, we could offer two different styles of worship but only record our sermons and liturgy once each Sunday. We would record our organist each week with a soloist and our contemporary worship leader each week doing an acoustic set and plug in each version of music, depending on which service we were leading.

The platform that we primarily utilized for worship each week was Facebook Live. We continued to also place audio content on our website as well. The only elements of our services that would stay up long term were our messages.

Many of our meetings and staff meetings utilized Zoom as a go-to that proved to be an incredible tool to help us navigate, plan, and strategize as a team.

Moving into our future, I really believe these tools, or ones that operate in a similar vein, could be a significant blessing to our churches. It always helps when people have shared experiences. No doubt, COVID-19 allowed room for a shared experience of receiving spiritual guidance, direction, leadership, preaching, and teaching from a screen rather than a live body in the room. There are a few trends that I believe are worth considering, including the continued implementation of this type of communication technology into our future.

The largest constituency of our people is Baby Boomers and older generations. More and more of our members will have a harder and harder time engaging in regular worship at the physical location of our churches. The necessity for a regular weekly rhythm of visitations that meet prayer and sacramental needs combined with enabling and equipping these generations to engage in worship online is most likely going to be the future reality in some way, shape, or form. We have several people in our congregation already who would love to be at our physical address on a Sunday morning, but they are no longer able to drive, suffer from severe chronic pain of one kind or another, or something like a pandemic comes along, and they become the most statistically vulnerable by even leaving their home or community.

In fact, our minister of care is doubling as an IT consultant to ensure that those individuals who may be elderly and want to engage with us on Facebook are adequately equipped to do so.

The one area I would stress, if you go this route, is the degree to which engagement with your online audience takes place. In our case, we have been intentional to make sure that those who connect to our online platform are acknowledged, welcomed, and interacted with so as to do everything we possibly can to deepen their connection with us during worship. I'm personally finding that this gap is quite a bit further apart than we tend to realize. To some degree, their feeling of separation can be deepened by a ninety-second or two-minute portion of the service that is carried out in person almost every Sunday. The segment I am speaking of is oftentimes labeled "passing the peace," "greeting time," or "welcome time." The vast majority of churches may not do this well, may not be intentional about it, and if people are already apt to feel disconnected or ignored when they are physically in our churches, the potential for it to be all the greater online is a reality we have to push through.

The anonymity factor and not physically being present in a church allows for people to simply switch off or tune out of worship. The human connection is absolutely critical. So while the online opportunity for a greater reach to the ends of the earth is heightened, your opportunity to leave people disconnected online is heightened as well.

And believe it or not, there are two critical elements to this that you may not think at first have anything to do with this topic. Number one, knowing yourself. Number two, knowing your team, staff, and volunteers. For example, I do like talking to people; I do like listening to their stories. I truly do, which is probably good since I am a pastor. But there are people that God has placed around me at our church that find the deepest passion in building deep relationships with individuals. One of the things that I have come to realize that is rarely understood between the megachurch world and small-church world, is depth and breadth of what is required of you at a small church.

I was on a staff as a youth minister right out of college at one of the biggest LCMS churches in the country. This particular church was and is a major player in our Synod. Did I work hard? Yes. Was my ministry pretty large and complex? Yes. But when I took my first call to be the senior pastor of a church that has, on some Sundays, fewer worshipers than I had in my youth group, I can tell you that while my role as a youth minister required a lot of me, it was only in a few categories that my time was concentrated. A small church, as many of you know, can be a mile wide and a mile deep. So for me, I love people, and I do what I can as often as I can to love people. At the same time, I must be prepared each and every Sunday to handle any staff issues and continue to move our church forward. This, as many of you know, is a delicate balance.

So this is where the turn happens in this conversation. How do we leverage technology that opens new doors and creates new possibilities, while at the same time somehow finding a way to be efficient as well?

A PROLONGED PANDEMIC

When COVID-19 stretched on, we had to make a massive shift in our thinking. This wasn't something that was going to stop any time soon. This isn't meant to be a political statement, but sadly, it will come off as one. With COVID-19, the best path forward, best practices and strategies became, well, politicized. It may sound crazy, and maybe this only applies to my state of Texas. But even wearing or not wearing a mask became political. I can't think of a time when pastors were walking in stranger waters. I'm sure it's happened before, but for my lifetime and my generation, this season of life and ministry is virtually unmatched. Not only a global pandemic, the adjustments necessary for the church to continue maximizing its reach to its total church family, but then throw in an election year, and racial tensions at a level that rivaled the early to late 1960s, as some of our cities burned. I mentioned earlier the politicization of wearing a mask; how about the politicization of Jesus. Yikes! Why is this relevant?

Well, because suddenly many of us pastors were forced—thrust—into our present-day town square. The Book of Acts tells us that Paul would do just that, engage in the town square. Our new town square, the agora of choice, our version of the great intersection of Rome's roads, would be called YouTube, Facebook, Instagram, .com, .org, and whatever else is next. Never before, like this season of ministry, were people looking for answers and asking questions that transcended the local or big network news.

Take away people's connection to their neighbors, limit their social interactions, have them lose their jobs, force them to become homeschool parents—then throw in the polarization factor of politics, a dishonest media, and the constant message that death is all around, but you might be able to prevent it. Understand what I'm saying—being a good steward of a situation is a very different thing than being able to or believing you can control a situation. Needless to say, we are in a season of ministry in which fear, anxiety, anger, doubt, vengeance, deception, intimidation, wrath, and hostility are in full effect. At the same time, patience, hope, grace, love, mercy, and forgiveness are in short supply.

Why does that matter for you? The moment you enter the new town square, there is potential for the reach of your church family, the message of Jesus, and your heart as a pastor to literally reach someone, impact someone, and transform the heart of someone on the other side of the globe, not to mention right down the street.

So what was our massive shift? We decided to take the first major step in staffing and adjusting our ministry focus to ensure that our presence online was greatly improved and our presence on social media reflected the heart of Jesus in the town square.

Before COVID-19, we were a church that was holding a 9 a.m. traditional service, 10 a.m. Bible class, and an 11 a.m. contemporary service. As COVID-19 dragged on, it became obvious this wasn't a matter of weeks or even months but could quite possibly be our new reality (or dare I even say it—new normal—how many times have you heard that?!) for the next year or, possibly, for the unforeseeable future. Once we honestly began to entertain the possibility that we may never be quite the same on the other side of this, we began to make considerable course changes in how we did what we did. Here are several examples.

We have an elderly ministry called Young at Heart. Before COVID-19, this ministry met one Thursday a month in our parish hall. This group, easily considered the most at-risk demographic, was almost completely cut off from community almost overnight. What's fascinating with this particular group is that as we were making the mental model shift, little did we realize they, too, were making similar shifts in their mindset. Suddenly, spiritual instruction, guidance, and even worship via media, which would have previously been considered a knockoff or "not a real worship service" if you are at home on your couch, quickly became acceptable and, in fact, embraced. If you think about people in their eighties, who have lived their entire existence believing that you not only attend church every Sunday, but you go to church in the physical building, making the mental model shift to embrace worship from home is huge and profound. I truly applaud this generation for the ability to adapt to the situation. We had people who, in some cases, had no internet—or at least no internet they ever used—and no computer. Three months later, they were on Zoom and telling people half their age how to navigate the program to unmute themselves! It was awesome to watch!

In lieu of Sunday morning Bible class, another member of the team and I began to provide devotions two days a week on Facebook Live. By far, the most engaged group in the live setting was again our elderly population, with many of our other generations catching it after it was already posted.

Our minister of care is my right-hand man when it comes to shut-ins, hospital visits, and funerals. He helps keep me on track and prioritize which visits we need to make each month or week. He walks with me with grieving families and ensures that their experience through the grieving process and experience before and after a funeral is thoughtful, personal, and consistent. He is truly a blessing to my ministry and a blessing to our community. When COVID-19 hit, he became a one-man telethon, making between seventy and eighty calls a week because he was limited in the level of personal interactions he was able to have with our elderly. In addition, he began to take on an IT support role for his ministry emphasis. He would help troubleshoot IT needs our elderly were having as they were going from no experience with a computer to taking in worship on Facebook. He would also manage the call-in system we had for those who were not willing or able to make the jump to online worship.

When we did finally have a Young at Heart meeting during COVID-19, those that wanted to attend in person were socially distanced, and for those not comfortable showing up in person, he had a full setup via Zoom for them to be a part of the gathering, exchange stories, and see one another. It had otherwise been months since some of them had even seen one another's faces in real-time.

When it came to worship, as I said before, we were a two-service church. Not to kick up the classic worship battle discussion, but for what it's worth, I must confess I was not a blended service fan. That is about the most PC way I know how to say that. Before COVID-19, I was sold out to either have traditional or contemporary. But please no trademporary or contemptional. Here's a grimace moment. I can remember early on in my ministry some people wanting a blended service as a last-ditch effort to get some traditional worship flavor in their late service experience before they made the inevitable decision to leave our church. Not necessarily proud of this (just giving context and hopefully credibility to the points that are coming), but I disliked blended so much that I was willing to let some people walk. Some of you may read this and think, "I would have done the same thing." Others may say, "What's wrong with this guy?"

COVID-19 flipped many of my priorities at a time when we also lost our associate pastor, our worship leader in our contemporary service, and closed our K–8 school that had existed for more than sixty years and that I even attended myself from kindergarten to fourth grade before we moved.

All of those things working together broke me of that issue. Suddenly I found myself championing a blended service. I just simply wanted our people together. Not all of it was my favorite; in fact, much of it wasn't my favorite, but for some reason, that just didn't matter to me. What mattered to me was being together. And that included our online presence as well. For a period of time, as I had pointed out before, we would record our sermons and liturgy ahead of time and then play the service as though it was live so that we could give and offer a higher quality worship service online from basically just using our cell phones.

But as this dragged on, we had a gift of five thousand dollars and finally had a new staff member who actually knew what to do with this gift to enhance what we were doing online. What we began to do was record a sermon three to four days ahead of the Sunday in question, and the contemporary worship music seven days in advance. We did this specifically with this service for two reasons. One, we wanted to try to engage a different set of hearers online than we felt would engage with us on our livestream service. Second, we knew that in order for our quality to be at the highest possible level, we would need to prerecord our elements for the service. This was a way to play to our strengths. One such strength is an amazing film editor. Thanks to her and the creativity of our worship leader, you would not only think the service was live, you would think our equipment was worth tens of thousands of dollars more than it is. This effort and compilation would form our contemporary worship service, which, for the time being, was exclusively online. On our social media platforms and website, we would replay just the sermon later in the day as well. Throughout the week, we would also isolate the music portion of the service and make that available. When it came to a live experience, albeit at home or in our sanctuary, 9 a.m. was when we would stream live for the people who were our members or actively engaging with our church.

Had you told me a year ago that having to be prepared enough to deliver a sermon on a Tuesday, Wednesday, or Thursday ahead of the Sunday service would not only be possible for me but I would also like it, I would have said you were crazy! Such an odd gift from COVID-19. Suddenly, I found that because I had to be prepared in advance and had to deliver a message under a certain amount of pressure, the sermon was locked into my mind the rest of the week. Which meant that Saturday night and Sunday night, my stress level was lowered considerably. It forced me into a mindset of preparation, execution, and discipline that has really blessed me, my marriage, and my family.

LIFE AFTER COVID-19

If I can encourage you to do anything, it is to seriously consider integrating quality online worship, devotions, and Bible studies into the life of your church. We have seen a major shift happen, and I don't believe we will ever go back. What do I mean? People of all ages walked through a shared experience together (that is almost always one of the strongest factors in moving a group of people forward or in any direction, really), in which there is now a precedent of receiving spiritual guidance, instruction, teaching, preaching, and worship online. And if your people are anything like mine, it is an experience that literally spans eighty-plus years (or four generations) in our churches.

We carefully considered how to navigate COVID and the Lord's Supper. We made a concerted effort to keep our congregation unified, which meant that even if we had differing opinions about what was safe and what wasn't, we still walked together through this season of life. As an example, for those who feared coming to the altar for Communion, we offered prepackaged communion sets each person could take with them into the sanctuary. Then during the Order of Holy Communion, when the Words of Institution were spoken over the bread and wine in their communion sets, they were able to eat the Lord's body and drink His blood from their pew, socially distanced with a clear conscience and yet still very much be a part of the body of believers. We also offered Communion to those who wanted to come up to the rail and receive the Sacrament as they had always done before the pandemic. We recognized that our people were getting hit from so many different directions, from the media to healthcare professionals and friends and family alike, that we didn't want receiving God's grace to become something that burdened their consciences.

Think of what is now possible moving into the future of our congregations. Even if you have an aging congregation, because of this experience and how we were all stretched, folks that transition to assisted living or a retirement community do not have to be shut out or cut off from actively participating in the life and worship life of their congregations. That would have been an almost impossible sell at any other time in our history. Our people were forced to embrace change and the potential of infusing technology into our worship lives. That certainly does not remove our pastoral obligation to bring Communion to our members confined to home or in nursing homes, but it provides them the wonderful opportunity to gather with their church family for weekly worship.

I think when it comes to future discussions and discernment surrounding the tension between what's appropriate to offer online and what must be reserved for in-person worship, the reality is, we were built for interaction, live and in-person with one another. And even if certain elements are delivered digitally, all our members still need physical and in-person experiences. Our Lord Jesus became incarnate to be God with us; we need to be with our people.

This was one of the trickiest parts of being a pastor through the heart of the pandemic. Even at the time of this writing, I can still say that a percentage of my people are still quite frightened and are being told by their doctors or friends and family that they trust to stay home. This season of life has even stifled our ability to do routine home visits and hospital visits in many cases. I can only encourage us to make pastoral decisions that are faithful and rooted in God-honoring intentions and motives as we address and maneuver through the coming challenges from COVID.

This season of COVID-19 may have presented another lingering issue, a new option and new opportunity to deal with the challenge before us. What is that issue? What is that challenge? Well, we have considerably more churches without pastors than the number of seminarians produced each year from our seminaries. In addition, over the next seven to ten years, I think we will see the vacancy rate of our church body increase exponentially because an entire generation of pastors will be stepping away from full-time ministry. Up to this point, and to our credit, we have sought a few different courses of action to help produce synodically trained pastors. The blessing of what we have now all experienced with COVID-19, the challenges it presented, and the opportunities it created, is that we may be able to introduce another option. While home visits, hospital visits, and the lion's share of ministry could and should be done in person, preaching, teaching, and even elements of liturgy can be done from a distance. In some cases, "from a distance" could be five states away. Once you are in the rhythm and comfort zone of preaching to a camera, especially prerecorded messages, if you have the structure and the team in place, it becomes relatively easy to adjust your greetings and opening statements to personalize a message to different congregations. Just food for thought and something to consider.

WESTCLIFFE

So back to October 2019. In the last two minutes of my time with Dr. Looney, I mentioned to him this dream I had about a ministry or a church that would almost exclusively be online. It would be a resource to congregations who are vacant and need preaching on Sunday mornings and would offer a weekly engaging and creative combination of counseling, preaching, music, question and answer reactions from each week's content, and the call to action to make Jesus known and be His hands and His feet to our world.

The first week of Advent 2020, "Westcliffe" officially launched. Before COVID-19 ever hit us all, the time spent in Westcliffe, Colorado, and the forty days of prayer with our church inspired this endeavor. Westcliffe attempts to reach people far from Jesus in a reverent and relevant way to the ends of the earth. At the same time, Pilgrim Lutheran Church continues to be a faithful, loyal, loving, multigenerational, Gospel-centered Lutheran Church in Houston.

CLOSING

Back in 2016, I had a crazy and what I felt was a Spirit-led idea. Our school was headed to serious financial issues. After much prayer, I believed that God was leading us in a new direction in education. I contacted five Concordia Universities, two of our national leading Lutheran high schools, and a blue-ribbon Lutheran school. The pitch and idea were simple. Pilgrim Lutheran School would become a hybrid of online education and in-person education. We would partner with Lutheran universities and leading Lutheran high schools to offer the most dynamic course offerings anywhere in the country, and we would, in the education offered, leverage not only university-level buy-in but also the marketing elements as well. We literally had a representative from every one of these schools show up on the birthday of our church—we had just turned seventy. It was a special assembly. Each person explained their contribution to Pilgrim, their passion for Pilgrim, and each shot a promotional video for the future of Pilgrim.

We went live with this concept in 2017. In some ways, it worked, and in other ways, it was a mess! Our learning curve was huge. We quickly learned what would be needed to record lessons, how teachers would have to be trained differently, and all of the challenges associated with this brave new venture all seemed to hit at once. We were criticized as experimenting with children's education. The principal I started with had left, and the next principal wasn't as pumped about the project. As a result, I let it die. Besides, not even our staff, by and large, were fans.

Can you imagine if we had stuck with it? I believed it was a prompting from God, rooted in prayer and affirmed from dialogue with other godly people in my life. I believed I was doing the right thing. But I allowed the peanut gallery, critics, cynics, and even members of my own team to talk me out of staying the course with something I believed in. And then in 2020, the world, literally the world, became online education-based or some kind of hybrid of online and live instruction. What would Pilgrim have been in 2020 after three years of perfecting and honing this vision while also being partnered with five universities, two high schools, and a blue-ribbon school?

What's my point? I can't answer either of the questions that I just asked. And I will never know. When you integrate something like technology in a new way into your ministry, expect pushback. Expect setbacks. If you move in a direction with technology that's new for your church, and it's something you believe in, I mean really believe in, see it through.

My dad and I would play baseball in the front yard (specifically Wiffle ball). Looking back, I now know that my dad followed the same pattern. He would start out throwing me easy pitches, straight stuff. I would start out hitting the ball. I would feel great. Then, he would inevitably start throwing me trash. Curveballs, knuckleballs, off-speed stuff, heat down the middle, all the while laughing at me and my frustration. I would eventually throw my bat down and start to storm off to go back inside. But here was the catch; he wouldn't let me go inside. Quitting wasn't an option.

Little did I know then, but now understand, he would start throwing me straight stuff again. In my mind as a kid back then, I wasn't catching necessarily what was changing in what was being thrown at me. All I knew was that I couldn't hit the ball. My dad wouldn't let me quit. He would bring me back and start throwing me straight stuff again, and I would start hitting the ball again. What was the lesson? Never, ever quit. Keep swinging. Never stop swinging.

Don't get me wrong, strategic planning is important. Having a plan that is Specific, Measurable, Attainable, Relevant, and Time Manageable (SMART) is necessary and a great way to increase buy-in of your members.

The tension is this: remember that time when a pandemic hit our planet and literally every single facet of every single nation under every single leader on the planet had to throw out their plans?

Whether it is a thoughtful, strategic plan or reacting to unprecedented situations, seek God's heart for the vision and trust God in the journey. If you are like me, ministry will push you to the very edge of what you think you can handle, and, in fact, may even push you beyond your limits. I almost broke. And it is by God's grace alone that my passion, my heart, my creativity, and my love for my church, my people, my community, and the ministry have been restored and even grown.

Hear me when you are in those dark moments: never, ever stop swinging. God is shaping you in those moments. He is building you in those moments. He's growing you and leading you into uncharted waters to transform you into the disciple and pastor He so deeply desires you to be in your life.

By the time you read this, I have no idea if Westcliffe will be successful or already be dead and gone. What I do know is that I have peace. I have peace because I know that I faithfully followed what I believed in my heart to be the will of God after meditating on His Word and praying through the spirit. I didn't stop. I didn't walk away. I didn't throw my bat down and quit. I kept swinging.

When it comes to taking risks in integrating technology in ministry and taking risks in general, just keep swinging. Never stop swinging.

Know that you are not alone. There's a pastor in Houston that can relate. If you need to talk, make your way down to Houston. The first round is on me.